Madam Padishal and Child.

Two Centuries of Costume in America

1620-1820

ALICE MORSE EARLE

In two volumes

VOL.

I

Dover Publications, Inc.

New York

Published in Canada by General Publishing Company, Ltd., 30 Lesmill Road, Don Mills, Toronto, Ontario.

Published in the United Kingdom by Constable and Company, Ltd., 10 Orange Street, London WC 2.

This Dover edition, first published in 1970, is an unabridged republication, with minor corrections, of the work originally published by The Macmillan Company, New York, in 1903.

International Standard Book Number: 0-486-22551-8
Library of Congress Catalog Card Number: 70-118167

Manufactured in the United States of America
Dover Publications, Inc.
180 Varick Street
New York, N.Y. 10014

Contents

VOL. I

To

George P. Brett

" *An honeſt Stationer (or Publisher) is he, that exercizeth his Myſtery (vvhether it be in printing, bynding or selling of Bookes) vvith more reſpect to the glory of God & the publike aduantage than to his ovvne Commodity & is both an ornament & a profitable member in a ciuill Commonvvealth. . . . If he be a Printer he makes conſcience to exemplefy his Coppy fayrely & truly. If he be a Booke-bynder, he is no meere Bookeſeller (that is) one vvho ſelleth meerely ynck & paper bundled up together for his ovvne aduantage only: but he is a Chapman of Arts, of vviſdome, & of much experience for a little money. . . . The reputation of Schollers is as deare unto him as his ovvne: For, he acknovvledgeth that from them his Myſtery had both begining and means of continuance. He heartely loues & seekes the Proſperity of his ovvne Corporation: Yet he vvould not iniure the Uniuerſityes to aduantage it. In a vvord, he is such a man that the State ought to cheriſh him; Schollers to loue him; good Cuſtomers to frequent his shopp; and the vvhole Company of Stationers to pray for him.*"

— GEORGE WITHER, 1625.

List of Illustrations

CHAPTER I

APPAREL OF THE PURITAN AND PILGRIM FATHERS

" Deep-skirted doublets, puritanic capes
Which now would render men like upright apes
Was comelier wear, our wiser fathers thought
Than the cast fashions from all Europe brought."

— "New England's Crisis," BENJAMIN TOMPSON, 1675.

" I am neither Niggard nor Cynic to the due Bravery of the
true Gentry." — "The Simple Cobbler of Agawam," J. WARD, 1713.

" Never was it happier in England than when an English-
man was known abroad by his own cloth ; and contented himself
at home with his fine russet carsey hosen, and a warm slop;
his coat, gown, and cloak of brown, blue or putre, with some
pretty furnishings of velvet or fur, and a doublet of sad-
tawnie or black velvet or comely silk, without such cuts and
gawrish colours as are worn in these dayes by those who think
themselves the gayest men when they have most diversities of
jagges and changes of colours."

— "Chronicles," HOLINSHED, 1578.

Two Centuries of Costume

CHAPTER I

APPAREL OF THE PURITAN AND PILGRIM FATHERS

IT is difficult to discover the reasons, to trace the influences which have resulted in the production in the modern mind of that composite figure which serves to the everyday reader, the heedless observer, as the counterfeit presentment of the New England colonist, — the Boston Puritan or Plymouth Pilgrim. We have a very respectable notion, a fairly true picture, of Dutch patroon, Pennsylvania Quaker, and Virginia planter; but we see a very unreal New Englishman. This " gray old Gospeller, sour as midwinter," appears with good-wife or dame in the hastily drawn illustrations of our daily press; we find him outlined with greater care but equal inaccuracy in our choicer periodical literature; we have him depicted by artists in our handsome books and on the walls of our art museums; he is cut in stone and cast in bronze for our halls and parks; he is dressed by actors for a part in some historical play; he is furbished up with conglomerate and makeshift garments by enthusiastic and confident young folk in tableau and fancy-dress party; he is richly and amply attired by portly, self-satisfied members of our patriotic-hereditary societies; we constantly see these figures garbed in semblance in some details, yet never in verisimilitude as a whole figure.

We are wont to think of our Puritan forbears, indeed we are determined to think of them, garbed in sombre sad-colored garments, in a life devoid of color, warmth, or fragrance. But sad color was not dismal and dull save in name; it was brown in tone, and brown is warm, and being a primitive color is, like many primitive things, cheerful. Old England was garbed in hearty honest russet, even in the days of our colonization. Read the list of the garments of any master of the manor, of the honest English yeoman, of our own sturdy English emigrants from manor and farm in Suffolk and Essex. What did they wear across seas? What did they wear in the New World? What they wore in England, namely: Doublets of leathers, all brown in tint; breeches of various tanned skins and hides; untanned leather shoes; jerkins of " filomot " or " phillymort " (feuille morte), dead-leaf color; buff-coats of fine buff leather; tawny camlet cloaks and jackets of " du Boys " (which was wood color); russet hose; horseman's coats of tan-colored linsey-woolsey or homespun ginger-lyne or brown perpetuana; fawn-colored mandillions and deer-colored cassocks — all brown; and sometimes a hat of natural beaver. Here is a " falding " doublet of " treen color " — and what is treen but wooden and wood color is brown again.

It was a fitting dress for their conditions of life. The colonists lived close to nature — they touched the beginnings of things; and we are close to nature when all dress in russet. The homely "butternuts" of the Kentucky mountains express this; so too does khaki, a good, simple native dye and stuff; so eagerly welcomed, so closely cherished, as all good and primitive things should be.

Governor John Endicott.

So when I think of my sturdy Puritan for-bears in the summer planting of Salem and of Boston, I see them in "honest russet ker-sey"; gay too with the bright stamell-red of their waistcoats and the grain-red linings of man-dillions; scarlet-capped are they, and enlivened with many a great scar-let-hooded cloak.   I see them in this attire on ship-board, where they were greeted off Salem with "a smell from the shore like the smell of a garden"; I see them landing in happy June amid "sweet wild strawberries and fair single roses." I see them walking along the little lanes and half-streets in which for many years bayberry and sweet-fern lingered in dusty fragrant clumps by the roadside.

" Scented with Cædar and Sweet Fern
From Heats reflection dry,"

wrote of that welcoming shore one colonist who came on the first ship, and noted in rhyme what he found and saw and felt and smelt.   And I see the forefathers standing under the hot little cedar trees of the Massachusetts coast, not sober in sad color, but cheery in russet and scarlet; and sweetbrier and strawberries, bayberry and cedar, smell sweetly and glow genially in that summer sunlight which shines down on us through all these two centuries.

We have ample sources from which to learn precisely what was worn by these first colonists — men and women — gentle and simple.   We have minute " Lists of Apparell " furnished by the Colonization Companies to the male colonists; we have also ample lists of apparel supplied to individual emigrants of varied degree; we have inventories in detail of the personal estates of all those who died in the colonies even in the earliest years — inventories wherein even a half-worn pair of gloves is gravely set down, appraised in value, sworn to, and entered in the town records; we have wills giving equal minuteness; we have even the articles of dress themselves preserved from moth and rust and mildew; we have private letters asking that supplies of clothing be sent across seas — clothing substantial and clothing fashionable; we have ships' bills of lading showing that these orders were carried out; we have curiously minute private letters giving quaint descriptions and hints of new and modish wearing apparel; we have sumptuary laws telling what articles of clothing must not be worn by those of mean estate; we have court records showing trials

under these laws; we have ministers' sermons denouncing excessive details of fashion, enumerating
and almost describing the offences; and we have also
a goodly number of portraits of men and a few of
women.   I give in this chapter excellent portraits
of the first governors, Endicott, Winthrop, Bradstreet, Winslow; and others could be added.   Having all these, do we need
fashion-plates or maga-
zines of the modes? We
have also for the early
years great instruction
through comparison and
inference in knowing
the English fashions of
those dates as revealed
through inventories,
compotuses, accounts,
diaries, letters, portraits,
prints, carvings, and
effigies; and American
fashions varied little
from English ones.

Governor Edward Winslow.

It is impossible to disassociate the history of costume from the general history of the country where
such dress is worn.   Nor could any one write upon
dress with discrimination and balance unless he knew
thoroughly the dress of all countries and likewise the
history of all countries.   Of the special country, he
must know more than general history, for the relations of small things to great things are too close.
Influences apparently remote prove vital.   At no

time was history told in dress, and at no period was
dress influenced by historical events more than during the seventeenth century and in the dress of
English-speaking folk.   The writer on dress should
know the temperament and character of the dress
wearer ; this was of special bearing in the seventeenth
century.   It would be thought by any one ignorant
of the character of the first Puritan settlers, and indifferent to or ignorant of historical facts, that in a
new world with all the hardships, restraints, lacks,
and inconveniences, no one, even the vainest woman,
would think much upon dress, save that it should
be warm, comfortable, ample, and durable.   But, in
truth, such was not the case.   Even in the first years
the settlers paid close attention to their attire, to its
richness, its elegance, its modishness, and watched
narrowly also the attire of their neighbors, not only
from a distinct liking for dress, but from a careful
regard of social distinctions and from a regard for
the proprieties and relations of life.   Dress was a
badge of rank, of social standing and dignity ; and
class distinctions were just as zealously guarded in
America, the land of liberty, as in England.   The
Puritan church preached simplicity of dress ; but the
church attendants never followed that preaching.
All believed, too, that dress had a moral effect, as it
certainly does ; that to dress orderly and well and
convenable to the existing fashions helped to pre-
serve the morals of the individual and general wel-
fare of the community.   Eagerly did the settlers
seek every year, every season, by every incoming
ship, by every traveller, to learn the changes of fash-

ions in Europe.   The first native-born poet, Benjamin Tompson, is quoted in the heading of this
chapter in a wail over thus following new fashions,
a wail for the " good old times," as has been the cry
of " old fogy " poets and philosophers since the days
of the ancient classics.

We have ample proof of the love of dignity, of
form, of state, which dominated even in the first
struggling days ; we can see the governor of Virginia when he landed, turning out his entire force
in most formal attire and with full company of forty
halberdiers in scarlet cloaks to attend in imposing
procession the church services in the poor little
church edifice — this when the settlement at Jamestown was scarce more than an encampment.

We can read the words of Winthrop, the governor of Massachusetts, in which he recounts his
mortification at the undignified condition of affairs
when the governor of the French province, the
courtly La Tour, landed unexpectedly in Boston
and caught the governor picnicking peacefully with
his family on an island in the harbor, with no attendants, no soldiers, no dignitaries.   Nor was there
any force in the fort, and therefore no salute could
be given to the distinguished visitors ; and still more
mortifying was the sole announcement of this important arrival through the hurried sail across the
bay, and the running to the governor of a badly
scared woman neighbor.   We see Winthrop trying to recover his dignity in La Tour's eyes (and
in his own) by bourgeoning throughout the remainder of the French governor's stay with an

imposing guard of soldiers in formal attendance at every step he took abroad; ordering them to wear, I am sure, their very fullest stuffed doublets and shiniest armor, while he displayed his best black velvet suit of garments. Fortunately for New England's appearance, Winthrop was a man of such aristocratic bearing and feature that no dress or lack of dress could lower his dignity.

Our forbears did not change their dress by emigrating; they may have worn heavier clothing in New England, more furs, stronger shoes, but I cannot find that they adopted simpler or less costly clothing; any change that may have been made through Puritan belief and teaching had been made in England. All the colonists

> "... studied after nyce array,
> And made greet cost in clothing."

Many persons preferred to keep their property in the form of what they quaintly called "duds." The fashion did not wear out more apparel than the man; for clothing, no matter what its cut, was worn as long as it lasted, doing service frequently through three generations. For instance, we find Mrs. Epes, of Ipswich, Massachusetts, when she was over fifty years old, receiving this bequest by will: "If she desire to have the suit of damask which was the Lady Cheynies her grandmother, let her have it upon appraisement." I have traced a certain flowered satin gown and "manto" in four wills; a dame to her daughter; she to her sister; then to the child of the last-named who was a granddaugh-

Governor John Winthrop.

ter of the first owner. And it was a proud posses-
sion to the last. The fashions and shapes then did
not change yearly. The Boston gentlewoman of

1660 would not have been ill dressed or out of the mode in the dress worn by her grandmother when she landed in 1625.

Petty details were altered in woman's dress — though but slightly; the change of a cap, a band, a scarf, a ruffle, meant much to the wearer, though it seems unimportant to us to-day. Men's dress, we know from portraits, was unaltered for a time save in neckwear and hair-dressing, both being of such importance in costume that they must be written upon at length.

Let us fix in our minds the limit of reign of each ruler during the early years of colonization and the dates of settlement of each colony. When Elizabeth died in 1603, the Brownist Puritans or Separatists were well established in Holland; they had been there twenty years. They were dissatisfied with their Dutch home, however, and had had internal quarrels — one, of petty cause, namely, a "topish Hatt," a "Schowish Hood," a "garish spitz-fashioned Stomacher," the vain garments of one woman; but the strife over these "abhominations" lasted eleven years.

James I was king when the Pilgrims came to America in 1620; but Charles I was on the throne in 1630 when John Winthrop arrived with his band of friends and followers and settled in Salem and Boston.

The settlement of Portsmouth and Dover in New Hampshire was in 1623, and in Maine the same year. The settlements of the Dutch in New Netherland were in 1614; while Virginia, named for Elizabeth, the Virgin Queen, and discovered in her day, was settled first of all at Jamestown in 1607. The Plymouth colony was poor. It came poor from Holland, and grew poorer through various misfortunes and set-backs — one being the condition of the land near Plymouth. The Massachusetts Bay Company was different. It came with properties estimated to be worth a million dollars, and it had prospered wonderfully after an opening year of want and distress. The relative social condition and means of the settlers of Jamestown, of Plymouth, of Boston, were carefully investigated from English sources by a thoughtful and fair authority, the historian Green. He says of the Boston settlers in his *Short History of the English People* : —

" Those Massachusetts settlers were not like the earlier colonists of the South; broken men, adventurers, bankrupts, criminals; or simply poor men and artisans like the Pilgrim Fathers of the *Mayflower*. They were in great part men of the professional and middle classes; some of them men of large landed estate, some zealous clergymen, some shrewd London lawyers or young scholars from Oxford. The bulk were God-fearing farmers from Lincolnshire and the Eastern counties."

A full comprehension of these differences in the colonies will make us understand certain conditions, certain surprises, as to dress; for instance, why so little of the extreme Puritan is found in the dress of the first Boston colonists.

There lived in England, near the close of Elizabeth's reign, a Puritan named Philip Stubbes, to whom we are infinitely indebted for our knowledge of English dress of his times. It was also the dress of the colonists; for details of attire, especially of men's wear, had not changed to any extent since the years in which and of which Philip Stubbes wrote.

He published in 1586 a book called *An Anatomie of Abuses*, in which he described in full the excesses of England in his day. He wrote with spirited, vivid pen, and in plain speech, leaving nothing unspoken lest it offend, and he used strong, racy English words and sentences. In his later editions he even took pains to change certain " strange, inkhorn terms " or complicate words of his first writing into simpler ones. Thus he changed *preter time* to *former ages; auditory* to *hearers; prostrated* to *humbled; consummate* to *ended;* and of course this was to the book's advantage. Unusual words still linger, however, but we must believe they are not intentionally " outlandish," as was the term of the day for such words.

The attitude of Stubbes toward dress and dress wearers is of great interest, for he was certainly one of the most severe, most determined, most conscientious of Puritans; yet his hatred of " corruptions desiring reformation " did not lead him to a hatred of dress in itself. He is careful to state in detail in the body of his book and in his preface that his attack is not upon the dress of people of wealth and station; that he approves of rich dress for the rich. His hatred is for the pretentious dress of the many men of low birth or of mean estate who lavish their all in dress ill suited to their station; and also his

Governor Simon Bradstreet.

reproof is for swindling in dress materials and dress-making; against false weights and measures, adulterations and profits; in short, against abuses, not uses.

His words run thus explicitly : —

" Whereas I have spoken of the excesse in apparell, and of the Abuse of the same as wel in Men as in Women, generally I would not be so understood as though my speaches extended to any either noble honorable or worshipful; for I am farre from once thinking that any kind of sumptuous or gorgeous Attire is not to be worn of them; as I suppose them rather Ornaments in them than otherwise. And therefore when I speak of excesse of Apparel

my meaning is of the inferiour sorte only who for the most
parte do farre surpasse either noble honorable or worshipful, ruffling in Silks Velvets, Satens, Damaske, Taffeties,
Gold Silver and what not; these bee the Abuses I speak
of, these bee the Evills that I lament, and these bee the
Persons my wordes doe concern."

There was ample room for reformation from
Stubbes's point of view.

" There is such a confuse mingle mangle of apparell and
such preponderous excess thereof, as every one is permitted
to flaunt it out in what apparell he has himself or can get
by anie kind of means.   So that it is verie hard to know
who is noble, who is worshipful, who is a gentleman, who
is not; for you shall have those who are neither of the
nobilytie, gentilitie, nor yeomanrie goe daylie in silks velvets
satens damasks taffeties notwithstanding they be base by
byrth, meane by estate and servyle by calling.   This a great
confusion, a general disorder.   God bee mercyfull unto us."

This regard of dress was, I take it, the regard of
the Puritan reformer in general; it was only excess
in dress that was hated. This was certainly the
estimate of the best of the Puritans, and it was certainly the belief of the New England Puritan. It
would be thought, and was thought by some men,
that in the New World liberty of religious belief and
liberty of dress would be given to all. Not at all!
—the Puritan magistrates at once set to work to
show, by means of sumptuary laws, rules of town
settlement, and laws as to Sunday observance and
religious services, that nothing of the kind was expected or intended, or would be permitted willingly.

No religious sects and denominations were welcome save the Puritans and allied forms — Brownists, Presbyterians, Congregationalists.   For a time none other were permitted to hold services ; no one could wear rich dress save gentlefolk, and folk of wealth or some distinction — as Stubbes said, "by being in some sort of office."

We shall find in the early pages of this book frequent references to Stubbes's descriptions of articles of dress, but his own life has some bearing on his utterances ; so let me bear testimony as to his character and to the absolute truth of his descriptions. He was held up in his own day to contempt by that miserable Thomas Nashe who plagiarized his title and helped his own dull book into popularity by calling it *The Anatomie of Absurdities;* and who further ran on against him in a still duller book, *An Almand for a Parrat.*   He called Stubbes " A Mar-Prelate Zealot and Hypocrite," and Stubbes has been held up by others as a morose man having no family ties and no social instincts.   He was in reality the tenderest of husbands to a modest, gentle, pious girl whom he married when she was but fourteen, and with whom he lived in ideal happiness until her death in child-birth when eighteen years old.   He bore testimony to his happiness and her goodness in a loving but sad and trying book " intituled" *A Christiall Glasse for Christian Women.*   It is a record of a life which was indeed pure as crystal ; a life so retiring, so quiet, so composed, so unvarying, a life so remote from any gentlewoman's life to-day that it seems of another ether, another planet, as well as of another century. But it is useful for us to know it, notwithstanding its background of gloomy religionism and its air of unreality ; for it helps us to understand the character of Puritan women and of Philip Stubbes. This fair young wife died in an ecstasy, her voice triumphant, her face radiant with visions of another and a glorious life. And yet she was not wholly happy in death ; for she had a Puritan conscience, and she thought she *must* have offended God in some way. She had to search far indeed for the offence ; and this was it — it would be absurd if it were not so true and so deep in its sentiment of regret. She and her husband had set their hearts too much in affection upon a little dog that they had loved well, and she found now that "it was a vanitye" ; and she repented of it, and bade them bear the dog from her bedside. Knowing Stubbes's love for this little dog (and knowing it must have been a spaniel, for they were then being well known and beloved and were called "Spaniel-gentles or comforters"—a wonderfully appropriate name), I do not much mind the fierce words with which he stigmatizes the vanity and extravagance of women. I have a strong belief too that if we knew the dress of his child-wife, we would find that he liked her bravely even richly attired, and that he acquired his wonderful mastery of every term and detail of women's dress, every term of description, through a very uxorious regard of his wife's apparel.

Of the absolute truth of every word in Stubbes's accounts we have ample corroborative proof. He

Sir Richard Saltonstall.

wrote in real earnest, in true zeal, for the reform
of the foolery and extravagance he saw around him,
not against imaginary evils.   There is ample proof
in the writings of his contemporaries — in Shakespere's comparisons, in Harrison's sensible *Description of England*, in Tom Coryat's *Crudities* — and
oddities — of the existence of this foolishness and
extravagance.   There is likewise ample proof in the
sumptuary laws of Elizabeth's day.

It would have been the last thing the solemn
Stubbes could have liked or have imagined, that he
should have afforded important help to future writers
upon costume, yet such is the case.   For he described
the dress of English men and women with as much
precision as a modern reporter of the modes.   No
casual survey of dress could have furnished to him
the detail of his description.   It required much examination and inquiry, especially as to the minutiæ
of women's dress.   Therefore when I read his bitter
pages (if I can forget the little pet spaniel) I have
always a comic picture in my mind of a sour, morose,
shocked old Puritan, "a meer, bitter, narrow-sould
Puritan," clad in cloak and doublet, with great horn
spectacles on nose, and ample note-book, penner, and
ink-horn in hand, agonizingly though eagerly sur-
veying the figure of one of his fashion-clad women
neighbors, walking around her slowly, asking as
he walked the name of this jupe, the price of that
pinner, the stuff of this sleeve, the cut of this cap,
groaning as he wrote it all down, yet never turning
to squire or knight till every detail of her extravagance and " greet cost " is recorded.   In spite of all

his moralizing his quill pen had too sharp a point, his scowling forehead and fierce eyes too keen a power of vision ever to render to us a dull page; even the author of *Wimples and Crisping Pins* might envy his powers of perception and description.

The bravery of the Jacobean gallant did not differ in the main from his dress under Elizabeth; but in details he found some extravagances. The love-locks became more prominent, and shoe-roses and garters both grew in size. Pomanders were carried by men and women, and " casting-bottles." Gloves and pockets were perfumed. As musk was the favorite scent this perfume-wearing is not over-alluring. As a preventive of the plague all perfumes were valued.

Since a hatred and revolt against this excess was one of the conditions which positively led to the formation of the Puritan political party if not of the Separatist religious faith, and as a consequence to the settlement of the English colonies in America, let us recount the conditions of dress in England when America was settled. Let us regard first the dress of a courtier whose name is connected closely and warmly in history and romance with the colonization of America; a man who was hated by the Pilgrim and Puritan fathers but whose dress in some degree and likeness, though modified and simplified, must have been worn by the first emigrants to Virginia across seas — let us look at the portrait of Sir Walter Raleigh. He was a hero and a scholar, but he was also a courtier; and of a court, too, where every court-attendant had to bethink himself much and ever of dress, for dress occupied vastly the thought and almost wholly the public conversation of his queen and her successor.

To understand Raleigh's dress, you must know the man and his life; to comprehend its absurdities and forgive its follies and see whence it originated, you must know Elizabeth and her dress; you must see her with " oblong face, eyes small, yet black; her nose a little hooked, her lips narrow, her teeth black;

Sir Walter Raleigh.

false hair and that red," — these are the striking and plain words of the German ambassador to her court. You must look at this queen with her colorless meagre person lost in a dress monstrous in size, yet hung, even in its enormous expanse of many square yards, with crowded ornaments, tags, jewels, laces, embroideries, gimp, feathers, knobs, knots, and aglets, with these bedizened rankly, embellished richly. You must see her talking in public of buskins and gowns, love-locks and virginals, anything but matters of seriousness or of state; you must note her at a formal ceremonial tickling handsome Dudley in the neck; watch her dancing, "most high and disposedly" when in great age; you must see her giving Essex a hearty boxing of the ear; hear her swearing at her ministers. You must remember, too, her parents, her heritage. From King Henry VIII came her love of popularity, her great activity, her extraordinary self-confidence, her indomitable will, her outbursts of anger, her cruelty, just as came her harsh, mannish voice. From her mother, Anne Boleyn, came her sensuous love of pleasure, of dress, of flattery, of gayety and laughter. Her nature came from her mother, her temper from her father. The familiarity with Robert Dudley was but a piece with her boisterous romps in her girlhood, and her flap in the face of young Talbot when he saw her "unready in my night-stuff." But she had more in her than came from Henry and Anne; she had her own individuality, which made her as hard as steel, made her resolute, made her live frugally and work hard, and, above all, made her know her limitations. The woman, be she queen or the plainest mortal, who can estimate accurately her own limitations, who is proof against enthusiasm, proof against ambition, and, at a climax, proof against flattery, who knows what she can *not* do, in that very thing finds success. Elizabeth was and ever will be a wonderful character-study; I never weary of reading or thinking of her.

The settlement of Massachusetts was under James I; but costume varied little, save that it became more cumbersome. This may be attributed directly to the cowardice of the king, who wore quilted and padded — dagger-proof — clothing; and thus gave to his courtiers an example of stuffing and padding which exceeded even that of the men of Elizabeth's day. "A great, round, abominable breech," did the satirists call it. Stays had to be worn beneath the long-waisted, peascod-bellied, stuffed doublet to keep it in shape; thus a man's attire had scarcely a single natural outline.

We have this description of Raleigh, courtier and "servant" of Elizabeth and victim of James, given by a contemporary, Aubrey:—

"He looked like a Knave with his gogling eyes. He could transform himself into any shape. He was a tall, handsome, bold man; but his næve was that he was damnably proud. A good piece of him is in a white satin doublet all embroidered with rich pearls, and a mighty rich chain of great pearls around his neck. The old servants have told me that the true pearls were nigh as big as the painted ones. He had a most remarkable aspect, an exceeding high forehead, long faced, and sour eie-lidded, a kind of pigge-eie."

We leave the choice of belief between one sentence of this personal description, that he was handsome, and the later plain-spoken details to the judgment of the reader. Certainly both statements cannot be

true.   As I look at his portrait, the "good piece of
him" on page 21, I wholly disbelieve the former.

Sir Walter Raleigh and Son.

His laced-in, stiffened waist, his absurd breeches,
his ruffs and sashes and knots, his great shoe-roses,

his jewelled hatband, make this a fantastic picture, one of little dignity, though of vast cost. The jewels on his shoes were said to have cost thirty thousand pounds; and the perfect pearls in his ear, as seen in another portrait, must have been an inch and a half long. He had doublets entirely covered with a pattern of jewels. In another portrait (on the opposite page) his little son, poor child, stands by his side in similar stiff attire. The famous portrait of Sir Philip Sidney and his brother is equally comic in its absurdity of costume for young lads.

Read these words descriptive of another courtier, of the reign of James; his favorite, the Duke of Buckingham:—

"With great buttons of diamonds, and with diamond hat bands, cockades and ear-rings, yoked with great and manifold knots of pearls. At his going over to Paris in 1625 he had twenty-seven suits of clothes made the richest that embroidery, gems, lace, silk, velvet, gold and stones could contribute; one of which was a white uncut velvet set all over suit and cloak with diamonds valued at £14,000 besides a great feather stuck all over with diamonds, as were also his sword, girdle, hat-band and spurs."

These were all courtiers, but we should in general think of an English merchant as dressed richly but plainly; yet here is the dress of Marmaduke Rawdon, a merchant of that day:—

"The apparell he rid in, with his chaine of gold and hat band was vallued in a thousand Spanish ducats; being two hundred and seventy and five pounds sterling. His hatband was of esmeralds set in gold; his suite was of a fine cloth trim'd with a small silke and gold fringe; the buttons of his suite fine gold — goldsmith's work; his rapier and dagger richly hatcht with gold."

The white velvet dress of Buckingham showed one of the extreme fashions of the day, the wearing of pure white. Horace Walpole had a full-length painting of Lord Falkland all in white save his black gloves. Another of Sir Godfrey Hart, 1600, is all in white save scarlet heels to the shoes. These scarlet heels were worn long in every court. Who will ever forget their clatter in the pages of Saint Simon, as they ran in frantic haste through hall and corridor — in terror, in cupidity, in satisfaction, in zeal to curry favor, in desire to herald the news, in hope to obtain office, in every mean and detestable spirit — ran from the bedside of the dying king? We can still hear, after two centuries, the noisy, heartless tapping of those hurrying red heels.

Look at the portrait of another courtier, Sir Robert Dudley, who died in 1639; not the Robert Dudley who was tickled in the neck by Queen Elizabeth while he was being dubbed earl; not the Dudley who murdered Amy Robsart, but his disowned son by a noble lady whom he secretly married and dishonored. This son was a brave sailor and a learned man. He wrote the *Arcana del Mare*, and he was a sportsman; "the first of all that taught a dog to sit in order to catch partridges." His portrait shows clumsy armor and showy rings, a great jewel and a vast tie of gauze ribbon on one arm; on the other a cord with many aglets; he

ROBERT DEVEREVX EARLE OF ESSEX HIS EXCEL
lency &c Generall of yᵉ Army

Pub April 1. 1799 by W. Richar ardson York House N° 31 Strand

wears marvellously embroidered, slashed, and bom-
basted breeches, tight hose, a heavily jewelled, broad
belt; and a richly fringed scarf over one shoulder,
and ridiculous garters at his calf. It is so absurd,
so vain a dress one cannot wonder that sensible
gentlemen turned away in disgust to so-called Puritan plainness, even if it went to the extreme of
Puritan ugliness.

But in truth the eccentrics and extremes of Puritan dress were adopted by zealots; the best of that
dress only was worn by the best men of the party.
All Puritans were not like Philip Stubbes, the
moralist; nor did all Royalists dress like Buckingham, the courtier.

I have spoken of the influence of the word "sad-
color." I believe that our notion of the gloom of
Puritan dress, of the dress certainly of the New
England colonist, comes to us through it, for the
term was certainly much used. A Puritan lover
in Dorchester, Massachusetts, in 1645, wrote to his
lass that he had chosen for her a sad-colored gown.
Winthrop wrote, " Bring the coarsest woolen cloth,
so it be not flocks, and of sad colours and some
red ; " and he ordered a "grave gown" for his wife,
" not black, but sad-colour." But while sad-colored
meant a quiet tint, it did not mean either a dull
stone color or a dingy grayish brown — nor even
a dark brown. We read distinctly in an English
list of dyes of the year 1638 of these tints in these
words, "Sadd-colours the following; liver colour,
De Boys, tawney, russet, purple, French green,
ginger-lyne, deere colour, orange colour." Of

these nine tints, five, namely, " De Boys," tawny, russet, ginger-lyne, and deer color, were all browns. Other colors in this list of dyes were called " light colours " and " graine colours." Light colors were named plainly as those which are now termed by shopmen " evening shades"; that is, pale blue, pink, lemon, sulphur, lavender, pale green, écru, and cream color. Grain colors were shades of scarlet, and were worn as much as russet. When dress in sad colors ranged from purple and French green through the various tints of brown to orange, it was certainly not a *dull*-colored dress.

Let us see precisely what were the colors of the apparel of the first colonists. Let us read the details of russet and scarlet. We find them in *The Record of the Governor and Company of the Massachusetts Bay in New England*, one of the incontrovertible sources which are a delight to every true historian. These records are in the handwriting of the first secretary, Washburn, and contain lists of the articles sent on the ships *Talbot*, *George*, *Lion's Whelp*, *Four Sisters*, and *Mayflower* for the use of the plantation at Naumkeag (Salem) and later at Boston. They give the amount of iron, coal, and bricks sent as ballast; the red lead, sail-cloth, and copper; and in 1629, at some month and day previous to 16th of March, give the order for the " Apparell for 100 men." We learn that each colonist had this attire : —

" 4 Pair Shoes.
  2 Pair Irish Stockings about 13*d*. a pair.
  1 Pair knit Stockings about 2*s*. 4*d*. a pair.

1 Pair Norwich Garters about 5s. a dozen.

4 Shirts.

2 Suits of Doublet and Hose; of leather lined with oiled skin leather, the hose and doublet with hooks and eyes.

1 Suit of Northern Dussens or Hampshire Kerseys lined, the hose with skins; the doublet with linen of Guildford or Gedleyman serges, 2s. 10d. a yard, 4½ to 5 yards a suit.

4 Bands.

2 Plain falling bands.

1 Standing band.

1 Waistcoat of green cotton bound about with red tape.

1 Leather Girdle.

2 Monmouth Cap, about 2s. apiece.

1 Black Hat lined at the brim with leather.

5 Red knit caps milled; about 5d. apiece.

2 Dozen Hooks and eyes and small hooks and eyes for mandillions.

1 Pair Calfs Leather gloves (and some odd pairs of knit and sheeps leather gloves).

A number of Ells Sheer Linen for Handkerchiefs."

On March 16th was added to this list a mandillion lined with cotton at 12d. a yard. Also breeches and waistcoats; a leather suit of doublet and breeches of oiled leather; a pair of breeches of leather, "the drawers to serve to wear with both their other suits." There was also full, yes, generous for the day, provision of rugs, bedticks, bolsters, mats, blankets, and sheets for the berths, and table linen. There were fifty beds; evidently two men occupied each bed. Folk, even of wealth and refinement, were not at all sensitive as to their mode

of sleeping or their bedfellows. The pages of
Pepys's *Diary* give ample examples of this carelessness.

Arms and armor were also furnished, as will be
explained in a later chapter.

A private letter written by an engineer, one Master Graves, the following year (1630), giving a list
of " such needful things as every planter ought to
provide," affords a more curt and much less expensive list, though this has three full suits, two
being of wool stuffs : —

" 1 Monmouth Cap.	1 Suit of Cloth.
3 Falling Bands.	3 Pair of Stockings.
3 Shirts.	4 Pair of Shoes.
1 Waistcoat.	Armour complete.
1 Suit Canvass.	Sword & Belt."
1 Suit Frieze.	

The underclothing in this outfit seems very
scanty.

I am sure that to some of the emigrants on these
ships either outfit afforded an ampler wardrobe than
they had known theretofore in England, though
English folk of that day were well dressed. With a
little consideration we can see that the Massachusetts Bay apparel was adequate for all occasions,
but it was far different from a man's dress to-day.
The colonist " hadn't a coat to his back " ; nor
had he a pair of trousers. Some had not even a
pair of breeches. It was a time when great changes
in dress were taking place. The ancient gown
had just been abandoned for doublet and long

hose, which were still in high esteem, especially among " the elder sort," with garters or points for the knees.   These doublets were both of leather and wool.   And there were also doublets to be worn by younger men with breeches and stockings.

When doublet and hose were worn, the latter were, of course, the long, Florentine hose, somewhat like our modern tights.

The jerkin of other lists varied little from the doublet; both were often sleeveless, and the cassock in turn was different only in being longer; buff-coat and horseman's coat were slightly changed. The evolution of doublet, jerkin, and cassock into a man's coat is a long enough story for a special chapter, and one which took place just while America was being settled.   Let me explain here that, while the general arrangement of this book is naturally chronological, we halt upon our progress at times, to review a certain aspect of dress, as, for instance, the riding-dress of women, or the dress of the Quakers, or to review the description of certain details of dress in a consecutive account.   We thus run on ahead of our story sometimes; and other times, topics have to be resumed and reviewed near the close of the book.

The breeches worn by the early planters were fulled at the waist and knee, after the Dutch fashion, somewhat like our modern knickerbockers or the English bag-breeches.

The four pairs of shoes furnished to the colonists were the best.   In another entry the specifications of their make are given thus: —

" Welt Neats Leather shoes crossed on the out-side with a seam.　To be substantial good over-leather of the best, and two soles; the under sole of Neats-leather, the outer sole of tallowed backs."

They were to be of ample size, some thirteen inches long; each reference to them insisted upon good quality.

There is plentiful head-gear named in these inventories, — six caps and a hat for each man, at a time when Englishmen thought much and deeply upon what they wore to cover their heads, and at a time when hats were very costly.　I give due honor to those hats in an entire chapter, as I do to the ruffs and bands supplied in such adequate and dignified numbers.　There was an unusually liberal supply of shirts, and there were drawers which are believed to have been draw-strings for the breeches.

In *New England's First Fruits* we read instructions to bring over " good Irish stockings, which if they are good are much more serviceable than knit ones."　There appears to have been much variety in shape as well as in material.　John Usher, writing in 1675 to England, says, " your sherrups stockings and your turn down stocking are not salable here."　Nevertheless, stirrup stockings and socks were advertised in the *Boston News Letter* as late as January 30, 1731.　Stirrup-hose are described in 1658 as being very wide at the top — two yards wide — and edged with points or eyelet holes by which they were made fast to the girdle or bag-breeches.　Sometimes they were allowed to bag

down over the garter.   They are said to have been
worn on horseback to protect the other garments.

Stockings at that time were made of cotton and
woollen cloth more than they were knitted.   Calico
stockings are found in inventories, and often stockings as well as hose with calico linings.   In the
clothing of William Wright of Plymouth, at his
death in 1633, were

> " 2 Pair Old Knit Stockins.
>   2 Pair Old Yrish Stockins.
>   2 Pair Cloth Stockins.
>   2 Pair Wadmoll Stockins.
>   4 Pair Linnen Stockins,"

which would indicate that Goodman Wright had
stockings for all weathers, or, as said a list of that
day, "of all denominations."   He had also two
pair of boot-hose and two pair of boot-briches ; evidently he was a seafaring man.   I must note that he
had more ample underclothing than many " plain
citizens," having cotton drawers and linen drawers
and dimity waistcoats.

That petty details of propriety and dignity of
dress were not forgotten ; that the articles serving
to such dignity were furnished to the colonists, and
the use of these articles was expected of them, is
shown by the supply of such additions to dress as
Norwich garters.   Garters had been a decorative
and elegant ornament to dress, as may be seen by
glancing at the portraits of Sir Walter Raleigh, Sir
Robert Orchard, and the *English Antick*, in this
book.   And they might well have been decried as

offensive luxuries unmeet for any Puritan and unnecessary for any colonist; yet here they are. The
settlers in one of the closely following ships had
points for the knee as well as garters.

From all this cheerful and ample dress, this might
well be a Cavalier emigration; in truth, the apparel
supplied as an outfit to the Virginia planters (who
are generally supposed to be far more given over to
rich dress) is not as full nor as costly as this apparel
of Massachusetts Bay. In this as in every comparison I make, I find little to indicate any difference
between Puritan and Cavalier in quantity of garments, in quality, or cost — or, indeed, in form.
The differences in England were much exaggerated
in print; in America they often existed wholly in
men's notions of what a Puritan must be.

At first the English Puritan reformers made
marked alterations in dress; and there were also
distinct changes in the soldiers of Cromwell's army,
but in neither case did rigid reforms prove permanent, nor were they ever as great or as sweeping
as the changes which came to the Cavalier dress.
Many of the extremes preached in Elizabeth's day
had disappeared before New England was settled;
they had been abandoned as unwise or unnecessary;
others had been adopted by Cavaliers, so that equal-
ized all differences. I find it difficult to pick out
with accuracy Puritan or Cavalier in any picture of
a large gathering. Let us glance at the Puritan
Roundhead, at Cromwell himself. His picture is
given on the following page, cut from a famous print
of his day, which represents Cromwell dissolving

the Long Parliament.   He and his three friends, all
Puritan leaders, are dressed in clothes as distinctly
Cavalier as the attire of the king himself.   The graceful hats with sweeping ostrich feathers are precisely
like the Cavalier hats still preserved in England ; like
one in the South Kensington Museum.   Cromwell's
wide boots and his short cape all have a Cavalier aspect.

Cromwell dissolving Parliament.

While Cromwell was steadily working for power,
the fashion of plain attire was being more talked
about than at any other time ; so he appeared in
studiously simple dress — the plainest apparel, indeed, of any man prominent in affairs in English history.   This is a description of his appearance
at a time before his name was in all Englishmen's
mouths.   It was written by Sir Philip Warwick : —

" The first time I ever took notice of him (Cromwell) was in the beginning of Parliament, November, 1640. I came into the house one morning, well-clad, and perceived a gentleman speaking whom I knew not, very ordinary apparelled, for it was a plain cloth suit which seemed to have been made by an ill country tailor. His linen was plain and not very clean, and I remember a speck or two of blood upon his band which was not much larger than his collar; his hat was without a hat-band; his stature was of good size; his sword stuck close to his side."

Lowell has written of what he terms verbal magic; the power of certain words and sentences, apparently simple, and without any recognizable quality, which will, nevertheless, fix themselves in our memory, or will picture a scene to us which we can never forget. This description of Cromwell has this magic. There is no apparent reason why these plain, commonplace words should fix in my mind this simple, rough-hewn form; yet I never can think of Cromwell otherwise than in this attire, and whatever portrait I see of him, I instinctively look for the spot of blood on his band. I know of his rich dress after he was in power; of that splendid purple velvet suit in which he lay majestic in death; but they never seem to me to be Cromwell — he wears forever an ill-cut, clumsy cloth suit, a close sword, and rumpled linen.

The noble portraits of Cromwell by the miniaturist, Samuel Cooper, especially the one which is at Sidney Sussex College, Cambridge, are held to be the truest likenesses. They show a narrow band, but the hair curls softly on the shoulders. The wonderful portrait of the Puritan General Ireton, in the National Portrait Gallery, has beautiful, long hair, and a velvet suit much slashed, and with many loops and buttons at the slashes. He wears mustache and imperial. We expect we may find that friend of Puritanism, Lucius Carey, Lord Falkland, in rich dress; and we find him in the richest of dress; namely, a doublet made, as to its body and large full sleeves, wholly of bands an inch or two wide of embroidery and gold lace, opening like long slashes from throat to waist, and from arm-scye to wrist over fine white lawn, and with extra slashes at various spots, with the full white lawn of his " habit-shirt " pulled out in pretty puffs. His hair is long and curling.

Sir William Waller.

General Waller of Cromwell's army, here shown, is the very figure of a Cavalier, as handsome a face, with as flowing hair and careful mustache, as the Duke of Buckingham, or Mr. Endymion Porter, — that courtier of courtiers, — gentleman of the bed-chamber to Charles I. Cornet Joyce, the sturdy personal custodian of the king in captivity, came the closest to being a Roundhead; but even his hair covers his ear and hangs over his collar — it would be deemed over-long to-day.

Here is Lord Fairfax in plain buff coat slightly laced and slashed with white satin. Fanshawe dressed — so his wife tells us — in " phillamot bro-cade with 9 Laces every one as broad as my hand, a little gold and silver lace between and both of curious workmanship." And his suit was gay with scarlet knots of ribbon ; and his legs were cased in white silk hose over scarlet ones ; and he wore black shoes with scarlet shoe strings and scarlet roses and garters ; and his gloves were trimmed with scarlet ribbon — a fine " gaybeseen " — to use Chaucer's words.

Surprising to all must be the portrait of that Puritan figurehead, the Earl of Leicester ; for he wears an affected double-peaked beard, a great ruff, feathered hat, richly jewelled hatband and collar, and an ear-ring. Facing page 26 is the dress he wore when masquerading in Holland as general dur-ing the Netherland insurrection against Philip II.

It is strange to find even writers of intelligence calling Winthrop and Endicott Roundheads. A recent magazine article calls Myles Standish a Roundhead captain. That term was not invented till a score of years after Myles Standish landed at Plymouth. A political song printed in 1641 is entitled *The Character of a Roundhead*. It be-gins : —

> " What creature's this with his short hairs
> His little band and huge long ears
> That this new faith hath founded ?

The right Honourable Ferdinand
Lord Fairfax

> The Puritans were never such,
> The saints themselves had ne'er as much.
>   Oh, such a knave's a Roundhead."

Mrs. Lucy Hutchinson was the wife of a Puritan gentleman, who was colonel in Cromwell's army, and one of the regicide judges. She wrote a history of her husband's life, which is one of the most valuable sources of information of the period wherein he lived, the day when Cromwell and Hampden acted, when Laud and Strafford suffered. In this history she tells explicitly of the early use of the word Roundhead : —

"The name of Roundhead coming so opportunely, I shall make a little digression to show how it came up : When Puritanism grew a faction, the Zealots distinguished themselves by several affectations of habit, looks and words, which had it been a real forsaking of vanity would have been most commendable. Among other affected habits, few of the Puritans, what degree soever they were, wore their hair long enough to cover their ears ; and the ministers and many others cut it close around their heads with so many little peaks — as was something ridiculous to behold. From this custom that name of Roundhead became the scornful term given to the whole Parliament Party, whose army indeed marched out as if they had only been sent out till their hair was grown. Two or three years later any stranger that had seen them would have inquired the meaning of that name."

It is a pleasure to point out Colonel Hutchinson as a Puritan, though there was little in his dress to indicate the significance of such a name for him, and certainly he was not a Roundhead, with his light

brown hair "softer than the finest silk and curling
in great loose rings at the ends — a very fine, thick-
set head of hair." He loved dancing, fencing,
shooting, and hawking; he was a charming musician; he had judgment in painting, sculpture, archi-
tecture, and the "liberal arts." He delighted in
books and in gardening and in all rarities; in
fact, he seemed to care for everything that was
"lovely and of good report." "He was wonderfully neat, cleanly and genteel in his habit, and had
a very good fancy in it, but he left off very early
the wearing of anything very costly, yet in his plainest habit appeared very much a gentleman." Such
dress was the *best* of Puritan dress; just as he was
the best type of a Puritan. He was cheerful, witty,
happy, eager, earnest, vivacious — a bit quick in
temper, but kind, generous, and good. He was, in
truth, what is best of all, — a noble, consistent,
Christian gentleman.

Those who have not acquired from accurate
modern portrayal and representation their whole
notion of the dress of the early colonists have, I
find, a figure in their mind's eye something like
that of Matthew Hopkins the witch-finder. Hogarth's illustrations of Hudibras give similar Puritans. Others have figures, dull and plainly dressed,
from the pictures in some book of saints and
martyrs of the Puritan church, such as were found
in many an old New England home. *My* Puritan
is reproduced on page 41. I have found in later
years that this Alderman Abel of my old print
was quite a character in English history; having

been given with Cousin Kilvert the monopoly of
the sale of wines at retail, one of those vastly lucrative privileges which brought forth the bitterest de-
nunciations from Sir John Eliot, who regarded them

*Mr. Alderman Abell and Richard Kilvert,
the two maine Projectors for Wine · 1641.*

as an infamous imposition upon the English people.
The site of Abel's house had once belonged to
Cardinal Wolsey; and it was popularly believed
that Abel found and used treasure of the cardinal
which had been hidden in his cellar.   He was called
the " Main Projector and Patentee for the Raising
of Wines."   Unfortunately for my theory that
Abel was a typical Puritan, he was under the protection of King Charles I; and Cromwell's Parliament put an end to his monopoly in 1641, and
his dress was simply that of any dull, uninterest-
ing, commonplace, and common Englishman of his
day.

Another New England man who is constantly called a Roundhead is Cotton Mather; with equal inconsequence and inaccuracy he is often referred to, and often stigmatized, as "the typical Puritan colonist," a narrow, bigoted Gospeller. I have open before me an editorial from a reputable newspaper which speaks of Cotton Mather dressed in dingy, skimped, sad-colored garments "shivering in the icy air of Plymouth as he uncovered his close-clipped Round-head when he landed on the Rock from the *Mayflower*." He was in fact born in America; he was not a Plymouth man, and did not die till more than a century after the landing of the *Mayflower*, and, of course, he was not a Round-head. Another drawing of Cotton Mather, in a

Reverend John Cotton.

respectable magazine, depicts him with clipped hair, emaciated, clad in clumsy garments, mean and haggard in countenance, raising a bundle of rods over a cowering Indian child. Now, Cotton Mather was distinctly handsome, as may be seen from his picture facing this page, which displays plainly the full, sensual features of the Cotton family, shown in John Cotton's portrait. And the Roundhead is in an elegant, richly curled periwig, such as was fashionable a hundred years after the *Mayflower*. And though he had the tormenting Puritan conscience he was not wholly a Puritan, for the world, the flesh, and the devil were

Reverend Cotton Mather.

strong in him.   He was much more gentle and
tender than men of that day were in general ; especially with all children, white and Indian, and was
most conscientious in his relations both to Indians
and negroes.   And in those days of universal whippings by English and American schoolmasters and
parents, he spoke in no uncertain voice his horror
and disapproval of the rod for children, and never
countenanced or permitted any whippings.

There was certainly great diversity in dress among
those who called themselves Puritans.   Some amusing stories are told of that strange, restless, brilliant
creature, the major-general of Cromwell's army, —
Harrison.   When the first-accredited ambassador
sent by any great nation to the new republic came
to London, there was naturally some stir as to the
wisdom of certain details of demeanor and dress.
It was a ticklish time.   The new Commonwealth
must command due honor, and the day before the
audience a group of Parliament gentlemen, among
them Colonel Hutchinson and one who was afterwards the Earl of Warwick, were seated together
when Harrison came in and spoke of the coming
audience, and admonished them all — and Hutchinson in particular, "who was in a habit pretty rich
but grave and none other than he usually wore" —
that, now nations sent to them, they must "shine in
wisdom and piety, not in gold and silver and worldly
bravery which did not become saints."   And he
asked them not to appear before the ambassador in
"gorgeous habits."   So the colonel — though he
was not "convinced of any misbecoming bravery in

a suit of sad-coloured cloth trimmed with gold and
with silver points and buttons " — still conformed
to his comrade's opinion, and appeared as did all the
other gentlemen in solemn, handsome black.   When
who should come in, "all in red and gold-a," — in
scarlet coat and cloak laden with gold and silver,
"the coat so covered with clinquant one could
scarcely discern the ground," and in this gorgeous
and glittering habit seat himself alone just under
the speaker's chair and receive the specially low respects and salutes of all in the ambassador's train,—
who should thus blazon and brazon and bourgeon
forth but Harrison !   I presume, though Hutchinson was a Puritan and a saint, he was a bit chagrined
at his black suit of garments, and a bit angered at
being thus decoyed ; and it touched Madam Hutchinson deeply.

    But Hutchinson had his turn to wear gay clothes.
A great funeral was to be given to Ireton, who was
his distant kinsman ; yet Cromwell, from jealousy,
sent no bidding or mourning suit to him.   A general invitation and notice was given to the whole
assembly, and on the hour of the funeral, within the
great, gloomy state-chamber, hung in funereal black,
and filled with men in trappings of woe, covered
with great black cloaks with long, weeping hatbands
drooping to the ground, in strode Hutchinson ;
this time he was in scarlet and cliquante, "such as
he usually wore," — so wrote his wife, — astonishing
the eyes of all, especially the diplomats and ambas-
sadors who were present, who probably deemed him
of so great station as to be exempt from wearing

black. The master of ceremonies timidly regretted
to him, in hesitating words, that no mourning had
been sent — it had been in some way overlooked ;
the General could not, thus unsuitably dressed,
follow the coffin in the funeral procession — it
would not look well ; the master of ceremonies
would be rebuked — all which proved he did not
know Hutchinson, for follow he could, and would,
and did, in this rich dress. And he walked through
the streets and stood in the Abbey, with his scarlet
cloak flaunting and fluttering like a gay tropical bird
in the midst of a slowly flying, sagging flock of de-
pressed black crows, — you have seen their dragging,
heavy flight, — and was looked upon with admiration
and love by the people as a splendid and soldierly
figure.

We must not forget that the years which saw the
settlement of Salem and Boston were not under
the riot of dress countenanced by James. Charles
I was then on the throne ; and the rich and beautiful dress worn by that king had already taken shape.

There has been an endeavor made to attribute this
dress to the stimulus, to the influence, of Puritan
feeling. Possibly some of the reaction against the
absurdities of Elizabeth and James may have helped
in the establishment of this costume ; but I think
the excellent taste of Charles and especially of his
queen, Henrietta Maria, who succeeded in making
women's dress wholly beautiful, may be thanked
largely for it. And we may be grateful to the
painter Van Dyck ; for he had not only great taste
as to dress, and genius in presenting his taste to the

public, but he had a singular appreciation of the pictorial quality of dress and a power of making dress appropriate to the wearer. And he fully understood its value in indicating character.

Since Van Dyck formed and painted these fine and elegant modes, they are known by his name, — it is the Van Dyck costume. We have ample exposition of it, for his portraits are many. It is told that he painted forty portraits of the king and thirty of the queen, and many of the royal children. There are nine portraits by his hand of the Earl of Strafford, the king's friend. He painted the Earl of Arundel seven times. Venetia, Lady Digby, had four portraits in one year. He painted all persons of fashion, many of distinction and dignity, and some with no special reason for consideration or portrayal.

The Van Dyck dress is a gallant dress, one fitted for a court, not for everyday life, nor for a strenuous life, though men of such aims wore it. The absurdity of Elizabeth's day is lacking; the richness remains. It is a dress distinctly expressive of dignity. The doublet is of some rich, silken stuff, usually satin or velvet. The sleeves are loose and graceful; at one time they were slashed liberally to show the fine, full, linen shirt-sleeve. Here are a number of slashed sleeves, from portraits of the day, painted by Van Dyck. The cuffs of the doublet are often turned back deeply to show embroidered shirt cuffs or lace ruffles, or even linen undersleeves. The collar of the doublet was wholly covered with a band or collar of rich lace and lawn, or all lace;

this usually with the pointed edges now termed
Vandykes.   Band strings of ribbon or "snake-
bone" were worn.   These often had jewelled tassels.   Rich tassels of pearl were the favorite.   A
short cloak was thrown gracefully on one shoulder
or hung at the back.   Knee-breeches edged with
points or fringes or ribbons met the tops of wide,
high boots of Spanish leather, which often also

Slashed Sleeves, temp. Charles I.

turned over with ruffles of leather or lace.   Within-
doors silken hose and shoes with rich shoe-roses of
lace or ribbon were worn.   A great hat, broad-
leafed, often of Flemish beaver, had a splendid
feather and jewelled hatband.   A rich sword-belt
and gauntleted and fringed gloves were added.
A peaked beard with small upturned mustache
formed a triangle, with the mouth in the centre,
as in the portrait of General Waller.   The hair
curled loosely in the neck, and was rarely, I think,
powdered.

Other great painters besides Van Dyck were fortunately in England at the time this dress was worn, and the king was a patron and appreciator of art. Hence they were encouraged in their work; and every form and detail of this beautiful costume is fully depicted for us.

CHAPTER II

DRESS OF THE NEW ENGLAND MOTHERS

" *Nowe my deare hearte let me parlye a little with thee about trifles, for when I am present with thee, my speeche is preiudiced by thy presence which drawes my mind from itselfe ; I suppose now, upon thy unkles cominge there wilbe advisinge & counsel-linge of all hands ; and amongst many I know there wilbe some, that wilbe provokinge thee, in these indifferent things, as matter of apparell, fashions and other circumstances ; I hould it a rule of Christian wisdome in all things to follow the soberest examples ; I confesse that there be some ornaments which for Virgins and Knights Daughters &c may be comly and tollerrable wch yet in soe great a change as thine is, may well admitt a change allso ; I will medle with noe particulars neither doe I thinke it shall be needfull ; thine own wisdome and godliness shall teach thee sufficiently what to doe in such things. I knowe thou wilt not grieve me for trifles. Let me intreate thee (my sweet Love) to take all in good part.*"

— JOHN WINTHROP TO MARGARET TYNDALE, 1616.

HAVE expressed a doubt that the dress of Cavalier and Puritan varied as much as has been popularly believed; I feel sure that the dress of Puritan women did not differ from the attire of women of quiet life who remained in the Church of England; nor did it vary materially either in form or quality from the attire of the sensible followers of court life. It simply did not extend to the extreme of the mode in gay color, extravagance, or grotesqueness. In the first severity of revolt over the dissoluteness of English life which had shown so plainly in the extravagance and absurdity of English court dress, many persons of deep thought (especially men), both of the Church of England and of the Puritan faith, expressed their feeling by a change in their dress. Doubtless also in some the extremity of feeling extended to fanaticism. It is always thus in reforms; the slow start becomes suddenly a violent rush which needs to be retarded and moderated, and it always is moderated. I have referred to one exhibition of bigotry in regard to dress which is found in the annals of Puritanism; it is detailed in the censure and attempt at restraint of the dress of Madam Johnson, the wife of the Rev. Francis Johnson, the pastor of the exiles to Holland.

There is a tradition that Parson Johnson was one of the Marprelate brotherhood, who certainly deserved the imprisonment they received, were it only for their ill-spelling and ill-use of their native tongue. The Marprelate pamphlet before me as I write had an author who could not even spell the titles of the prelates it assailed; but called them "parsones, fyckers and currats," the latter two names being intended for vicars and curates. The story of Madam Johnson's revolt, and her triumph, is preserved to us in such real and earnest language, and was such a vital thing to the actors in the little play, that it seems almost irreverent to regard it as a farce, yet none to-day could read of it without a sense of absurdity, and we may as well laugh frankly and freely at the episode.

When the protagonist of this Puritan comedy entered the stage, she was a widow — Tomison or Thomasine Boyes, a "warm" widow, as the saying of the day ran, that is, warm with a comfortable legacy of ready money. She was a young widow, and she was handsome. At any rate, it was brought up against her when events came to a climax; it was testified in the church examination or trial that "men called her a bouncing girl," as if she could help that! Husband Boyes had been a haberdasher, and I fancy she got both her finery and her love of finery in his shop. And it was told with all the petty terms of scandal-mongering that might be heard in a small shop in a small English town to-day;

it was told very gravely that the "clarkes in the shop" compared her for her pride in apparel to the wife of the Bishop of London, and it was affirmed that she stood "gazing, braving, and vaunting in shop doores."

Now this special complaint against the Widow Boyes, that she stood braving and vaunting in shop doors, was not a far-fetched attack brought as a novelty of tantalizing annoyance; it touches in her what was one of the light carriages of the day, which were so detestable to sober and thoughtful folk, an odious custom specified by Stubbes in his *Anatomy of Abuses*. He writes thus of London women, the wives of merchants : —

> "Othersome spend the greater part of the daie in sittyng at the doore, to shewe their braveries, to make knowen their beauties, to behold the passers by; to view the coast, to see fashions, and to acquaint themselves of the bravest fellows — for, if not for these causes, I know no other causes why they should sitt at their doores — as many doe from Morning till Noon, from Noon till Night."

Other writers give other reasons for this "vaunting." We learn that "merchants' wives had seats built a purpose" to sit in, in order to lure customers. Marston in *The Dutch Courtesan* says : —

> "His wife's a proper woman — that she is! She has been as proper a woman as any in the Chepe. She paints now, and yet she keeps her husband's old customers to him still. In troth, a fine-fac'd wife in a wainscot-carved seat, is a worthy ornament to any tradesman's shop. And an attractive one I'le warrant."

This handsome, buxom, bouncing widow fell in love with Pastor Johnson, and he with her, while he was "a prisoner in the Clink," he having been thrown therein by the Archbishop of Canterbury for his persistent preaching of Puritanism.   Many of his friends " thought this not a good match " for him at any time ; and all deemed it ill advised for a man in prison to pledge himself in matrimony to any one.   And soon zealous and meddlesome Brother George Johnson took a hand in advice and counsel, with as high a hand as if Francis had been a child instead of a man of thirty-two, and a man of experience as well, and likewise older than George.

George at first opened warily, saying in his letters that " he was very loth to contrary his brother ; " still Brother Francis must be sensible that this widow was noted for her pride and vanity, her light and garish dress, and that it would give great offence to all Puritans if he married her, and " it (the vanity and extravagance, etc.) should not be refrained." There was then some apparent concession and yielding on the widow's part, for George for a time " sett down satysfyed " ; when suddenly, to his " great grief " and discomfiture, he found that his brother had been " inveigled and overcarried," and the sly twain had been married secretly in prison.

It must be remembered that this was in the last years of Elizabeth's reign, in 1596, when the laws were rigid in attempts at limitation of dress, as I shall note later in this chapter.   But there were certain privileges of large estate, even if the owner were of mean birth ; and Madam Johnson certainly had money enough to warrant her costly apparel, and in ready cash also, from Husband Boyes. But in the first good temper and general good will of the honeymoon she "obeyed"; she promised to dress as became her husband's condition, which would naturally mean much simpler attire. He was soon in very bad case for having married without permission of the archbishop, and was still more closely confined withinwalls; but even while he lingered in prison, Brother George saw with anguish that the bride's short obedience had ended. She appeared in " more garish and proud apparell" than he had ever before seen upon the widow, — naturally enough for a bride, — even the bride of a bridegroom in prison; but he "dealt with her that she would refrain" — poor, simple man! She dallied on, tantalizing him and daring him, and she was very "bold in inviting proof," but never quitting her bridal finery for one moment; so George read to her with emphasis, as a final and unconquerable weapon, that favorite wail of all men who would check or reprove an extravagant woman, namely, Isaiah iii, 16 *et seq.*, the chapter called by Mercy Warren

> " . . . An antiquated page
> That taught us the threatenings of an Hebrew sage
> Gainst wimples, mantles, curls and crisping pins."

I wonder how many Puritan parsons have preached fatuously upon those verses! how many defiant women have had them read to them — and how many meek ones! I knew a deacon's wife in Worcester, some years ago, who asked for a new pair of India-rubber overshoes, and in pious response her frugal partner slapped open the great Bible at this favorite third chapter of the lamenting and threatening prophet, and roared out to his poor little wife, sitting meekly before him in calico gown and checked apron, the lesson of the haughty daughters of Zion walking with stretched-forth necks and tinkling feet; of their chains and bracelets and mufflers ; their bonnets and rings and rich jewels ; their mantles and wimples and crisping-pins ; their fair hoods and veils — oh, how she must have longed for an Oriental husband !

Petulant with his new sister-in-law's successful evasions of his readings, his letters, and his advice, his instructions, his pleadings, his commands, and "full of sauce and zeal" like Elnathan, George Johnson, in emulation of the prophet Isaiah, made a list of the offences of this London "daughter of Zion," wrote them out, and presented them to the congregation. She wore " 3, 4, or even 5 gold rings at one time." Then likewise "her Busks and ye Whalebones at her Brest were soe manifest that many of ye Saints were greeved thereby." She was asked to " pull off her Excessive Deal of Lace." And she was fairly implored to " exchange ye Schowish Hatt for a sober Taffety or Felt." She was ordered severely "to discontinue Whalebones," and to " quit ye great starcht Ruffs, ye Muske, and ye Rings." And not to wear her bodice tied to her petticoat " as men do their doublets to their hose contrary to 1 Thessalonians, V, 22." And a certain stomacher or neckerchief he plainly called "abominable and loathsome."

A " schowish Velvet Hood," such as only " the richest, finest and proudest sort should use," was likewise beyond endurance, almost beyond forgiveness, and other " gawrish gear gave him grave greevance."

Mrs. William Clark.

But here the young husband interfered, as it was high time he should; and he called his brother " fantasticall, fond, ignorant, anabaptisticall and such like," though what the poor Anabaptists had to do with such dress quarrels I know not.   George's cautious reference in his letter to the third verse of the third chapter of Jeremiah made the parson call

it "the Abhominablest Letter ever was written."
George, a bit frightened, answered pacificatorily
that he noted of late that "the excessive lace upon
the sleeve of her dress had a Cover drawn upon
it;" that the stomacher was not "so gawrish, so low,
and so spitz-fashioned as it was wont to be"; nor
was her hat "so topishly set," — and he expressed
pious gladness at the happy change, "hoping more
would follow,"—and for a time all did seem subdued.
But soon another meddlesome young man became
"greeved" (did ever any one hear of such a set of
silly, grieving fellows?); and seeing "how heavily the
young gentleman took it," stupid George must in-
terfere again, to be met this time very boldly by the
bouncing girl herself, who, he writes sadly, answered
him in a tone "very peert and coppet." "Coppet"
is a delightful old word which all our dictionaries
have missed; it signifies impudent, saucy, or, to be
precise, "sassy," which we all know has a shade
more of meaning. "Peert and coppet" is a delightful
characterization. George refused to give the sad
young complainer's name, who must have been well
ashamed of himself by this time, and was then re-
proached with being a "forestaller," a "picker," and
a "quarrelous meddler" — and with truth.

During the action of this farce, all had gone from
London into exile in Holland. Then came the
sudden trip to Newfoundland and the disastrous
and speedy return to Holland again. And through
the misfortunes and the exiles, the company drew
more closely together, and gentle words prevailed;
George was "sorie if he had overcarried himself";

Madam "was sure if it were to do now, she would not so wear it." Still, she did not offer her martinet of a brother-in-law a room to lodge in in her house, though she had many rooms unused, and he needed shelter, whereat he whimpered much; and soon he was charging her again "with Muske as a sin" (musk was at that time in the very height of fashion in France) and cavilling at her unbearable "topish hat." Then came long argument and sparring for months over "topishness," which seems to have been deemed a most offensive term. They told its nature and being; they brought in Greek derivatives, and the pastor produced a syllogism upon the word. And they declared that the hat in itself was not topish, but only became so when she wore it, she being the wife of a preacher; and they disputed over velvet and vanity; they bickered over topishness and lightness; they wrangled about lawn coives and busks in a way that was sad to read. The pastor argued soundly, logically, that both coives and busks might be lawfully used; whereat one of his flock, Christopher Dickens, rose up promptly in dire fright and dread of future extravagance among the women-saints in the line of topish hats and coives and busks, and he "begged them not to speak so, and *so loud*, lest it should bring *many inconveniences among their wives*." Finally the topish head-gear was demanded in court, which the parson declared was "offensive"; and so they bickered on till a most unseemly hour, till *ten o'clock at night*, as "was proved by the watchman and rattleman coming about." Naturally they wished to go to bed at an early hour, for religious services began at nine; one of the complaints against the topish bride was that she was a " slug-a-bed," flippantly refused to rise and have her house ordered and ready for the

Lady Mary Armine.

nine o'clock public service.   The meetings were then held in the parson's house, and held every day; which may have been one reason why the settle- ment grew poorer.   It matters little what was said, or how it ended, since it did not disrupt and disband the Holland Pilgrims.   For eleven years this stupid wrangling lasted; and it seemed imminent that the settlement would finish with a separation, and a return of many to England.   Slight events have great power — this topish hat of a vain and pretty, a peert and coppet young Puritan bride came near to hindering and changing the colonization of America.

I have related this episode at some length because its recounting makes us enter into the spirit of the first Separatist settlers.   It shows us too that dress conquered zeal; it could not be "forborne" by entreaty, by reproof, by discipline, by threats, by example.   An influence, or perhaps I should term it an echo, of this long quarrel is seen plainly by the thoughtful mind in the sumptuary laws of the New World.   Some of the articles of dress so dreaded, so discussed in Holland, still threatened the peace of Puritanical husbands in New England; they still dreaded "many inconveniences."   In 1634, the general court of Massachusetts issued this edict: —

"That no person, man or woman, shall hereafter make or buy any Apparell, either Woolen, or Silk, or Linen, with any Lace on it, Silver, Gold, or Thread, under the penalty of forfeiture of said clothes.   Also that no person either man or woman, shall make or buy any Slashed Clothes, other than one Slash in each Sleeve and another in the Back. Also all Cut-works, embroideries, or Needlework Caps, Bands or Rails, are forbidden hereafter to be made and worn under the aforesaid Penalty; also all gold or silver Girdles Hat bands, Belts, Ruffs, Beaver hats are prohibited to be bought and worn hereafter."

Fines were stated, also the amount of estate which released the dress-wearer from restriction. Liberty was given to all to wear out the apparel which they had on hand except "immoderate great sleeves, slashed apparell, immoderate great rails, and long wings" — these being beyond endurance.

In 1639 "immoderate great breeches, knots of riban, broad shoulder bands and rayles, silk roses, double ruffles and capes" were forbidden to folk of low estate. Soon the court expressed its "utter detestation and dislike," that men and women of "mean condition, education and calling" should take upon themselves "the garb of gentlemen" by wearing gold and silver lace, buttons and points at the knee, or "walk in great boots," or women of the same low rank to wear silk or tiffany hoods or scarfs. There were likewise orders that no short sleeves should be worn "whereby the nakedness of the arms may be discovered"; women's sleeves were not to be more than half an ell wide; long hair and immodest laying out of the hair and wearing borders of hair were abhorrent. Poor folk must not appear with "naked breasts and arms; or as it were pinioned with superstitious ribbons on hair and apparell." Tailors who made garments for servants or children, richer than the garments of the parents or masters of these juniors, were to be fined. Similar laws were passed in Connecticut and Virginia. I know of no one being "psented" under these laws in Virginia, but in Connecticut and Massachusetts both men and women were fined. In 1676, in Northampton, thirty-six young women at one time were brought

The Tub-preacher.

up for overdress chiefly in hoods; and an amusing
entry in the court record is that one of them, Hannah Lyman, appeared in the very hood for which
she was fined; and was thereupon censured for
"wearing silk in a fflonting manner, in an offensive
way, not only before but when she stood Psented.
Not only in Ordinary but Extraordinary times."
These girls were all fined; but six years later, when
a stern magistrate attempted a similar persecution,
the indictments were quashed.

It is not unusual to find the careless observer or
the superficial reader — and writer — commenting
upon the sumptuary laws of the New World as
if they were extraordinary and peculiar. There
appeared in a recent American magazine a long
rehearsal of the unheard-of presumption of Puritan
magistrates in their prohibition of certain articles of
dress. This writer was evidently wholly ignorant
of the existence of similar laws in England, and even
of like laws in Virginia, but railed against Winthrop
and Endicott as monsters of Puritanical arrogance
and impudence.

In truth, however, such laws had existed not only
in France and England, but since the days of the
old Locrian legislation, when it was ordered that no
woman should go attended with more than one
maid in the street "unless she were drunk." Ancient Rome and Sparta were surrounded by dress
restrictions which were broken just as were similar
ones in more modern times. The Roman could
wear a robe but of a single color; he could wear
in embroideries not more than half an ounce of

Old Venice Point Lace.

gold; and with what seems churlishness he was
forbidden to ride in a carriage.   At that time, just
as in later days, dress was made to emphasize class
distinction, and the clergy joined with the magistrates in denouncing extravagant dress in both men
and women.   The chronicles of the monks are ever
chiding men for their peaked shoes, deep sleeves
and curled locks like women, and Savonarola out-
did them all in severity.   The English kings and
queens, jealous of the rich dress of their opulent
subjects, multiplied restrictions, and some very
curious anecdotes exist of the calm assumption
by both Elizabeth and Mary to their own wardrobe of the rich finery of some lady at the court
who displayed some new and too becoming fancy.

Adam Smith declared it "an act of highest im-
pertinence and presumption for kings and rulers to

pretend to watch over the earnings and expenditure of private persons," nevertheless this public interference lingered long, especially under monarchies.

These sumptuary laws of New England followed in spirit and letter similar laws in England. Winthrop had seen the many apprentices who ran through London streets, dressed under laws as full of details of dress as is a modern journal of the modes. For instance, the apprentice's head-covering must be a small, flat, round cap, called often a bonnet — a hat like a pie-dish. The facing of the hat could not exceed three inches in breadth in the head; nor could the hat with band and facing cost over five shillings. His band or collar could have no lace edge; it must be of linen not over five shillings an ell in price; and could have no other work or ornament save "a plain hem and one stitch" — which was a hemstitch. If he wore a ruff, it must not be over three inches wide before it was gathered and set into the "stock." The collar of his doublet could have neither "point, well-bone or plait," but must be made "close and comely." The stuff of his doublet and breeches could not cost over two shillings and sixpence a yard. It could be either cloth, kersey, fustian, sackcloth, canvas, or "English stuff"; or leather could be used. The breeches were generally of the shape known as "round slops." His stockings could be knit or of cloth; but his shoes could have no polonia heels. His hair was to be cut close, with no "tuft or lock."

Queen Elizabeth stood no nonsense in these

things ; finding that London 'prentices had adopted
a certain white stitching for their collars, she put a
stop to this mild finery by ordering the first trans-
gressor to be whipped publicly in the hall of his
company. These same laws, tinkered and altered
to suit occasions, appear for many years in English
records, for years after New England's sumptuary
laws were silenced.

Notwithstanding Hannah Lyman and the thirty-
six vain Northampton girls, we do not on the whole
hear great complaint of extravagance in dress or de-
portment. At any rate none were called bouncing
girls. The portraits of men or women certainly
show no restraint as to richness in dress. Their
sumptuary laws were of less use to their day than
to ours, for they do reveal to us what articles of
dress our forbears wore.

While the Massachusetts magistrates were fussing
a little over woman's dress, the parsons, as a whole,
were remarkably silent. Of course two or three of
them could not refrain from announcing a text from
Isaiah iii, 16 *et seq.*, and enlarging upon the well-
worn wimples and nose jewels, and bells on their
feet, which were as much out of fashion in Massachusetts then as now. It is such a well-rounded,
ringing, colorful arraignment of woman's follies
you couldn't expect a parson to give it up. Every
evil predicted of the prophet was laid at the door of
these demure Puritan dames, — fire and war, and
caterpillars, and even baldness, which last was really
unjust. Solomon Stoddard preached on the " Intol-
erable Pride in the Plantations in Clothes and Hair,"

Rebecca Rawson.

that his parishioners " drew iniquity with a cord of vanity and sin with a cart-rope." The apostle Paul also furnished ample texts for the Puritan preacher.

In the eleventh chapter of Corinthians wise Paul delivered some sentences of exhortation, of re-proof, of warning to Corinthian women which I presume he understood and perhaps Corinthian dames did, but which have been a dire puzzle since to parsons and male members of their congregations. (I cannot think that women ever bothered much about his words.) For instance, Archbishop Lati-mer, in one of the cheerful, slangy rallies to his hearers which he called sermons, quotes Paul's sen-tence that a woman ought to have a power on her head, and construes positively that a power is a French hood. This is certainly a somewhat sur-prising notion, but I presume he knew. However, Roger Williams deemed a power a veil; and being somewhat dictatorial in his words, albeit the tender-est of creatures in his heart, he bade Salem women come to meeting in a veil, telling them they should come like Sarah of old, wearing this veil as a token of submission to their husbands. The text saith this exactly, " A woman ought to have power on her head because of the angels," which seems to me one of those convenient sayings of Paul and others which can be twisted to many, to any meanings, even to Latimer's French hood. Old John Cotton, of course, found ample Scripture to prove Salem women should not wear veils, and so here in this New World, as in the Holland sojourn, the head-covering of the mothers rent in twain the meetings

of the fathers, while the women wore veils or no
veils, French hoods or beaver hats, in despite of
Paul's opinions and their husbands' constructions of
his opinions.

An excellent description of the Puritan women
of a dissenting congregation is in *Hudibras Redivivus;* it reads : —

> "The good old dames among the rest
>   Were all most primitively drest
>   In stiffen-bodyed russet gowns
>   And on their heads old steeple crowns
>   With pristine pinners next their faces
>   Edged round with ancient scallop-laces,
>   Such as, my antiquary says,
>   Were worn in old Queen Bess's days,
>   In ruffs ; and fifty other ways
>   Their wrinkled necks were covered o'er
>   With whisks of lawn by granmarms wore."

The "old steeple crowns" over "pristine pinners" were not peculiar to the Puritans. There
was a time, in the first years of the seventeenth
century, when many Englishwomen wore steeple-
crowned hats with costly hatbands. We find them
in pictures of women of the court, as well as upon
the heads of Puritans. I have a dozen prints and
portraits of Englishwomen in rich dress with these
hats. The Quaker Tub-preacher, facing page 62,
wears one. Perhaps the best known example to
Americans may be seen in the portrait of Pocahontas facing page 122.

Authentic portraits of American women who came
in the *Mayflower* or in the first ships to the Massa-

chusetts Bay settlement, there are none to my knowledge. Some exist which are doubtless of that day, but cannot be certified. One preserved in Connecticut in the family of Governor Eaton shows a brown old canvas like a Rembrandt. The subject is believed to be of the Yale family, and the chief and most distinct feature of dress is the ruff.

It was a time of change both of men's and women's neckwear. A few older women clung to the ruffs of their youth; younger women wore bands, falling-bands, falls, rebatoes, falling-whisks and whisks, the "fifty other ways" which could be counted everywhere. Carlyle says : —

"There are various traceable small threads of relation, interesting reciprocities and mutabilities connecting the poor young Infant, New England, with its old Puritan mother and her affairs, which ought to be disentangled, to be made conspicuous by the Infant herself now she has grown big."

These traceable threads of relation are ever of romantic interest to me, and even when I refer to the dress of English folk I linger with pleasure with those whose lives were connected even by the smallest thread with the Infant, New England. One such thread of connection was in the life of Lady Mary Armine; so I choose to give her picture on page 60, to illustrate the dress, if not of a New Englander, yet of one of New England's closest friends. She was a noble, high-minded English gentlewoman, who gave "even to her dying day" to the conversion of poor tawny heathen of New England. A churchwoman by open profession, she was a Puri-

tan in her sympathies, as were many of England's
best hearts and souls who never left the Church of
England.   She gave in one gift £500 to families
of ministers who had been driven from their pulpits
in England.   The Nipmuck schools at Natick and
Hassamanesit (near Grafton) were founded under
her patronage.   The life of this "Truly Honourable, Very Aged and Singularly Pious Lady who dyed
1675," was written as a "pattern to Ladies."   Her
long prosy epitaph, after enumerating the virtues of
many of the name of Mary, concludes thus : —

> "The Army of such Ladies so Divine
>   This Lady said 'I'll follow, they Ar-mine.'
>   Lady Elect ! in whom there did combine
>   So many Maries, might well say All Ar-mine."

A pun was a Puritan's one jocularity; and he
would pun even in an epitaph.

It will be seen that Lady Mary Armine wears the
straight collar or band, and the black French hood
which was the forerunner, then the rival, and at last
the survivor of the "sugar-loaf" beaver or felt hat, —
a hood with a history, which will have a chapter for
the telling thereof.   Lady Mary wears a peaked
widow's cap under her hood ; this also is a detail of
much interest.

Another portrait of this date is of Mrs. Clark (see
page 57).   This has two singular details ; namely,
a thumb-ring, which was frequently owned but in-
frequently painted, and a singular bracelet, which is
accurately described in the verse of Herrick, written
at that date : —

> "I saw about her spotless wrist
> Of blackest silk a curious twist
> Which circumvolving gently there
> Enthralled her arm as prisoner."

I may say in passing that I have seen in portraits knots of narrow ribbon on the wrists, both of men and women, and I am sure they had some mourning significance, as did the knot of black on the left arm of the queen of King James of England.

We have in the portrait shown as a frontispiece an excellent presentment of the dress of the Puritan woman of refinement; the dress worn by the wives of Winthrop, Endicott, Leverett, Dudley, Saltonstall, and other gentlemen of Salem and Boston and Plymouth. We have also the dress worn by her little child about a year old. This portrait is of Madam Padishal. She was a Plymouth woman; and we know from the inventories of estates that there were not so many richly dressed women in Plymouth as in Boston and Salem. This dress of Madam Padishal's is certainly much richer than the ordinary attire of Plymouth dames of that generation.

This portrait has been preserved in Plymouth in the family of Judge Thomas, from whom it descended to the present owner. Madam Padishal was young and handsome when this portrait was painted. Her black velvet gown is shaped just like the gown of Madam Rawson (facing page 66), of Madam Stoddard (facing page 76), both Boston women; and of the English ladies of her times. It is much richer than that of Lady Mary Armine or Mrs. Clark.

The gown of Madam Padishal is varied pleasingly from that of Lady Mary Armine, in that the body is low-necked, and the lace whisk is worn over the bare neck. The pearl necklace and ear-rings likewise show a more frivolous spirit than that of the English dame.

Another Plymouth portrait of very rich dress, that of Elizabeth Paddy, Mrs. John Wensley, faces this page. The dress in this is a golden-brown brocade under-petticoat and satin overdress. The stiff, busked stays are equal to Queen Elizabeth's. Revers at the edge of overdress and on the virago sleeves are now of flame color, a Spanish pink, but were originally scarlet, I am sure. The narrow stomacher is a beaded galloon with bright spangles and bugles. On the hair there shows above the ears a curious ornament which resembles a band of this galloon. There are traces of a similar ornament in Madam Rawson's portrait (facing page 66); and Madam Stoddard's (facing page 76) has some ornament over the ears. This may have been a modification of a contemporary Dutch head-jewel. The pattern of the lace of Elizabeth Paddy's whisk is most distinct; it was a good costly Flemish parchment lace like Mrs. Padishal's. She carries a fan, and wears rings, a pearl necklace, and ear-rings. I may say here that I have never seen other jewels than these, —a few rings, and necklace and ear-rings of pearl. Other necklaces seem never to have been worn.

We cannot always trust that all the jewels seen in these portraits were real, or that the sitter owned as many as represented. A bill is in existence where

Elizabeth Paddy Wensley.

a painter charged ten shillings extra for bestowing a gold and pearl necklace upon his complaisant subject.   In this case, however, the extra charge was to pay for the gold paint or gold-leaf used for gilding the painted necklace.   In the amusing letters of Lady Sussex to Lord Verney are many relating to her portrait by Van Dyck.   She consented to the painting very unwillingly, saying, "it is money ill bestowed."   She writes : —

"Put Sr Vandyke in remembrance to do my pictuer well. I have seen sables with the clasp of them set with diamonds — if those I am pictured in were done so, I think it would look very well in the pictuer.   If Sr Vandyke thinks it would do well I pray desier him to do all the clawes so.   I do not mene the end of the tales but only the end of the other peces, they call them clawes I think."

This gives a glimpse of a richness of detail in dress even beyond our own day, and one which I commend to some New York dame of vast wealth, to have the claws of her sables set with diamonds. She writes later in two letters of some weeks' difference in date : —

"I am glad you have prefalede with Sr Vandyke to make my pictuer leaner, for truly it was too fat.   If he made it farer it will bee to my credit.   I am glad you have made Sr Vandyke mind my dress." . . .

"I am glad you have got home my pictuer, but I doubt he has made it lener or farer, but too rich in jewels, I am sure ; but 'tis no great matter for another age to thinke mee richer than I was.   I wish it could be mended in the face for sure 'tis very ugly.   The pictuer is very ill-favourede, makes me quite out of love with myselfe, the face is so bigg and so fat it pleases mee not at all. It looks like one of the Windes puffinge — (but truly I think it is lyke the original)."

I am struck by a likeness in workmanship in the portraits of these two Plymouth dames, and the portrait of Madam Stoddard (facing page 76), and succeeding illustrations of the Gibbes children. I do wish I knew whether these were painted by Tom Child — a painter-stainer and limner referred to by Judge Samuel Sewall in his Diary, who was living in Boston at that time. Perhaps we may find something, some day, to tell us this. I feel sure these were all painted in America, especially the portraits of the Gibbes children. A great many coats-of-arms were made in Boston at this time, and I expect the painter-stainer made them. All painting then was called coloring. A man would say in 1700, " Archer has set us a fine example of expense; he has colored his house, and has even laid one room in oils; he had the painter-stainer from Boston to do it — the man who limns faces, and does pieces, and tricks coats." This was absolutely correct English, but we would hardly know that the man meant: " Archer has been extravagant enough; he has painted his house, and even painted the woodwork of one room. He had the artist from Boston to do the work — the painter of faces and full-lengths, who makes coats-of-arms."

It is hard to associate the very melancholy countenance shown facing page 66 with a tradition of youth and beauty. Had the portrait been painted after a romance of sorrow came to this young maid, Rebecca Rawson, we could understand her expression; but it was painted when she was young and beautiful, so beautiful that she caught the eye and the wandering affections of a wandering gentleman, who announced himself as the son of one nobleman and kinsman of many others, and persuaded this daughter of Secretary Edward Rawson to marry him, which she did in the presence of forty witnesses. This young married pair then went to London, where the husband deserted Rebecca, who found to her horror that she was not his wife, as he had at least one English wife living. Alone and proud, Rebecca Rawson supported herself and her child by painting on glass; and when at last she set out to return to her childhood's home, her life was lost at sea by shipwreck.

The portrait of another Boston woman of distinction, Mrs. Simeon Stoddard, is given facing page 76. I will attempt to explain who Mrs. Simeon Stoddard was. She was Mr. Stoddard's third widow and the third widow also of Peter Sergeant, builder of the Province House. Mr. Sergeant's second wife had been married twice before she married him, and Simeon Stoddard's father had four wives, all having been widows when he married them. Lastly, our Mrs. Simeon Stoddard, triumphing over death and this gallimaufry of Boston widows, took a fourth husband, the richest merchant in town, Samuel Shrimpton. Having had in all four husbands of wealth, and with them and their accumulation of widows there must have been as a widow's mite an immense increment and inheritance of clothing (for clothing we know was a valued bequest), it is natural that we find her very richly dressed and with a distinctly haughty look upon her handsome face as becomes a conqueror both of men and widows.

The straight, lace collar, such as is worn by Madam Padishal and shown in all portraits of this date, is, I believe, a whisk.

The whisk was a very interesting and to us a puzzling article of attire, through the lack of precise description. It was at first called the falling-whisk, and is believed to have been simply the handsome, lace-edged, stiff, standing collar turned down over the shoulders. This collar had been both worn with the ruff and worn after it, and had been called a fall. Quicherat tells that the "whisk" came into universal use in 1644, when very low-necked gowns were worn, and that it was simply a kerchief or fichu to cover the neck.

We have a few side-lights to help us, as to the shape of the whisk, in the form of advertisements of lost whisks. In one case (1662) it is "a cambric whisk with Flanders lace, about a quarter of a yard broad, and a lace turning up about an inch broad, with a stock in the neck and a strap hanging down before." And in 1664 "A Tiffany Whisk with a great Lace down and a little one up, of large Flowers, and open work; with a Roul for the Head and Peak." The roll and peak were part of a cap.

Mrs. Simeon Stoddard.

These portraits show whisks in slightly varying forms. We have the "broad Lace lying down" in the handsome band at the shoulder; the "little lace standing up" was a narrow lace edging the whisk at the throat or just above the broad lace. Sometimes the whisk was wholly of mull or lawn. The whisk was at first wholly a part of woman's attire, then for a time it was worn, in modified form, by men.

Madam Pepys had a white whisk in 1660 and then a "noble lace whisk." The same year she bought hers in London, Governor Berkeley paid half a pound for a tiffany whisk in Virginia. Many American women, probably all well-dressed women, had them. They are also seen on French portraits of the day. One of Madam de Maintenon shows precisely the same whisk as this of Madam Padi-shal's, tied in front with tiny knots of ribbon.

It will be noted that Madam Padishal has black lace frills about the upper portion of the sleeve, at the arm-scye. English portraits previous to the year 1660 seldom show black lace, and portraits are not many of the succeeding forty years which have black lace, so in this American portrait this detail is un-usual. The wearing of black lace came into a short popularity in the year 1660, through compliment to the Spanish court upon the marriage of the young French king, Louis XIV, with the Infanta. The English court followed promptly. Pepys gloried in "our Mistress Stewart in black and white lace." It interests me to see how quickly American women had the very latest court fashions and wore them

even in uncourtlike America; such distinct novelties
as black lace.   Contemporary descriptions of dress
are silent as to it by the year 1700, and it disappears
from portraits until a century later, when we have
pretty black lace collars, capes and fichus, as may be
seen on the portraits of Mrs. Sedgwick, Mrs. Waldo,
and others later in this book.   These first black laces
of 1660 are Bayeux laces, which are precisely like

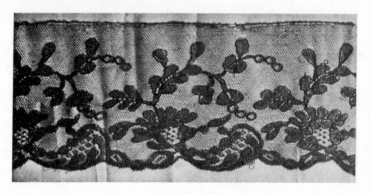

Ancient Black Lace.

our Chantilly laces of to-day.   This ancient piece of
black lace has been carefully preserved in an old New
York family.   A portrait of the year 1690 has a
black lace frill like the Maltese laces of to-day, with
the same guipure pattern.   But such laces were not
made in Malta until after 1833.   So it must have
been a guipure lace of the kind known in England
as parchment lace.   This was made in the environs
of Paris, but was seldom black, so this was a rare bit.
It was sometimes made of gold and silver thread.
Parchment lace was a favorite lace of Mary, Queen

of Scots, and through her good offices was peddled in England by French lace-makers. The black moiré hoods of Italian women sometimes had a narrow edge of black lace, and a little was brought to England on French hoods, but as a whole black lace was seldom seen or known.

An evidence of the widespread extent of fashions even in that day, a proof that English and French women and American women (when American women there were other than the native squaws) all dressed alike, is found in comparing portraits. An interesting one from the James Jackson Jarvis Collection is now in the Boston Museum of Fine Arts. It is of an unknown woman and by an unknown artist, and is simply labelled " Of the School of Susteman." But this unknown Frenchwoman has a dress as precisely like Madam Padishal's and Madam Stoddard's as are Doucet's models of to-day like each other. All have the whisk of rich straight-edged lace, and the tiny knots of velvet ribbon. All have the sleeve knots, but the French portrait is gay in narrow red and buff ribbon.

Doubtless many have formed their notion of Puritan dress from the imaginary pictures of several popular modern artists. It can plainly be seen by any one who examines the portraits in this book that they are little like these modern representations. The single figures called " Priscilla" and " Rose Standish " are well known. The former is the better in costume, and could the close dark cloth or velvet hood with turned-back band, and plain linen edge displayed beneath, be exchanged for the horseshoe shaped French hood which was then and many years later the universal head-wear, the verisimilitude would be increased. This hood is shown on the portraits of Madam Rawson, Madam Stoddard, Mistress Paddy, and others in this book. Rose Standish's cap is a very pretty one, much prettier than the French hood, but I do not find it like any cap in English portraits of that day. Nor have I seen her picturesque sash. I do not deny the existence in portraits of 1620 of this cap and sash; I simply say that I have never found them myself in the hundreds of English portraits, effigies, etc., that I have examined.

It will be noted that the women in the modern pictures all wear aprons. I think this is correct as they are drawn in their everyday dress, but it will be noted that none of these portraits display an apron; nor was an apron part of any rich dress in the seventeenth century. The reign of the apron had been in the sixteenth century, and it came in again with Anne. Of course every woman in Massachusetts used aprons.

Early inventories of the effects of emigrant dames contain many an item of those housewifely garments. Jane Humphreys, of Dorchester, Massachusetts, had in her good wardrobe, in 1668, " 2 Blew aprons, A White Holland Apron with a Small Lace at the bottom. A White Holland Apron with two breathes in it. My best white apron. My greene apron."

In the pictures, *The Return of the Mayflower* and *The Pilgrim Exiles*, the masculine dress therein displayed is very close to that of the real men of the times. The great power of these pictures is, after all, not in the dress, but in the expression of the faces. The artist has portrayed the very spirit of pure religious feeling, self-denial, home-longing, and sadness of exile which we know must have been imprinted on those faces.

The lack of likeness in the women's dress is more through difference of figure and carriage and an indescribable cut of the garments than in detail, except in one adjunct, the sleeve, which is wholly unlike the seventeenth-century sleeve in these portraits. I have ever deemed the sleeve an important part both of a man's coat and a woman's gown. The tailor in the old play, *The Maid of the Mill*, says, " O Sleeve ! O Sleeve ! I'll study all night, madam, to magnify your sleeves!" By its inelegant shape a garment may be ruined. By its grace it accents the beauty of other portions of the apparel. In these pictures of Puritan attire, it has proved able to make or mar the likeness to the real dress. It is now a component part of both outer and inner garment. It was formerly extraneous.

In the reign of Henry VIII, the sleeve was generally a separate article of dress and the most gorgeous and richly ornamented portion of the dress. Outer and inner sleeves were worn by both men and women, for their doublets were sleeveless. Elizabeth gradually banished the outer hanging sleeve, though she retained the detached sleeve.

Sleeves had grown gravely offensive to Puritans ; the slashing was excessive. A Massachusetts statute of 1634 specifies that " No man or woman shall

make or buy any slashed clothes other than one
slash in each sleeve and another in the back. Men
and women shall have liberty to wear out such
apparell as they now are provided of except the
immoderate great sleeves and slashed apparel."

Size and slashes were both held to be a waste of
good cloth. "Immoderate great sleeves" could
never be the simple coat sleeve with cuff in which our
modern artists are given to depicting Virginian and

Virago-sleeve.

New England dames. Doubtless
the general shape of the dress was
simple enough, but the sleeve was
the only part which was not close
and plain and unornamented. I
have found no close coat sleeves
with cuffs upon any old American
portraits. I recall none on English
portraits. You may see them,
though rarely, in England under
hanging sleeves upon figures which
have proved valuable conservators
of fashion, albeit sombre of design
and rigid of form, namely, effigies in stone or metal
upon old tombs; these not after the year 1620, though
these are really a small "leg-of-mutton" sleeve being gathered into the arm-scye. A beautiful brass in
a church on the Isle of Wight is dated 1615. This
has long, hanging sleeves edged with leaflike points
of cut-work; cuffs of similar work turn back from
the wrists of the undersleeves. A *Satyr* by Fitz-
geffrey, published the same year, complains that the
wrists of women and men are clogged with bush-

points, ribbons, or rebato-twists. " Double cufts " is
an entry in a Plymouth inventory — which explains
itself.   In the hundreds of inventories I have investigated I have never seen half a dozen entries of
cuffs.   The two or three I have found have been
specified as " lace cuffs."

George Fox, the founder of Quakerism, wrote
with a vivid pen ; one of his own followers said with
severity, " He paints high."   Some of his denuncia-
tions of the dress of his day afford a very good
notion of the peculiarities of contemporary costume ;
though he may be read with this caution in mind.
He writes deploringly of women's sleeves (in the
year 1654) ; it will be noted that he refers to double
cuffs: —

> " The women having their cuffs double under and above,
> like a butcher with his white sleeves, their ribands tied
> about their hands, and three or four gold laces about their
> clothes."

There were three generations of English heralds
named Holme, all genealogists, and all artists ; they
have added much to our knowledge of old English
dress.   Randle Holme, the Chester herald, lived in
the reign of Charles II, and increased a collection of
manuscript begun by his grandfather and now forming part of the Harleian Collection in the British
Museum.   He wrote also the *Academy of Armoury*,
published in 1688, and made a vast number of
drawings for it, as well as for his other works.   His
note-books of drawings are preserved.   In one of
them he gives drawings of the sleeve which is found

on every seventeenth-century portrait of American women which I have ever seen. He calls this a virago-sleeve. It was worn in Queen Elizabeth's day, but was a French fashion. It is gathered very full in the shoulder and again at the wrist, or at the forearm. At intervals between, it is drawn in by gathering-strings of narrow ribbons, or ferret, which are tied in a pretty knot or rose on the upper part of the sleeve. One from a French portrait is given on page 82. Madam Ninon de l'Enclos also wears one. This gathering may be at the elbow, forming thus two puffs, or there may be several such drawing-strings. I have seen a virago-sleeve with five puffs. It is a fine decorative sleeve, not always shapely, perhaps, but affording in the pretty knots of ribbon some relief to the severity of the rest of the dress.

Ninon de l'Enclos.

Stubbes wrote, " Some have sleeves cut up the arm, drawn out with sundry colours, pointed with silk ribbands, and very gallantly tied with love knotts." It was at first a convention of fashion, and it lingered long in some modification, that wherever there was a slash there was a knot of ribbon or a bunch of tags or aglets.   This in its origin was really that the slash might be tied together.   Ribbon knots were much worn; the early days of the great court of Louis XIV saw an infinite use of ribbons for men and women.   When, in the closing years of the century, rows of these knots were placed on either side of the stiff busk with bars of ribbon forming a stomacher, they were called *echelles*, ladders.   The *Ladies' Dictionary* (1694) says they were "much in request."

This virago-sleeve was worn by women of all ages and by children, both boys and girls.   A virago-sleeve is worn by Rebecca Rawson (facing page 66), and by Mrs. Simeon Stoddard (facing page 76), by Madam Padishal and by her little girl, and by the Gibbes child shown later in the book.

A carved figure of Anne Stotevill (1631) is in Westminster Abbey.   Her dress is a rich gown slightly open in front at the foot.   It has ornamental hooks, or frogs, with a button at each end — these are in groups of three, from chin to toe.   Four groups of three frogs each, on both sides, make twenty-four, thus giving forty-eight buttons.   A stiff ruff is at the neck, and similar smaller ones at the wrist.   She wears a French hood with a loose scarf over it.   She has a very graceful virago-sleeve with handsome knots of ribbon.

It is certain that men's sleeves and women's sleeves kept ever close company.   Neither followed the other; they walked abreast.   If a woman's sleeves

were broad and scalloped, so was the man's.   If the
man had a tight and narrow sleeve, so did his wife.
When women had virago-sleeves, so did men.   Even
in the nineteenth century, at the first coming of leg-
of-mutton sleeves in 1830 *et seq.*, dandies' sleeves
were gathered full at the armhole.   In the second
reign of these vast sleeves a few years ago, man
had emancipated himself from the reign of woman's
fashions, and his sleeves remained severely plain.

Small invoices of fashionable clothing were constantly being sent across seas.   There were sent to
and from England and other countries " ventures,"
which were either small lots of goods sent on speculation to be sold in the New World, or a small
sum given by a private individual as a " venture,"
with instructions to purchase abroad anything of
interest or value that was salable.   To take charge
of these petty commercial transactions, there existed
an officer, now obsolete, known as a supercargo.   It
is told that one Providence ship went out with the
ventures of one hundred and fifty neighbors on
board — that is, one hundred and fifty persons had
some money or property at stake on the trip.   Three
hundred ventures were placed with another supercargo.   Sometimes women sent sage from their
gardens, or ginseng if they could get it.   A bunch
of sage paid in China for a porcelain tea-set.   Along
the coast, women ventured food-supplies, — cheese,
eggs, butter, dried apples, pickles, even hard ginger-
bread ; another sent a barrel of cider vinegar.
Clothes in small lots were constantly being bought
and sold on a venture.   From London, in Novem-

ber, 1667, Walter Banesely sent as a venture to William Pïtkin in Hartford these articles of clothing with their prices : —

		£.	s.
" 1 Paire Pinck Colour'd mens hose		1	6
10 " Mens Silke Hose, 17s per pair . . .		8	10
2 " Womens " " 16s " " . . .		1	12
10 " " Green Hose		6	10
1 Pinck Colour'd Stomacher made of Knotts .		3	10

1 Pinck Colour'd Wastcote
A Black Sute of Padisuay.   Hatt,
    Hatt band, Shoo knots & trunk.
The wastcote and stomacher are a
Venture of my wife's ; the Silke Stockens mine own."

There remains another means of information of the dress of Puritan women in what was the nearest approach to a collection of fashion-plates which the times afforded.

In the year 1640 a collection of twenty-six pictures of Englishwomen was issued by one Wenceslas Hollar, an engraver and drawing-master, with this title, *Ornatus Muliebris Anglicanus. The severall Habits of Englishwomen, from the Nobilitie to the Country Woman As they are in these Times.* These bear the same relation to portraits showing what was really worn, as do fashion-plates to photographs. They give us the shapes of gowns, bonnets, etc., yet are not precisely the real thing. The value of this special set is found in three points : First, the drawings confirm the testimony of Lely, Van Dyck, and other artists ; they prove how slightly Van Dyck idealized the costume of his sitters.   Second, they give

representations of folk in the lower walks of life;
such folk were not of course depicted in portraits.
Third, the drawings are full length, which the portraits are not.   Four of these drawings are reduced

Lady Catharina Howard.

facing page 96. I give on page 142 the one entitled
The Puritan Woman, though it is one of the most
disappointing in the whole collection. It is such
a negative presentation; so little marked detail or
even associated evidence is gained from it. I had
a baffled thought after examining it that I knew less

of Puritan dress than without it.   I see that they
gather up their gowns for walking after a mode
known in later years as washerwoman style.   And
by that very gathering up we lose what the drawing
might have told us; namely, how the gowns were
shaped in the back; how attached to the waist or
bodice; and how the bodice was shaped at the waist,
whether it had a straight belt, whether it was pointed,
whether slashed in tabs or laps like a samare.   The
sleeve, too, is concealed, and the kerchief hides
everything else.   We know these kerchiefs were worn
among the "fifty other ways," for some portraits
have them; but the whisk was far more common.
Lady Catharina Howard, aged eleven in the year
1646, was drawn by Hollar in a kerchief.

There had been some change in the names of
women's attire in twenty years, since 1600, when
the catalogue of the Queen's wardrobe was made.
Exclusive of the Coronation, Garter, Parliament, and
mourning robes, it ran thus : —

" Robes.	Petticoats.
French gowns.	Cloaks.
Round gowns.	Safeguards.
Loose gowns.	Jupes.
Kirtles.	Doublets.
Foreparts.	Lap mantles."

In her New Year's gifts were also, "strayt-
bodyed gowns, trayn-gowns, waist-robes, night rayls,
shoulder cloaks, inner sleeves, round kirtles."   She
also had nightgowns and jackets, and underwear,
hose, and various forms of foot-gear.

Many of these garments never came to America. Some came under new names. Many quickly disappeared from wardrobes. I never read in early American inventories of robes, either French robes or plain robes. Round gowns, loose gowns, petticoats, cloaks, safeguards, lap mantles, sleeves, nightgowns, nightrails, and night-jackets continued in wear.

I have never found the word forepart in this distinctive signification nor the word kirtle; though our modern writers of historical novels are most liberal of kirtles to their heroines. It is a pretty, quaint name, and ought to have lingered with us; but " what a deformed thief this Fashion is " — it will not leave with us garment or name that we like simply because it pleases us.

Doublets were worn by women.

" The Women also have doublets and Jerkins as men have, buttoned up the brest, and made with Wings, Welts and Pinions on shoulder points as men's apparell is for all the world, & though this be a kind of attire appropriate only to Man yet they blush not to wear it."

Anne Hibbins, the *witch*, had a black satin doublet among other substantial attire.

A fellow-barrister of Governor John Winthrop, Sergeant Erasmus Earle, a most uxorious husband, was writing love-letters to his wife Frances, who lived out of London, at the same time that Winthrop was writing to Margaret Winthrop. Earle was much concerned over a certain doublet he had ordered for his wife. He had bought the blue bayes for this garment in two pieces, and he could not decide

whether the shorter piece should go into the sleeve
or the body, whether it should have skirts or not.
If it did not, then he had bought too much silver
lace, which troubled him sorely.

Margaret Winthrop had better instincts; to her
husband's query as to sending trimming for her
doublet and gown, she answers, "*When I see the
cloth* I will send word what trimming will serve;"
and she writes to London, insisting on " the civilest
fashion now in use," and for Sister Downing, who is
still in England, to give Tailor Smith directions
"that he may make it the better."   Mr. Smith sent
scissors and a hundred needles and the like homely
gifts across seas as " tokens " to various members of
the Winthrop household, showing his friendly inti-
macy with them all.   For many years after America
was settled we find no evidence that women's garments were ever made by mantua-makers.   All the
bills which exist are from tailors.   One of William
Sweatland for work done for Jonathan Corwin of
Salem is in the library of the American Antiquarian
Society: —

	£	s.	d.
" Sept. 29, 1679. To plaiting a gown for Mrs.		3	6
To makeing a Childs Coat		6	
To makeing a Scarlet petticoat with Silver Lace for Mrs.		9	
For new makeing a plush somar for Mrs .		6	
Dec. 22, 1679. For makeing a somar for your Maide		10	
Mar. 10, 1679. To a yard of Callico . .		2	
To 1 Douzen and ½ of silver buttons .		1	6
To Thread		4	

	£	s.	d.
To makeing a broad cloth hatte		14	
To makeing a haire Camcottcoat		9	
To makeing new halfsleeves to a silk Coascett		1	
March 25. To altering and fitting a paire of Stays for Mrs.		1	
Ap. 2, 1680, to makeing a Gowne for ye Maide		10	
May 20. For removing buttons of yr coat .			6
Juli 25, 1630. For makeing two Hatts and Jacketts for your two sonnes		19	
Aug. 14. To makeing a white Scarsonnett plaited Gowne for Mrs.		8	
To makeing a black broad cloth Coat for your-selfe		9	
Sept. 3, 1868. To makeing a Silke Laced Gowne for Mrs.	1	8	
Oct. 7, 1860, to makeing a Young Childs Coate		4	
To faceing your Owne Coat Sleeves . . .		1	
To new plaiting a petty Coat for Mrs. . .		1	6
Nov. 7. To makeing a black broad Cloth Gowne for Mrs.		18	
Feb. 26, 1680–1. To Searing a Petty Coat for Mrs.		6	

Sum is, £8   4s. 10d."

From many bills and inventories we learn that the time of the settlement of Plymouth and Boston reached a transitional period in women's dress as it did in men's. Mrs. Winthrop had doublets as had Governor Winthrop, but I think her daughter wore gowns when her sons wore coats. The doublet for a woman was shaped like that of a man, and was of double thickness like a man's. It might be sleeve-

less, with a row of welts or wings around the armhole ;
or if it had sleeves the welts, or a roll or cap, still remained. The trimming of the arm-scye was universal,
both for men and women. A fuller description of
the doublet than has ever before been written will be
given in the chapter upon the Evolution of the Coat.
The " somar " which is the samare, named also in
the bill of the Salem tailor, seems to have been a
Dutch garment, and was so much worn in New York
that I prefer to write of it in the following chapter.
We are then left with the gown ; the gown which
took definite shape in Elizabeth's day. Of course
no one could describe it like Stubbes. I frankly
confess my inability to approach him. Read his
words, so concise yet full of color and conveying
detail ; I protest it is wonderful.

" Their Gowns be no less famous, some of silk velvet
grogram taffety fine cloth of forty shillings a yard. But
if the whole gown be not silke or velvet then the same
shall be layed with lace two or three fingers broade all over
the gowne or the most parte. Or if not so (as Lace is
not fine enough sometimes) then it must be garded with
great gardes of costly Lace, and as these gowns be of
sundry colours so they be of divers fashions changing with
the Moon. Some with sleeves hanging down to their
skirts, trayling on the ground, and cast over the shoulders
like a cow's tayle. These have sleeves much shorter, cut
up the arme, and pointed with Silke-ribons very gallantly
tyed with true loves knottes — (for soe they call them).
Some have capes fastened down to the middist of their
backs, faced with velvet or else with some fine wrought
silk Taffeetie at the least, and fringed about Bravely, and

(to sum up all in a word) some are pleated and ryveled down the back wonderfully with more knacks than I can declare."

The guards of lace a finger broad laid on over the seams of the gown are described by Pepys in his day. He had some of these guards of gold lace taken from the seams of one of his wife's old gowns to overlay the seams of one of his own cassocks and rig it up for wear, just as he took his wife's old muff, like a thrifty husband, and bought her a new muff, like a kind one. Not such a domestic frugalist was he, though, as his contemporary, the great political economist, Dudley North, Baron Guildford, Lord Sheriff of London, who loved to sit with his wife ripping off the old guards of lace from her gown, "unpicking" her gown, he called it, and was not at all secret about it. Both men walked abroad to survey the gems and guards worn by their neighbors' wives, and to bring home word of new stuffs, new trimmings, to their own wives. Really a seventeenth-century husband was not so bad. Note in my *Life of Margaret Winthrop* how Winthrop's fellow-barrister, Sergeant Erasmus Earle, bought camlet and lace, and patterns for doublets for his wife Frances Fontayne, and ran from London clothier to London mantua-maker, and then to London haberdasher and London tailor, to learn the newest weaves of cloth, the newest drawing in of the sleeves. I know no nineteenth-century husband of that name who would hunt materials and sleeve patterns, and buy doublet laces and find gown-guards for his wife. And then the gown sleeves! What a description by Stubbes of the virago-sleeve "tied in and knotted with silk ribbons in love-knots!" It is all wonderful to read.

We learn from these tailors' bills that tailors' work embraced far more articles than to-day; in the *Orbis Sensualium Pictus*, 1659, a tailor's shop has hanging upon the wall woollen hats, breeches, waist-coats, jackets, women's cloaks, and petticoats. There are also either long hose or lasts for stretching hose, for they made stockings, leggins, gaiters, buskins; also a number of boxes which look like muff-boxes. One tailor at work is seated upon a platform raised about a foot from the floor. His seat is a curious bench with two legs about two feet long and two about one foot long. The base of the two long legs are on the floor, the other two set upon the platform. The tailor's feet are on the platform, thus his work is held well up before his face. Sometimes his legs are crossed upon the platform in front of him. The platform was necessary, or, at any rate, advisable for another reason. The habits of Englishmen at that time, their manners and customs, I mean, were not tidy; and floors were very dirty. Any garment resting on the floor would have been too soiled for a gentleman's wear before it was donned at all.

I have discovered one thing about old-time tailors, — they were just as trying as their successors, and had as many tricks of trade. A writer in 1582 says, " If a tailor makes your gown too little, he covers his fault with a broad stomacher; if too great, with a number of pleats; if too short, with a fine guard; if too long with a false gathering."

In several of the household accounts of colonial dames which I have examined I have found the prices and items very confusing and irregular when compared with tailors' bills and descriptive notes and letters accompanying them. And in one case I was fain to believe that the lady's account-book had been kept upon the plan devised by the simple Mrs. Pepys, — a plan which did anger her spouse Samuel "most mightily." He was filled with admiration of her household-lists — her kitchen accounts. He admired in the modern sense of the word "admire"; then he admired in the old-time meaning — of suspicious wonder. For albeit she could do through his strenuous teaching but simple sums in "Arithmetique," had never even attempted long division, yet she always rendered to her husband perfectly balanced accounts, month after month. At last, to his angry queries, she whimpered that "whenever she doe misse a sum of money, she do add some sums to other things," till she made it perfectly correct in her book — a piece of such simple duplicity that I wonder her husband had not suspected it months before. And she also revealed to him that she "would lay aside money for a necklace" by pretending to pay more for household supplies than she really had, and then tying up the extra amount in a stocking foot. He writes, "I find she is very cunning and when she makes least show hath her wits at work; and *so* to my office to my accounts."

English Gentlewoman

Lady of the Court of England

Country Servant

Costumes of Englishwomen of the Seventeenth Century.

CHAPTER III

ATTIRE OF VIRGINIA DAMES AND THEIR NEIGHBORS

" *Two things I love, two usuall thinges they are:*
The Firste, New-fashioned cloaths I love to wear,
Newe Tires, newe Ruffes; aye, and newe Gestures too
In all newe Fashions I do love to goe.
    The Second Thing I love is this, I weene
    To ride aboute to have those Newe Cloaths seene.

" *At every Gossipping I am at still*
And ever wilbe — maye I have my will.
For at ones own Home, praie — who is't can see
How fyne in new-found fashioned Tyres we bee?
Vnless our Husbands — Faith! but very fewe! —
And whoo'd goe gaie, to please a Husband's view?
    Alas! wee wives doe take but small Delight
    If none (besides our husbands) see that Sight."

— "The Gossipping Wives Complaint," 1611 (circa).

CHAPTER III

IT is a matter of deep regret that no "Lists of Apparel" were made out for the women emigrants in any of the colonies. Doubtless many came who had a distinct allotment of clothing, among them the redemptioners. We know one case, that of the "Casket Girls," of Louisiana, where a group of "virtuous, modest, well-carriaged young maids" each had a casket or box of clothing supplied to her as part of her payment for emigration. I wish we had these lists, not that I should deem them of great value or accuracy in one respect since they would have been made out naturally by men, but because I should like to read the struggles of the average shipping-clerk or supercargo, or even shipping-master or company's president, over the items of women's dress. One reason why the lists we have in the court records are so wildly spelled and often vague is, I am sure, because the recording-clerks were always men. Such hopeless puzzles as droll or drowlas, cale or caul or kail, chatto or shadow, shabbaroon or chaperone, have come to us through these poor struggling gentlemen.

There are not to my knowledge any portraits in existence of the wives of the first Dutch settlers of New Netherland. They would have been dressed, I am sure, in the full dress of Holland vrouws. We can turn to the court records of New Netherland to learn the exact item of the dress of the settlers. Let me give in full this inventory of an exceptionally rich and varied wardrobe of Madam Jacob de Lange of New Amsterdam, 1662 : —

	£	s.	d.
One under petticoat with a body of red bay .	1	7	
One under petticoat, scarlet	1	15	
One petticoat, red cloth with black lace . .	2	15	
One striped stuff petticoat with black lace .	1	8	
Two colored drugget petticoats with gray linings	1	2	
Two colored drugget petticoats with white linings		18	
One colored drugget petticoat with pointed lace		8	
One black silk petticoat with ash gray silk lining	1	10	
One potto-foo silk petticoat with black silk lining	2	15	
One potto-foo silk petticoat with taffeta lining	1	13	
One silk potoso-a-samare with lace	3		
One tartanel samare with tucker	1	10	
One black silk crape samare with tucker . .	1	10	
Three flowered calico samares	2	17	
Three calico nightgowns, one flowered, two red		7	
One silk waistcoat, one calico waistcoat . .		14	
One pair of bodices		4	
Five pair white cotton stockings		9	
Three black love-hoods		5	

	£	s.	d.
One white love-hood		2	6
Two pair sleeves with great lace	1	3	
Four cornet caps with lace	3		
One black silk rain cloth cap		10	
One black plush mask		1	6
Four yellow lace drowlas		2	

This is a most interesting list of garments. The sleeves with great lace must from their price have been very rich articles of dress. The yellow lace drowlas, since there were four of them (and no other neckerchiefs, such as gorgets, piccadillies, or whisks are named), must have been neckwear of some form. I suspect they are the lace drowls or drolls to which I refer in a succeeding chapter on A Vain Puritan Grandmother. The rain cloth cap of black silk is curious also, being intended to wear over another cap or a love-hood. The cornet caps with lace are a Dutch fashion. The "lace" was in the form of lappets or pinners which flapped down at the side of the face over the ears and almost over the cheeks. Evelyn speaks of a woman in "a cornet with the upper pinner dangling about her cheeks like hound's ears." Cotgrave tells in rather vague definition that a cornet is "a fashion of Shadow or Boone Grace used in old time and to this day by old women." It was not like a bongrace, nor like the cap I always have termed a shadow, but it had two points like broad horns or ears with lace or gauze spread over both and hanging from these horns. Cornets and corneted caps are often in Dutch inventories in early New York. And they can be seen in old Dutch pictures. They were one of the few distinctly Dutch modes that lingered in New Netherland; but by the third generation from the settlement they had disappeared.

Mrs. Livingstone.

What the words "potto-foo" and "potoso-a-samare" mean I cannot decipher. I have tried to find Dutch words allied in sound but in vain. I believe the samare was a Dutch fashion. We rarely find samares worn in Virginia and Maryland, but the name frequently occurs in the first Dutch inventories in New Netherland and occasionally in the

Connecticut valley, where there were a few Dutch settlers; occasionally also in Plymouth, whose first settlers had been for a number of years under Dutch influences in Holland; and rarely in Salem and Boston, whose planters also had felt Dutch influences through the settling in Essex and Suffolk of opulent Flemish and Dutch " clothiers " — cloth-workers. These Dutchmen had married English-women, and their presence in English homes was distinctly shown by the use then and to the present day of Dutch words, Dutch articles of dress, furniture, and food. From these Dutch-settled shires of Essex and Suffolk came John Winthrop and all the so-called Bay Emigration.

I am convinced that a samare was a certain garment which I have seen in French, Dutch, and English portraits of the day. It is a tight-fitting jacket or waist or bodice — call it what you will; its skirt or portion below the belt-line is four to eight inches deep, cut up in tabs or oblong flaps, four on each side. These slits are to the belt line. It is, to explain further, a basque, tight-fitting or with the waist laid in plaits, and with the basque skirt cut in eight tabs. These laps or tabs set out rather stiffly and squarely over the full-gathered petticoats of the day.

I turn to a Dutch dictionary for a definition of the word " samare," though my Dutch dictionary being of the date 1735 is too recent a publication to be of much value. In it a samare is defined simply as a woman's gown. Randle Holme says, rather vaguely, that it is a short jacket for women's wear

with four side-laps, reaching to the knees. In this
rich wardrobe of the widow De Lange, twelve petticoats are enumerated and no overdress-jacket or
doublet of any kind except those samares. Their
price shows that they were not a small garment.
One "silk potoso-a-samare with lace" was worth
£3. One "tartanel samare with tucker" was worth
£1 10s. One "black silk crape samare with tucker"
was worth £1 10s., and three "flowered calico"
samares were worth £2 10s. They were evidently
of varying weights for summer and winter wear, and
were worn over the rich petticoat.

The bill of the Salem tailor, William Sweatland
(1679), shows that he charged 9s. for making a
scarlet petticoat with silver lace; for making a
black broadcloth gown 18s.; while "new-makeing
a plush somar for M^{rs.}" (which was making over)
was 6s.; "making a somar for your Maide" was
10s., which was the same price he charged for
making a gown for the maid.

The colors in the Dutch gowns were uniformly
gay. Madam Cornelia de Vos in a green cloth petticoat, a red and blue "Haarlamer" waistcoat, a
pair of red and yellow sleeves, a white cornet cap,
green stockings with crimson clocks, and a purple
"Pooyse" apron was a blooming flower-bed of
color.

I fear we have unconsciously formed our mental
pictures of our Dutch forefathers through the vivid
descriptions of Washington Irving. We certainly
cannot improve upon his account of the Dutch
housewife of New Amsterdam : —

Mrs. Magdalen Beekman.

" Their hair, untortured by the abominations of art, was scrupulously pomatumed back from their foreheads with a candle, and covered with a little cap of quilted calico, which fitted exactly to their heads. Their petticoats of linsey-woolsey were striped with a variety of gorgeous dyes, though I must confess those gallant garments were rather short, scarce reaching below the knee; but then they made up in the number, which generally equalled that of the gentlemen's small-clothes; and what is still more praise-worthy, they were all of their own manufacture, — of which circumstance, as may well be supposed, they were not a little vain.

" Those were the honest days, in which every woman stayed at home, read the Bible, and wore pockets, — ay, and that, too, of a goodly size, fashioned with patchwork into many curious devices, and ostentatiously worn on the outside. These, in fact, were convenient receptacles where all good housewives carefully stored away such things as they wished to have at hand; by which means they often came to be incredibly crammed.

" Besides these notable pockets, they likewise wore scissors and pincushions suspended from their girdles by red ribbons, or, among the more opulent and showy classes, by brass and even silver chains, indubitable tokens of thrifty housewives and industrious spinsters. I cannot say much in vindication of the shortness of the petticoats; it doubtless was introduced for the purpose of giving the stockings a chance to be seen, which were generally of blue worsted, with magnificent red clocks; or perhaps to display a well-turned ankle and a neat though serviceable foot, set off by a high-heeled leathern shoe, with a large and splendid silver buckle.

" There was a secret charm in those petticoats, which no doubt entered into the consideration of the prudent gallants. The wardrobe of a lady was in those days her only fortune; and she who had a good stock of petticoats and stockings was as absolutely an heiress as is a Kamtschatka damsel with a store of bear-skins, or a Lapland belle with plenty of reindeer."

A Boston lady, Madam Knights, visiting New York in 1704, wrote also with clear pen:—

"The English go very fashionable in their dress. But the Dutch, especially the middling sort, differ from our women, in their habitt go loose, wear French muches wch are like a Capp and headband in one, leaving their ears bare, which are sett out with jewells of a large size and many in number; and their fingers hoop't with rings, some with large stones in them of many Coullers, as were their pendants in their ears, which you should see very old women wear as well as Young."

The jewels of one settler of New Amsterdam were unusually rich (in 1650), and were enumerated thus:—

	£	s.	d.
One embroidered purse with silver bugle and chain to the girdle and silver hook and eye		1	4
One pair black pendants, gold nocks . . .			10
One gold boat, wherein thirteen diamonds & one white coral chain		16	
One pair gold stucks or pendants each with ten diamonds		25	
Two diamond rings		24	
One gold ring with clasp beck			12
One gold ring or hoop bound round with diamonds	2	10	

These jewels were owned by the wife of an English-born citizen; but some of the Dutch

dames had handsome jewels, especially rich chate-
laines with their equipages and etuis with rich and
useful articles in variety.   When we read of such
articles, we find it difficult to credit the words of an
English clergyman who visited Albany about the
year 1700; namely, that he found the Dutch
women of best Albany families going about their
homes in summer time and doing their household
work while barefooted.

Many conditions existed in Maryland which were
found nowhere else in the colonies.   These were
chiefly topographical.   The bay and its many and
accommodative tide-water estuaries gave the planters
the means, not only of easy, cheap, and speedy
communication with each other, but with the whole
world.   It was a freedom of intercourse not given
to any other *agricultural* community in the whole
world.   It was said that every planter had salt
water within a rifle-shot of his front gate — therefore the world was open to him.   The tide is
never strong enough on this shore to hinder a sail-
boat nor is the current of the rivers perceptible.
The crop of the settlers was wholly tobacco — indeed, all the processes of government, of society, of
domestic life, began and ended with tobacco.   It
was a wonderfully lucrative crop, but it was an un-
happy one for any colony; for the tobacco ships
arrived in fleets only in May and June, when the
crops were ready for market.   The ships could come
in anywhere by tide-water.   Hence there were two
or three months of intense excitement, or jollity,
lavishness, extravagance, when these ships were in;

a regular Bartholomew Fair of disorder, coarse wit, and rough fun; and the rest of the year there was nothing; no business, no money, no fun.   Often the planter found himself after a month of June gambling and fun with three years' crops pledged in

advance to his creditors. The factor then played his part; took a mortgage, perhaps, on both crops and plantation; and invariably ended in owning everything. A striking but coarse picture of the traffic and its evils is given in *The Sot-weed Factor*, a poem of the day.

Land and living were cheap in this tobacco

Lady Anne Clifford.

land, but labor was needed for the sudden crops; so negro slaves were bought, and warm invitations were sent back to England for all and every kind of labor. Convicts were welcomed, redemptioners were eagerly sought for; and the scrupulous laws which were made for their protection were blazoned in England. Many laborers were "crimped," too, in England, and brought of course, willy-nilly, to Maryland. Landlords were even granted lands in proportion to their number of servants; a hundred acres per capita was the allowance. It can readily be seen that an ambitious or unscrupulous planter would gather in in some way as many heads as possible.

Maryland under the Baltimores was the only colony that then admitted convicts — that is, admitted them openly and legally. She even greeted them warmly, eager for the labor of their hands, which was often skilled labor; welcomed them for their wits, albeit these had often been ill applied; welcomed them for their manners, often amply refined; welcomed them for their possibilities of rehabilitation of morals and behavior.

The kidnapped servants did not fare badly. Many examples are known where they worked on until they had acquired ample means; still the literature of the day is full of complaints such as this in *The Sot-weed Factor* : —

> " Not then a slave ; for twice two years
> My clothes were fashionably new.
> Nor were my shifts of linen blue.
> But Things are Changed.   Now at the Hoe
> I daily work ; and Barefoot go.
> In weeding Corn, or feeding Swine
> I spend my melancholy time.''

Cheap ballads were sold in England warning English maidens against kidnapping.

In the collection of Old Black Letter Ballads in the British Museum is one entitled *The Trappan'd Maiden or the Distress'd Damsel*.   Its date is believed to be 1670.

> " The Girl was cunningly trappan'd
> Sent to Virginny from England.

> Where she doth Hardship undergo ;
> There is no cure, it must be so ;
> But if she lives to cross the Main
> She vows she'll ne'er go there again.
>   Give ear unto a Maid
>   That lately was betray'd
>   And sent unto Virginny O.
>   In brief I shall declare
>   What I have suffered there
>   When that I was weary, O.
>   The cloathes that I brought in
>   They are worn so thin
>   In the Land of Virginny O.
>   Which makes me for to say
>   Alas ! and well-a-day
>   When that I was weary, O."

The indentured servant, the redemptioner, or free-willer saw before him, at the close of his seven years term, a home in a teeming land ; he would own fifty acres of that land with three barrels, an axe, a gun, and a hoe — truly, the world was his. He would have also a suit of kersey, strong hose, a shirt, French fall shoes, and a good hat, — a Monmouth cap, — a suit worthy any man. Abigail had an equal start, a petticoat and waistcoat of strong wool, a perpetuana or callimaneo, two blue aprons, two linen caps, a pair of new shoes, two pairs of new stockings and a smock, and three barrels of Indian corn.

We find that many of these redemptioners became soldiers in the colonial wars, often distinguished for bravery. This was through a law passed by the British government that all who enlisted in military service in the colonies were released by that act from further bondage.

In the year 1659, on an autumn day, two white
men with an Indian guide paddled swiftly over the
waters of Chesapeake Bay on business of much im-
port.   They had come from Manhattan, and bore

Lady Herrman.

despatches from Governor Stuyvesant to the governor of Maryland, relating to the ever troublesome
query of those days, namely, the exact placing of
boundary lines.   One of these men was Augustine
Herrman, a man of parts, who had been ambassador to Rhode Island, a ship-owner, and man of

executive ability, which was proven by his offer to
Lord Baltimore to draw a map of Maryland and
the surrounding country in exchange for a tract of
land at the head of the bay. He was a land-sur-
veyor, and drew an excellent map; and he received
the four thousand acres afterwards known as Bohe-
mia Manor. His portrait and that of his wife exist;
they are wretched daubs, as were many of the portraits of the day, but, nevertheless, her dress is
plainly revealed by it. You can see a copy of it
on page 111. The overdress, pleated body, and
upper sleeve are green. The little lace collar is
drawn up with a tiny ribbon just as we see collars
to-day. Her hair is simplicity itself. The full
undersleeves and heavy ear-rings give a little richness to the dress, which is not English nor is it
Dutch.

It is easy to know the items of the dress of the
early Virginian settlers, where any court records exist.
Many, of course, have perished in the terrible devas-
tations of two long wars; but wherever they have
escaped destruction all the records of church and
town in the various counties of Virginia have been
carefully transcribed and certified, and are open to
consultation in the Virginia State Library at Rich-
mond, where many of the originals are also preserved. Many have also been printed. Mr. Bruce,
in his fine book, *The Economic History of Virginia in the Seventeenth Century*, has given frequent extracts from these certified records. From
them and from the originals I gain much knowledge of the dress of the planters at that time. It

varied little from dress in the New England colonies save that Virginians were richer than New Englanders, and so had more costly apparel. Almost nothing was manufactured in Virginia. The plainest and simplest articles of dress, save those of homespun stuffs, were ordered from England, as well as richer garments. We see even in George Washington's day, until he was prevented by war, that he sent frequent orders, wherein elaborately detailed attire was ordered with the pettiest articles for household and plantation use.

Elizabeth Cromwell.

Mrs. Francis Pritchard of Lancaster, Virginia (in 1660), we find had a representative wardrobe. She owned an olive-colored silk petticoat, another of silk tabby, and one of flowered tabby, one of velvet, and one of white striped dimity. Her printed calico gown was lined with blue silk, thus proving how much calico was valued. Other bodices were a striped dimity jacket and a black silk waistcoat. To wear with these were a pair of scarlet sleeves and other sleeves of ruffled holland. Five aprons, various neckwear of Flanders lace, and several rich handkerchiefs completed a gay costume to which green silk stockings gave an additional touch of color. Green was distinctly the favorite color for hose among all the early settlers ; and nearly all the inventories in Virginia have that entry.

Mrs. Sarah Willoughby of Lower Norfolk, Virginia, had at the same date a like gay wardrobe, valued, however, at but £14. Petticoats of calico, striped linen, India silk, worsted prunella, and red, blue, and black silk were accompanied with scarlet waistcoats with silver lace, a white knit waistcoat, a "pair of red paragon bodices," and another pair of sky-colored satin bodices. She had also a striped stuff jacket, a worsted prunella mantle, and a black silk gown. There were distinctions in the shape of the outer garments — mantles, jackets, and gowns. Hoods, aprons, and bands completed her comfortable attire.

Though so much of the clothing of the Virginia planters was made in England, there was certain work done by home tailors ; such work as repairs, alterations, making children's common clothing, and the like, also the clothing of upper servants. Often the tailor himself was a bond-servant. Thus, Luke Mathews, a tailor from Hereford, England, was bound to Thomas Landon for a term of two years from the day he landed. He was to have sixpence a day while working for the Landon family, but when working for other persons half of whatever he earned. In the Lancaster County records is a tailor's account (one Noah Rogers) from the year 1690 to 1709 ; it was paid, of course, in tobacco. We may set the tobacco as worth about twopence a pound. It will be thus seen from the following items that prices in Virginia were higher than in New England : —

Pounds

For making seven womens' Jacketts	70
For making a Coat for y^r Wife	60
For altering a Plush Britches.	20
For Y^r Wife & Daughturs Jackett	30
For y^r Britches	20
Coat	40
Y^r Boys Jacketts	20
Y^r Sons britches	25
Y^r Eldest Sons Ticking Suite	60
To making 1 Dimity Waistcoat, Serge suite 2 Cotton Waistcoats and y^r Dimity Coat	185
For a pr of buff Gloves	100
For 1 Neck Cloth	12
A pr of Stockings	120
A pr Callimmaneo britches	60

Another bill of the year 1643 reads : —

Pounds

To making a suit with buttons to it	80
1 ell canvas	30
for dimothy linings	30
for buttons & silke	50
for points	50
for taffeta	58
for belly pieces	40
for hooks & eies	10
for ribbonin for pockets	20
for stiffinin for a collar	10
	___
Sum	378

The extraordinary prices of one hundred and twenty pounds of tobacco for making a pair of stockings, and one hundred for a pair of gloves, when making a coat was but forty, must remain a seventeenth-century puzzle. This coat was probably a petticoat. It is curious, too, to find a tailor making gloves and stockings at any price. I think both buff gloves and stockings were of leather. Perhaps he charged thus broadly because it was " not in his line." Work in leather was always well paid. We find tailors making leather breeches and leather drawers ; the latter could not be the garments thus named to-day. Tailors became prosperous and well-to-do, perhaps because they worked in winter when other Virginia tradesfolk were idle ; and they acquired large tracts of land.

The conditions of settlement of Virginia were somewhat different from those of the planting of New England. We find the land of many Massachusetts towns wholly taken up by a group of settlers who emigrated together from the Old World and gathered into a town together in the New. It was like the transferal of a neighborhood. It brought about many happy results of mutual helpfulness and interdependence. From it arose that system of domestic service in which the children of friends rendered helpful duty in other households and were called help. Nothing of the kind existed in Virginia. There was far less neighborhood life. Plantations were isolated. Lines of demarcation in domestic service were much more definite where black life slaves and white bond-servants for a term of years performed all household service. For the daughter of one Virginia household to " help " in the work in another household was unknown. Each system had its benefits; each had its drawbacks. Neither has wholly survived; but something better has been evolved, in spite of our lamentations for the good old times.

Life is better ordered, but it is not so picturesque as when negro servants swarmed in the kitchen, and German, Scotch, and Irish redemptioners served in varied callings. There was vast variety of attire to be found on the Virginia and Maryland plantations and in the few towns of these colonies. The black slaves wore homespun cloths and homespun stuff, crocus and Virginia cloth; and the women were happy if they could crown their simple attire with gay turbans. Indians stalked up to the plantation doors, halted in silence, and added their gay dress of the wild woods. German sectaries and mystics fared on garbed in their simple peasant dress. Irish sturdy beggars idled and fiddled through existence, in dress of shabby gentility, with always a wig. " Wild-Irish " came in brogues and Irish trousers. Sailors and pirates came ashore gayly dressed in varied costume, with gay sashes full of pistols and cutlasses, swaggering from wharf to plantation. Queer details of dress had all these varied souls; some have lingered to puzzle us.

A year ago I had sent to me, by a descendant of an old Virginia family, a photograph of a curious gold medal or disk, a family relic which was evidently a token of some importance, since it bore tiny holes and had marks of having been affixed as an insignia. Though I could decipher the bold initials, cut in openwork, I could judge little by the colorless

photograph, and finally with due misgivings and
great precautions in careful packing, insurance, etc.,
the priceless family relic was intrusted to an express
company for transmission to my inspection. Glad
indeed was I that the owner had not presented it
in person ; for the decoration of honor, the insignia
of rank, the trophy of prowess in war or emblem of
conquest in love, was the pauper's badge of a Maryland or Virginia parish. It was not a pleasant task
to write back the mortifying news ; but I am proud
of the letter which I composed ; no one could have
done the deed better.

There was an old law in Virginia which ran thus : —

"Every person who shall receive relief from the parish
and be sent to the said alms-house, shall, upon the shoulder
of the right sleeve of his uppermost garment in an open and
visible manner, wear a badge with the name of the parish
to which he or she belongs, cut in red, blue or green cloth,
as the vestry or church wardens shall direct. And if any
poor person shall neglect or refuse to wear such badge, such
offense may be punished either by ordering his or her allowance to be abridged, suspended or withdrawn, or the offender
to be whipped not exceeding five lashes for one offense ;
and if any person not entitled to relief as aforesaid, shall
presume to wear such badge, he or she shall be whipped
for every such offense."

This law did not mean the full name of the parish,
but significant initials. Sometimes the initials "P P"
were employed, standing for public pauper. In
other counties a metal badge was ordered, often cast
in pewter. In one case a die-cutter was made by
which an oblong brass badge could be cut, and

stamps of letters to stamp the badges accompanied
it.   Sometimes these badges were three inches long.

The expression, " the badge of poverty," became
a literal one when all persons receiving parochial
relief had to wear a large Roman " P " with the initial
of their parish set on the right sleeve of the uppermost garment in an open and visible manner.   Likewise all pensioners were ordered to wear their badges
" so they may be seen."   A pauper who refused to
do this might be whipped and imprisoned for twenty-
one days.   Moreover, if the parish beadle neglected
to spy out that the badge was missing from some
poor pensioner, he had to pay half a crown himself.
This legality was necessitated by actions like that
of the English goody, who, when ordered to wear
this pauper's badge, demurely fastened it to her
flannel petticoat.   For this law, like all the early
Virginia statutes, was simply a transcript of English
laws.   In New York, for some years in the eighteenth century, the parish poor — there were no
paupers — were ordered to wear these badges.

This mode of stigmatizing offenders as well as
paupers was in force in the earlier days of all the
colonies.   Its existence in New England has been
immortalized in *The Scarlet Letter*.   I have given
in my book, *Curious Punishments of By-gone Days*,
many examples of the wearing of significant letters
by criminals in various New England towns, in
Plymouth, Salem, Taunton, Boston, Hartford, New
London, also in New York.   It offered a singular
and striking detail of costume to see William
Bacon in Boston, and Robert Coles in Roxbury,

wearing " hanged about their necks on their outerd
garment a D made of Ridd cloth sett on white."
A Boston woman wore a great " B," not for Boston,
but for blasphemy. John Davis wore a " V " for
viciousness. Others were forced to wear for years
a heavy cord around the neck, signifying that the
offender lived under the shadow of the gallows and
its rope.

But return we to the metal badge which has caused
this diversion to so gloomy a subject as crime and
punishment. It was simply an oblong plate about
three and one-half inches long, of humble metal —
pinchbeck, or alchemy — but plated heavily with gold,
therefore readily mistaken for solid gold ; upon it the
telltale initials " P P " had been stamped with a die,
while smaller letters read " St. J. Psh." These con-
firmed my immediate suspicions, for I had seen an
order of relief for a stricken wanderer — an order for
two weeks' relief, where the wardens of " St. J. Psh."
ordered the sheriff to send the pauper on — to make
him " move along " to some other parish. This gold
badge was not unlike the metal badges worn on the
left arm by " Bedlam beggars," the licensed beggars
of Bethlehem Hospital, the half-cured patients of
that asylum for lunatics.

The owner of this badge with ancient letters had
not idly accepted them, or jumped at the conclu-
sion that it was a decoration of honor for his ancestor. He had searched its history long, and he
had found in Hall's *Chronicles of the Pageants and
Progress of the English Kings* ample reference to
similar letters, but not as pauper's badges. Indeed,

like many another well-read and intelligent person, he had never heard of pauper's badges. He read:—

"In this garden was the King and five with him apparyelled in garments of purpull satyn, every edge garnished with frysed golde and every garment full of posyes made of letters of fine gold, of bullion as thick as might be. And six Ladyes wore rochettes rouled with crymosyn velvet and set with lettres like Carettes. And after the Kyng and his compaignions had daunsed, he appointed the Ladies, Gentlewomen, and Ambassadours to take the lettres off their garments in token of liberalyte. Which thing the common people perceiving, ranne to them and stripped them. And at this banket a shypman of London caught certayn lettres which he sould to a goldsmith for £3. 14s. 8d."

All this was pleasing to the vanity of our friend, who fancied his letters as having taken part in a like pageant; perhaps as a gift of the king himself. We must remember that he believed his badge of pure gold. He did not know it was a base metal, plated. He proudly pictured his forbears taking part in some kingly pageant. He scorned so modern and commonplace a possibility as a society like Knights of the Golden Horseshoe, which was formed of Virginian gentlefolk.

It plainly was a relic of some romance, and in the strangely picturesque events of the early years in this New World need not, though a pauper's badge, have been a badge of dishonor. What strange event or happening, or scene had it overlooked? Why had it been covered with its golden sheet? Was it in defiance or in satire, in remorse, or in revenge, or in humble and grateful recognition

of some strange and protecting Providence? We
shall never know. It was certainly not an agreeable
discovery, to think that your great-grandmother or
grandfather had probably been branded as a public
pauper; but there were strange exiles and strange
paupers in those days, exiles through political parties,
through the disfavor of kings, through religious
conviction, and the pauper of the golden badge, the
pauper of " St. J. Psh.," may have ended his days as
vestryman of that very church. Certain it was, that
no ordinary pauper would have, or could have, thus
preserved it; and from similar reverses and glorify-
ing equally base objects came the subjects of half
the crests of English heraldry.

The likeness of Pocahontas (facing this page)
is dated 1616. It is in the dress of a well-to-do
Englishwoman, a woman of importance and means.
This portrait has been a shock to many who idealized the Indian princess as " that sweet American
girl," as Thackeray called her. Especially is it
disagreeable in many of the common prints from
it. One flippant young friend, the wife of an army
officer, who had been stationed in the far West,
said of it, in disgust, remembering her frontier
residence, " With a man's hat on! just like every
old Indian squaw!" This hat is certainly displeasing, but it was not worn through Indian taste; it
was an English fashion, seen on women of wealth
as well as of the plainer sort. I have a score of
prints and photographs of English portraits, wherein
this mannish hat is shown. In the original of this
portrait of Pocahontas, the heavy, sombre effect is

Pocahontas.

much lightened by the gold hatband. These rich hatbands were one of the articles of dress prohibited as vain and extravagant by the Massachusetts magistrates. They were costly luxuries. We find them named and valued in many inventories in all the colonies, and John Pory, secretary of the Virginia colony, wrote about that time to a friend in England a sentence which has given, I think to all who read it, an exaggerated notion of the dress of Virginians : —

"Our cowekeeper here of James citty on Sundays goes accoutred all in ffreshe fflaminge silke, and a wife of one that had in England professed the blacke arte not of a Scholler but of a Collier weares her rough beaver hatt with a faire perle hatband, and a silken sute there to correspond."

Corroborative evidence of the richness and great cost of these hatbands is found in a letter of Susan Moseley to Governor Yardley of Virginia, telling of the exchange of a hatband and jewel for four young cows, one older cow and four oxen, on account of her "great want of cattle." She writes on "this Last July 1650, at Elizabeth River in Virginia" : —

"I had rayther your wife should weare them then any gentle woman I yet know in ye country; but good Sir have *no* scruple concerninge their rightnesse, for I went my selfe from Rotterdam to ye haugh (The Hague) to inquire of ye gould smiths and found y't they weare all Right, therefore thats without question, and for ye hat band y't alone coste five hundred gilders as my husband knows verry well and will tell you soe when he sees you; for ye Juell and

ye ringe they weare made for me at Rotterdam and I paid
in good rex dollars sixty gilders for ye Juell and fivety and
two gilders for ye ringe, which comes to in English monny
eleaven poundes fower shillings.   I have sent the sute and
Ringe by your servant, and I wish Mrs. Yeardley health
and prosperity to weare them in, and give you both thanks
for your kind token.   When my husband comes home we
will see to gett ye Cattell home, in ye meantime I present
my Love and service to your selfe & wife, and commit
you all to God, and remaine,

"Your friend and servant,
                "Susan Moseley."

The purchasing value of five hundred guilders,
the cost of the hatband, would be equal to-day to
nearly a thousand dollars.

In the portrait of Pocahontas in the original,
there is also much liveliness of color, a rich scarlet
with heavy braidings ; these all lessen somewhat the
forbidding presence of the stiff hat.   She carries a
fan of ostrich feathers, such as are depicted in portraits of Queen Elizabeth.

These feather fans had little looking-glasses of
silvered glass or polished steel set at the base of the
feathers.   Euphues says, " The glasses you carry
in fans of feathers show you to be lighter than
feathers ; the new-found glass chains that you wear
about your necks, argue you to be more brittle than
glass."

These fans were, in the queen's hands, as large
as hand fire-screens ; many were given to her as
New Year's gifts or other tokens, one by Sir Francis
Drake.   This makes me believe that they were a

fashion taken from the North American Indians and eagerly adopted in England; where, for two centuries, everything related to the red-men of the New World was seized upon with avidity — except their costume.

The hat worn by Pocahontas, or a lower crowned form of it, is seen in the Hollar drawing of Puritan women (facing page 96), where it seems specially ugly and ineffective, and on the Quaker Tub-preacher. It lingered for many years, perched on top of French hoods, close caps, kerchiefs, and other variety of head-gear worn by women of all ranks; never elegant, never becoming. I can think of no reason for its long existence and dominance save its costliness. It was not imitated, so it kept its place as long as the supply of beaver was ample. This hat was also durable. A good beaver hat was not for a year nor even for a generation. It lasted easily half a century. But we all know that the beaver disappeared suddenly from our forests; and as a sequence the beaver hat was no longer available for common wear. It still held its place as a splendid, feather-trimmed, rich article of dress, a hat for dress wear, and it was then comely and becoming. Within a few years, through national and state protection, the beaver, most interesting of wild creatures, has increased and multiplied in North America until it has become in certain localities a serious pest to lumbermen. We must revive the fashion of real beaver hats — that will speedily exterminate the race.

It always has seemed strange to me that, in the prodigious interest felt in England for the American

Indian, an interest shown in the thronging, gaping sight-seers that surrounded every taciturn red-man who visited the Old World, no fashions of ornament or dress were copied as gay, novel, or becoming. The Indian afforded startling detail to interest

Duchess of Buckingham and her Two Children.

the most jaded fashion-seeker. The *Works of Captain John Smith*, Strachey's *Historie of Travaile into Virginia*, the works of Roger Williams, of John Josselyn, the letters of various missionaries, give full accounts of their brilliant attire; and many of these works were illustrated. The beautiful mantles of the Virginia squaws, made of carefully dressed skins, were tastefully fringed and embroidered with tiny white beads and minute disks of copper, like spangles, which, with the buff of the dressed skin, made a charming color-study — copper and buff — picked out with white. Sometimes small brilliant shells or feathers were added to the fringes. An Indian princess, writes one chronicler, wore a fair white deer-skin with a frontal of white coral and pendants of "great but imperfect-colored and worse-drilled pearls" — our modern baroque pearls. A chain of linked copper encircled her neck; and her maid brought to her a mantle called a "puttawas" of glossy blue feathers sewed so thickly and evenly that it seemed like heavy purple satin.

A traveller wrote thus of an Indian squaw and brave : —

"His wife was very well favored, of medium stature and very bashful. She had on her back a long cloak of leather, with the fur side next to her body. About her forehead she had a band of white coral. In her ears she had bracelets of pearls hanging down to her waist. The rest of her women of the better sort had pendants of copper hanging in either ear, and some of the children of the King's brother and other noblemen, had five or six in either ear. He himself had upon his head a broad plate of gold or copper, for being unpolished we knew not which metal it might be, neither would he by any means suffer us to take it off his head. His apparel was like his wife's, only the women wear their hair long on both sides of the head, and the men on but one side. They are of color yellowish, and their hair black for the most part, and yet we saw children who had very fine auburn and chestnut colored hair."

John Josselyn wrote of tawny beauties : —

" They are girt about the middle with a Zone wrought
with Blue and White Beads into Pretty Works. Of these
Beads they have Bracelets for the Neck and Arms, and
Links to hang in their Ears, and a Fair Table curiously
made up with Beads Likewise to wear before their Breast.
Their Hair they combe backward, and tye it up short with
a Border about two Handsfull broad, wrought in works as
the Other with their Beads.

Powhatan's " Habit " still exists. It is in England, in the Tradescant Collection which formed
the nucleus of the Ashmolean Collection. It was
probably presented by Captain John Smith himself.
It is made of two deerskins ornamented with " roanoke " shell-work, about seven feet long by five feet
wide. Roanoke is akin to wampum, but this is made
of West Indian shells. The figures are circles, a
crude human figure and two mythical composite animals. He also wore fine mantles of raccoon skins.
A conjurer's dress was simply a girdle with a single
deerskin, while a great blackbird with outstretched
wings was fastened to one ear — a striking ornament.
I am always delighted to read such proof as this of
a fact that I have ever known, namely, that the
American Indian is the most accomplished, the
most telling *poseur* the world has ever known.
The ear of the Indian man and woman was pierced
along the entire outer edge and filled with long
drops, a fringe of coral, gold, and pearl. The wives
of Powhatan wore triple strings of great pearls close
around their throats, and a long string over one

shoulder, while their mantles were draped to show
their full handsome neck and arms. Altogether,
with their carefully dressed hair, they would have
made in full dress a fine show in a modern opera-
box, and, indeed, the Indian squaws did cause vast
exhibition of curiosity and delight when they visited
London and were taken sight-seeing and sight-seen.

As early as 1629 an Indian chief with his wife and
son came from Nova Scotia to England. Lord
Poulet paid them much attention in Somersetshire,
and Lady Poulet took Lady Squaw up to London
and gave her a necklace and a diamond, which I
suppose she wore with her blue and white beads.

Be the story of the saving of John Smith by
Pocahontas a myth or the truth, it forever lives a
beautiful and tender reality in the hearts of American children. Pocahontas was not the only Indian
squaw who played a kindly part in the first colonization of this country. There were many, though
their deeds and names are forgotten ; and there was
one Indian woman whose influence was much greater
and more prolonged than was that of Pocahontas,
and was haloed with many years of exciting adventure
as well as romance. Let me recount a few details
of her life, that you may wonder with me that the
only trace of Indian life marked indelibly on England was found on the swinging signs of inns known
by the name of " The Bell Savage," " La Belle Sau-
vage," and even " The Savage and Bell."

This second Indian squaw was a South Carolina
neighbor of our beloved Pocahontas ; she had not,
alas, the lovely disposition and noble character of

Powhatan's daughter. She was systematically and constitutionally mischievous, like a rogue elephant, so I call her a rogue squaw. Her name was Coosaponakasee. The name is too long and too hard to say with frequency, so we will do as did her English friends and foes — call her Mary. Indeed, she was baptized Mary, for she was a half-breed, and her white father had her reared like a Christian, had her educated like an English girl as far as could be done in the little primitive settlement of Ponpon, South Carolina. It will be shown that the attempt was not over-successful.

She was a princess, the niece of crafty old Brim, the king of two powerful tribes of Georgia Indians, the Creeks and Uchees. In 1715, when she was about fifteen years old, a fierce Indian war broke out in the early spring, and at the defeat of the Indians she promptly left her school and her church and went out into the wilds, a savage among savages, preferring defeat and a wild summer in the woods with her own people to decorous victory within doors with her fellow Christians.

The following year an Englishman, Colonel John Musgrove, accompanied by his son, went out as a mediator to the Creek Indians to secure their friendship, or at any rate their neutrality. The young squaw, Mary, served as interpreter, and the younger English pacificator promptly proved his amicable disposition by falling in love with her. He did what was more unusual, he married her; and soon they set up a large trading-house on the Savannah River, where they prospered beyond belief. On the arrival

A Woman's Doublet. Mrs. Anne Turner.

of the shipload of emigrants sent out by the Trustees of Georgia the English found Mary Musgrove and her husband already carrying on a large trade, in securing and transacting which she had served as interpreter. When Oglethorpe landed, he at once went to her, and asked permission to settle near her trading-station. She welcomed him, helped him, interpreted for him, and kept things in general running smoothly in the settlement between the English and the Indians. The two became close friends, and as long as generous but confiding Oglethorpe remained, all went well in the settlement; but in time he returned to England, giving her a handsome diamond ring in token of his esteem. Her husband died soon after and she removed to a new station called Mount Venture. Oglethorpe shortly wrote of her : —

" I find that there is the utmost endeavour by the Spaniards to destroy her because she is of consequence and in the King's interests ; therefor it is the business of the King's friends to support her ; besides which I shall always be desirous to serve her out of the friendship she has shown me as well as the colony."

In a letter of John Wesley's written to Lady Oglethorpe, and now preserved in the Georgia Historical Society, he refers frequently to Mary Musgrove, saying : —

" I had with me an interpreter the half-breed, Mary Musgrove, and daily had meetings for instruction and prayer. One woman was baptized. She was of them who came out of great tribulation, her husband and all her three chil-

dren having been drowned four days before in crossing the
Ogeechee River.   Her happiness in the gospel caused me
to feel that, like Job, the widow's heart had been caused to
sing for joy.   She was married again the day following her
baptism.   I suggested longer days of mourning.   She replied that her first husband was surely dead; and that his
successor was of much substance, owning a cornfield and
gun.   I doubt the interpreter Mary Musgrove, that she is
yet in the valley and shadow of darkness."

One can picture the excitement of the Choctaw
squaw to lose her husband and children, and to get
another husband and religion in a week's time.
Her reply that her husband " was surely dead "
bears a close resemblance to the hackneyed story of
the response to a charivari query of the Dutch
bridegroom who had been a widower but a week,
" Ain't my vife as deadt as she ever vill be? "

Her usefulness continued.   If a " talk " were had
with the Indians in Savannah, Fredonia, or any
other settlement, Mary had to be sent for; if
Indian warriors had to be hired, to keep an army
against the Spanish or marauding Indians, Mary
obtained them from her own people.   If land were
bought of the Indians, Mary made the trade.   She
soon married Captain Matthews, who had been sent
out with a small English troop to protect her trad-
ing-post; he also speedily died, leaving her free,
after alliances with trade and war, to find a third
husband in ecclesiastical circles, in the person of one
Chaplain Bosomworth, a parson of much pomposity
and ambition, and of liberal education without a liberal brain.   He had had a goodly grant of lands

to prompt and encourage him in his missionary
endeavors; and he was under the direction and protection of the Society for the Propagation of the Gospel. His mission was to convert the Indians, and he
began by marrying one; he then proceeded to break
the law by bringing in the first load of negro slaves
in that colony, a trade which was positively prohibited by the conditions and laws of the colony.
When his illegal traffic was stopped, he got his wife
to send in back claims to the colony of Georgia
for $25,000 as interpreter, mediator, agent, etc.,
for the English. She had already been paid
about a thousand dollars. This demand being
promptly refused, the hitherto pacific and friendly
Mary, edged on by that sorry specimen of a parson,
her husband, began a series of annoying and extraordinary capers. She declared herself empress of
Georgia, and after sending her half-brother, a full-
blooded Indian, as an advance-courier, she came
with a body of Indians to Savannah. The Rev.
Thomas Bosomworth, decked in full canonical robes,
headed the Indians by the side of his empress wife,
dressed in Indian costume; and an imposing procession they made, with plenty of theatrical color.
At first the desperate colonists thought of seizing
Mary and shipping her off to England to Oglethorpe, but this notion was abandoned. As the
English soldiers were very few at that special time,
and the Indian warriors many, we can well believe
that the colonists were well scared, the more so that
when the Indians were asked the reason of their
visit, " their answers were very trifling and very

dark." So a feast was offered them, but Mary and her brother refused to come and to eat; and the dinner was scarcely under way when more armed Indians appeared from all quarters in the streets, running up and down in an uproar, and the town was in great confusion. The alarm drums were beaten, and it was reported that the Indians had cut off the head of the president as they sat together at the feast. Every man in the colony turned out in full arms for duty, the women and children gathered in groups in their homes in unspeakable terror. Then the president and his assistants who had been at the dinner, and who had gone unarmed to show their friendly intent, did what they should have done in the beginning, seized that disreputable specimen of an English missionary, the Rev. Mr. Bosom-worth, and put him in prison; and we wonder they kept their hands off him as long as they did. Still trying to settle the matter without bloodshed, the president asked the Indian chiefs to adjourn to his house " to drink a glass of wine and talk the matter over." Into this conference came Mary, bereft of her husband, raging like a madwoman, threatening the lives of the magistrates, swearing she would annihilate the colony. "A fig for your general," screamed she, " you own not a foot of land in this colony. The whole earth is mine." Whereupon the Empress of Georgia, too, was placed under military guard.

Then a harassing week of apprehension ensued; the Indians were fed, and parleyed with, and reasoned with, and explained to. At last Mary's brother Malatche, at a conference, presented as a final demand a paper setting forth plainly the claims of the Indians. The sequel of this presentation is almost comic. The paper was so evidently the production of Bosomworth, and so wholly for his own personal benefit and not for that of the Indians, and the astonishment of the president and his council was so great at his vast and open assumption, that the Indians were bewildered in turn by the strange and unexpected manner of the white men upon reading the paper; and childishly begged to have the paper back again "to give to him who made it." A plain exposition of Bosomworth's greed and craft followed, and all seemed amicably explained and settled, and the Creeks offered to smoke the pipe of peace; when in came Mary, having escaped her guards, full of rum and of rancor. The president said to her in a low voice that unless she ceased brawling and quarrelling he would at once put her into close confinement; she turned in a rage to her brother, and translated the threat. He and every Indian in the room sprang to their feet, drew tomahawks, and for a short time a complete massacre was imminent. Then the captain of the guard, Captain Noble Jones, who had chafed under all this explaining diplomacy, lost his much-tried patience, and like a brave and fearless English soldier ordered the Indians to surrender arms. Though far greater in number than the English, they yielded to his intrepidity and wrath; and the following night and day they sneaked out of the town, as ordered, by twos and threes.

For one month this fright and commotion and expense had existed; and at last wholly alone were left the two contemptible malcontents and instigators of it all.   Mr. and Mrs. Bosomworth thereafter ate very humble pie; he begged sorely and cried tearfully to be forgiven; and he wailed so deeply and promised so broadly that at last the two were publicly pardoned.

Yet, after all, they had their own way; for they soon went to London and cut an infinitely fine figure there.   Mary was the top of the mode, and there Bosomworth managed to get for his wife lands and coin to the amount of about a hundred thousand dollars.

The prosperous twain returned to America in triumph, and built a curious and large house on an island they had acquired; in it the Empress did not long reign; at her death the Rev. Mr. Bosomworth married his chambermaid.

Such is the sorry tale of the Indian squaw and the English parson, a tale the more despicable because, though she had been reared in English ways, baptized in the English faith, had been the friend of English men and women, and married three English husbands; yet when fifty years old she returned at vicious suggestion with promptitude and fierceness to violent savage ways, to incite a massacre of her friends.   And that suggestion came not from her barbarian kin, but from an English gentleman — a Christian priest.

CHAPTER IV

A VAIN PURITAN GRANDMOTHER

" *Things farre-fetched and deare-bought are good for Ladies.*"
— " Arte of English Poesie," G. PUTTENHAM, 1589.

" *I honour a Woman that can honour herself with her Attire. A good Text deserves a Fair Margent.*"

— " The Simple Cobbler of Agawam," J. WARD, 1713.

CHAPTER IV

A VAIN PURITAN GRANDMOTHER

HERE was a certain family prominent in affairs in the seventeenth and eighteenth centuries, with members resident in England, New England, and the Barbadoes. They were gentlefolk — and gentle folk; they were of birth and breeding; and they were kindly, tender, affectionate to one another. They were given to much letter-writing, and better still to much letter-keeping. Knowing the quality of their letters, I cannot wonder at either habit; for the prevalence of the letter-keeping was due, I am sure, to the perfection of the writing. Their letters were ever lively in diction, direct and lucid in description, and widely varied in interest; therefore they were well worthy of preservation, simply for the owner's re-reading. They have proved so for all who have brushed the dust from the packages and deciphered the faded words. Moreover, these letters are among the few family letters of our two centuries which convey, either to the original reader or to his successor of to-day, anything that could, by most generous construction or fullest imagination, be deemed equivalent to what we now term News.

Of course their epistles contained many moral reflections and ample religious allusions and aspirations; and they even transcribed to each other, in full, long Biblical quotations with as much exactness and length as if each deemed his correspondent a benighted heathen, with no Bible to consult, instead of being an equally pious kinsman with a Bible in every room of his house.

Their name was Hall. The heads of the family in early colonial days were the merchants John Hall and Hugh Hall; these surnames have continued in the family till the present time, as has the cunning of hand and wit of brain in letter-writing, even into the seventh and eighth generation, as I can abundantly testify from my own private correspondence. I have quoted freely in several of my books from old family letters and business letter-books of the Hall family. Many of these letters have been intrusted to me from the family archives; others, especially the business letters, have found their way, through devious paths, to our several historical societies; where they have been lost in oblivion, hidden through churlishness, displayed in pride, or offered in helpfulness, as suited the various humors of their custodians. To the safe, wise, and generous guardianship of the American Antiquarian Society fell a collection of letters of the years 1663 to 1684, written from London by the merchant John Hall to his mother, Madam Rebekah Symonds, who, after a fourth matrimonial venture, — successful, as were all her marriages, — was living, in what must have seemed painful seclusion to any Londoner, in the struggling little New England hamlet of Ipswich, Massachusetts.

I wish to note as a light-giving fact in regard to these letters that the Halls were as happy in marrying as in letter-writing, and as assiduous. They married early; they married late. And by each marriage increased wonderfully either the number of descendants, or of influential family connections, who were often also business associates.

Madam Symonds had four excellent husbands, more than her share of good fortune. She married Henry Byley in 1636; John Hall in 1641; William Worcester in 1650; and Deputy Governor Symonds in 1663. She was, therefore, in 1664, scarcely more than a bride (if one may be so termed for the fourth time), when many costly garments were sent to her by her devoted and loving son, John Hall; she was then about forty-eight years of age. Her husband, Governor Symonds, was a gentle and noble old Puritan gentleman, a New Englishman of the best type; a Christian of missionary spirit who wrote that he "could go singing to his grave" if he felt sure that the poor benighted Indians were won to Christ. His stepson, John Hall, never failed in respectful and affectionate messages to him and sedately appropriate gifts, such as "men's knives." Governor Symonds had two sons and six married daughters by two — or three — previous marriages. He died in Boston in 1678.

A triangle of mutual helpfulness and prosperity was formed by England, New England, and the

A Puritan Dame.

Barbadoes in this widespread relationship of the Hall family in matrimony, business, kin, and friendly allies. England sent to the Barbadoes English trading - stuffs and judiciously cheap and attractive trinkets. The islands sent to New England sugar and molasses, and also the young children born in the islands, to be educated in Boston schools ere they went to English universities, or were presented in the English court and London society. There was one school in Boston established expressly for the children of the Barbadoes planters. You may read in a later chapter upon the dress of old-time children of some naughty grandchildren of John Hall who were sent to this Boston school and to the care of another oft-married grandmother. In this triangle, New England returned to the Barbadoes non-perishable and most lucrative rum and salt codfish — codfish for the many fast-days of the Roman Catholic Church ; New England rum to exchange with profit for slaves, coffee, and sugar. The Barbadoes and New England sent good, solid Spanish coin to England, both for investment and domestic purchases ; and England sent to New England what is of value to us in this book — the latest fashions.

When I ponder on the conditions of life in Ipswich at the time these letters were written — the few good houses, the small amount of tilled land, the entire lack of all the elegancies of social life ; when I think upon the proximity and ferocity of the Indian tribes and the ever present terror of their invasion ; when I picture the gloom, the dread, the oppression of the vast, close-lying, primeval forest, —then the rich articles of dress and elaborate explanation of the modes despatched by John Hall to his mother would seem more than incongruous, they would be ridiculous, did I not know what a factor dress was in public life in that day.

Poor Madam Symonds dreaded deeply lest The Plague be sent to her in her fine garments from London ; and her dutiful son wrote her to have no fear, that he bought her finery himself, in safe shops, from reliable dealers, and kept all for a month in his own home where none had been infected. But she must have had fear of disaster and death more intimately menacing to her home than was The Plague.

She had seen the career of genial Master Rowlandson, a neighbor's son, full of naughtiness, fun, and
life. While an undergraduate at Harvard College
he had written in doggerel what was termed pom-
pously a " scandalous libell," and he had pinned it
on the door of Ipswich Meeting-house, along with
the tax-collector's and road-mender's notices and
the announcement of intending marriages, and the
grinning wolves' heads brought for reward. For this
prank he had been soundly whipped by the college
president on the College Green ; but it did not prevent his graduating with honor at the head of his
class. He was valedictorian, class-orator, class-poet
— in fact, I may say that he had full honors. (I
have to add also that in his case honors were easy ;
for his class, of the year 1652, had but one graduate,
himself.) The gay, mischievous boy had become a
faithful, zealous, noble preacher to the Puritan church
in the neighboring town of Lancaster ; and in one
cruel night, in 1676, his home was destroyed, the
whole town made desolate, his parishioners slaugh-
tered, and his wife, Esther Rowlandson, carried off
by the savage red-men, from whom she was bravely
rescued by my far-off grandfather, John Hoar.
Read the thrilling story of her " captivation " and
rescue, and then think of Madam Symonds's finery
in her gilt trunk in the near-by town. For four years
the valley of the Nashua — blood-stained, fire-black-
ened — lay desolate and unsettled before Madam Symonds's eyes ; then settlers slowly crept in. But for
fifty years Ipswich was not deemed a safe home nor
free from dread of cruel Indians ; " Lovewell's War "

dragged on in 1726. But mantuas and masks, whisks and drolls, were just as eagerly sought by the governor's wife as if Esther Rowlandson's capture had been a dream.

There was a soured, abusive, intolerant old fellow in New England in the year 1700, a "vituperative epithetizer," ready to throw mud on everything around him (though not working — to my knowledge — in cleaning out any mud-holes). He was not abusive because he was a Puritan, but because "it was his nature to." He styled himself a "Simple Cobbler," and he announced himself "willing to Mend his Native Country, lamentably tattered both in the upper Leather and in the Sole, with all the Honest Stitches he can take," but he took out his aid in loud hammering of his lapstone and noisy protesting against all other footwear than his own. I fancy he thought himself another Stubbes. I know of no whole soles he set, nor any holes he mended, and his "Simple" ideas are so involved in expression, in such twisted sentences, and with such "strange Ink-pot termes" and so many Latin quotations and derivatives, that I doubt if many sensible folk knew what he meant, even in his own day. His words have none of the directness, the force, the interest that have the writings of old Stubbes. Such words as nugiperous, perquisquilian, ill-shapen-shotten, nudistertian, futulous, overturcased, quaematry, surquedryes, prodromie, would seem to apply ill to woman's attire; they really fall wide of the mark if intended as weapons, but it was to such vain dames as the governor's wife that the Simple Cobbler applied them. Some of the ministers of the colony, terrified by the Indian outbreaks, gloomily held the vanity and extravagance of dames and goodwives as responsible for them all. Others, with broader minds, could discern that both the open and the subtle influence of good clothes was needed in the new community. They gave an air of cheerfulness, of substance, of stability, which is of importance in any new venture. For the governor's wife to dress richly and in the best London modes added lustre to the governor's office. And when the excitement had quieted and the sullen Indian sachem and his tawny braves stalked through the little town in their gay, barbaric trappings, they were sensible that Madam Symonds's embroidered satin manteau was rich and costly, even if they did not know what we know, that it was the top of the mode.

Governor Symonds's home in Ipswich was on the ground where the old seminary building now stands ; but the happy married pair spent much of the time at his farm-house on Argilla Farm, on Heart-Break Hill, by Labor-in-vain Creek, which was also in Ipswich County. This lonely farm, so sad in name, was the only dwelling-place in that region ; it was so remote that when Indian assault was daily feared, the general court voted to station there a guard of soldiers at public expense because the governor was " so much in the country's service." He says distinctly, however, concerning the bargain in the purchase of Argilla Farm, that his wife was well content with it.

There were also intimate personal considerations which would apparently render so luxurious a ward-

Penelope Winslow.

robe unnecessary and unsuitable. The age and
health of the wearer might generally be held to be
sufficient reason for indifference to such costly, delicate, and gay finery. When Madam Symonds was
fifty-eight years old, in 1674, her son wrote, " Oh,
Good Mother, grieved am I to learn that Craziness
creeps upon you, yet am I glad that you have Faith
to look beyond this Life." Craziness had originally
no meaning of infirmity of mind ; it meant feeble-
ness, weakness of body. Her letters evidently in-
formed him of failing health, but even that did not
hinder the export of London finery.

Governor Symonds's estate at his death was under
£3000, and Argilla Farm was valued only at
£150 ; yet Madam had a " Manto " which is
marked distinctly in her son's own handwriting as
costing £30. She had money of her own, and estates in England, of which John Hall kept an account,
and with the income of which he made these purchases. This manteau was of flowered satin, and
had silver clasps and a rich pair of embroidered satin
sleeves to wear with it ; it was evidently like a sleeveless cape. We must always remember that seventeenth-century accounts must be multiplied by five
to give twentieth-century values. Even this valua-
tion is inadequate. Therefore the £30 paid for the
manteau would to-day be £150 ; $800 would nearly
represent the original value. As it was sent in early
autumn it was evidently a winter garment, and it
must have been furred with sable to be so costly.

In the early inventories of all the colonies " a pair
of sleeves " is a frequent item, and to my delight —

when so seldom color is given — I have more than
once a pair of green sleeves.

> " Thy gown was of the grassy green
>   Thy sleeves of satin hanging by,
> Which made thee be our harvest queen
>   And yet thou wouldst not love me.
>   Green sleeves was all my joy,
>   Green sleeves was my delight,
>   Green sleeves was my Heart of Gold,
>   And who but Lady Green-sleeves ! "

Let me recount some of " My Good Son's labors
of love and pride in London shops " for his vain
old mother. She had written in the year 1675 for
lawn whisks, but he is quick to respond that she has
made a very countrified mistake.

" Lawn whisks is not now worn either by Gentil or
simple, young or old.   Instead whereof I have bought a
shape and ruffles, what is now the ware of the bravest as
well as the young ones.   Such as goe not with naked neckes,
wear a black whisk over it.   Therefore I have not only
bought a plain one you sent for, but also a Lustre one, such
as are most in fashion."

John Hall's " lustre for whisks" was of course
lustring, or lutestring, a soft half-lustred pure silk
fabric which was worn constantly for two centuries.
He sent his mother many yards of it for her wear.

We have ample proof that these black whisks
were in general wear in England.   In an account-
book of Sarah Fell of Swarthmoor Hall in 1673,
are these items : " a black alamode whiske for Sister
Rachel ; a round whiske for Susanna ; a little black

whiske for myself." This English Quaker sends also a colored stuff manteo to her sister; scores of English inventories of women's wardrobes contain precisely similar items to those bought by Son Hall. And it is a tribute to the devotion of American women to the rigid laws of fashion, even in that early day, to find that all whisks, save black whisks and lustring ones, disappear at this date from colonial inventories of effects.

She wrote to him for a "side of plum colored leather" for her shoes. This was a matter of much concern to him, not at all because this leather was a bit gay or extravagant, or frail wear for an elderly grandmother, but because it was not the very latest thing in leather. He writes anxiously:—

"Secondly you sent for Damson-Coloured Spanish Leather for Womans Shoes. But there is noe Spanish Leather of that Colour; and Turkey Leather is coloured on the grain side only, both of which are out of use for Women's Shoes. Therefore I bought a Skin of Leather that is all the mode for Women's Shoes. All that I fear is, that it is too thick. But my Coz. Eppes told me yt such thin ones as are here generally used, would by rain and snow in N. England presently be rendered of noe service and therefore persuaded me to send this, which is stronger than ordinary. And if the Shoemaker fit it well, may not be uneasy."

Perhaps his anxious offices and advices in regard to fans show more curiously than other quotations, the insistent attitude of the New England mind in regard to the latest fashions. I cannot to-day conceive why any woman, young or old, could have

been at all concerned in Ipswich in 1675 as to which
sort of fan she carried, or what was carried in London, yet good Son John writes : —

" As to the feathered fan, I should also have found it in
my heart to let it alone, because none but very grave persons (and of them very few) use it.   That now 'tis grown
almost as obsolete as Russets and more rare to be seen than
a yellow Hood.   But the Thing being Civil and not very
dear, Remembering that in the years 64 and 68, if I mistake not, you had Two Fans sent, I have bought one now
on purpose for you, and I hope you will be pleased."

Evidently the screen-fan of Pocahontas's day was
no longer a novelty.   His mother had had far more
fans that he remembered.   In 1664 two " Tortis
shell fanns " had gone across seas ; one had cost five
shillings, the other ten shillings.   The following
year came a black feather fan with silver handle, and
two tortoise-shell fans ; in 1666 two more tortoise-
shell fans ; in 1688 another feather fan, and so on.
These many fans may have been disposed of as gifts
to others, but the entire trend of the son's letters, as
well as his express directions, would show that all
these articles were for his mother's personal use.
When finery was sent for madam's daughter, it was
so specified ; in 1675, when the daughter became a
bride, Brother John sent her her wedding gloves,
ever a gift of sentiment.   A pair of wedding gloves
of that date lies now before me.   They are mitts
rather than gloves, being fingerless.   They are of
white kid, and are twenty-two inches long.   They
are very wide at the top, and have three drawing-

strings with gilt tassels ; these are run in welts about two inches apart, and were evidently drawn into puffs above the elbow when worn. A full edging of white Swiss lace and a pretty design of dots made in gold thread on the back of the hand, form altogether a very costly, elegant, and decorative article of dress. I should fancy they cost several pounds. Men's gloves were equally rich. Here are the gold-fringed gloves of Governor Leverett worn in 1640.

Gold-fringed Gloves of Governor Leverett.

Of course the only head-gear of Madam Symonds for outdoor wear was a hood. Hats were falling in disfavor. I shall tell in a special chapter of the dominance at this date and the importance of the French hood. Its heavy black folds are shown in the portraits of Rebecca Rawson (facing page 66), of Madam Simeon Stoddard (facing page 76), and on other heads in this book. Such a hood probably covered Madam Symonds's head heavily and fully, whene'er she walked abroad; certainly it did when she rode a pillion-back. She had other fashionable hoods — all the fashionable hoods, in fact, that were worn in England at that time; hoods of lustring, of tiffany, of " bird's-eye " — precisely the same as had Madam Pepys, and one of spotted gauze, the last a pretty vanity for summer wear. We may remember, in fact, that Madam Symonds was a contemporary — across-seas — of Madam Pepys, and wore the same garments; only she apparently had richer and more varied garments than did that beautiful young woman whose husband was in the immediate employ of the king.

Arthur Abbott was the agent in Boston through whom this London finery and flummery was delivered to Madam Symonds in safety; and it is an amusing side-light upon social life in the colony to know that in 1675 Abbott's wife was " presented before the court " for wearing a silk hood above her station, and her husband paid the fine. Knowing womankind, and knowing the skill and cunning in needlework of women of that day, I cannot resist building up a little imaginative story around this " presentment " and fine. I believe that the pretty young woman could not put aside the fascination of all the beautiful London hoods consigned to her husband for the old lady at Ipswich; I suspect she tried all the finery on, and that she copied one hood for herself so successfully and with such telling effect that its air of high fashion at once caught the eye and met with the reproof of the severe Boston magistrates. She was the last woman, I believe, to be fined under the colonial sumptuary laws of Massachusetts.

The colors of Madam Symonds's garments were seldom given, but I doubt that they were " sad-coloured " or "grave of colour" as we find Governor Winthrop's orders for his wife.   One lustring hood was brown ; and frequently green ribbons were sent ; also many yards of scarlet and pink gauze, which seem the very essence of juvenility.   Her son writes a list of gifts to her and the members of her family from his own people : —

" A light violet-colored Petti-Coat is my wife's token to you.   The Petti-Coat was bought for my wife's mother and scarcely worn.   This my wife humbly presents to you, requesting your acceptance of it, for your own wearing, as being Grave and suitable for a Person of Quality."

Even a half-worn petticoat was a considerable gift ; for petticoats were both costly and of infinite needlework.   Even the wealthiest folk esteemed a gift of partly worn clothing, when materials were so rich.   Letters of deep gratitude were sent in thanks.

The variety of stuffs used in them was great. Some of these are wholly obsolete ; even the meaning of their names is lost.   In an inventory of 1644, of a citizen of Plymouth there was, for instance, " a petticoate of phillip & cheny " worth £1.   Much of the value of these petticoats was in the handwork bestowed upon them ; they were both embroidered and elaborately quilted.   About 1730, in the Van Cortlandt family, a woman was paid at one time £2 5s. for quilting, a large amount for that

Embroidered Petticoat Band.

day. Often we find items of fifteen or twenty
shillings for quilting a petticoat.

The handsomest petticoats were of quilted silk
or satin. No pattern was so elaborate, no amount
of work so large, that it could dismay the heart or
tire the fingers of an eighteenth-century needle-
woman. One yellow satin petticoat has a lining of
stout linen. These are quilted together in an exquisite irregular design of interlacing ribbons, slender vines, and long, narrow leaves, all stuffed with
white cord. Though the general effect of this
pattern is very regular, an examination shows it is
not a set design, but must have been drawn as well
as worked by the maker. Another petticoat has a

curious design made with two shades of blue silk
cord sewed on in a pattern.   Another of infinite
work has a design outlined in tiny rolls of satin.

These petticoats had many flat trimmings ; laces
of silver, gold, or silk thread were used, galloons and
orrice.   Tufts of fringed silk were dotted in clusters
and made into fly-fringe.   Bridget Neal, writing in
1685 to her sister, says : —

"I am told las is yused on petit-coats.   Three fringes
is much yused, but they are not set on the petcot strait,
but in waves ; it does not look well, unless all the fringes
yused that fashion is the plane twisted fring not very deep.
I hear some has nine fringes sett in this fashion."

Anxiety to please his honored mother, and desire
that she should be dressed in the top of the mode,
show in every letter of John Hall : —

"I bought your muffs of my Coz. Jno. Rolfe who tells
me they are worth more money than I gave for them.   You
desired yours Modish yet Long ; but here with us they are
now much shorter.   These were made a Purpose for you.
As to yr Silk Flowered Manto, I hope it may please you ;
Tis not the Mode to lyne you now at all ; but if you like
to have it soe, any silke will serve, and may be done at yr
pleasure."

In 1663 Pepys notes (with his customary delight
at a new fashion, mingled with fear that thereby he
might be led into more expense) that ladies at the
play put on " vizards which hid the whole face, and
had become a great fashion ; and *so* to the Exchange
to buy a Vizard for my wife."   Soon he added a

French mask, which led to some unpleasant encoun-
ters for Mrs. Pepys with dissolute courtiers on the
street. The plays in London were then so bold
and so bad that we cannot wonder at the masks
of the play-goers. The masks concealed constant
blushes; but wearers and hearers did not stay away,
for neither eyes nor ears were covered by the mask.
Busino tells of a woman at the theatre all in yellow
and scarlet, with two masks and three pairs of gloves,
worn one pair over the other. Suddenly out came
disappointing Queen Anne with her royal command that the plays be refined and reformed, and
then masks were abandoned.

Masks were in those years in constant wear in
the French court and society, as a protection to the
complexion when walking or riding. Sometimes
plain glass was fitted in the eye-holes. French
masks had wires which fastened behind the ears,
or a mouthpiece of silver; or they had an ingenious
and simple stay in the form of two strings at the
corners of the mouth-opening of the mask. These
strings ended in a silver button or glass bead.
With a bead held firmly in either corner of her
mouth, the mask-wearer could talk. These vizards
are seen in old English wood-cuts, often hanging
by the side, fastened to the belt with a small cord
or chain. They brought forth the bitter denuncia-
tions of the old Puritan Stubbes. He writes in
his *Anatomie of Abuses*: —

"When they vse to ride abroad, they haue visors made
of ueluet (or in my iudgment they may rather be called
inuisories) wherewith they couer all their faces, hauing

Blue Brocade Gown and Quilted Satin Petticoat.

holes made in them agaynst their eies, whereout they looke. So that if a man that knew not their guise before, shoulde chaunce to meete one of theme, he would thinke he mette a monster or a deuill; for face he can see none, but two broad holes against their eyes with glasses in them."

Masks were certainly worn to a considerable extent in America. As early as 1645, masks were forbidden in Plymouth, Massachusetts, "for improper purposes." When you think of the Plymouth of that year, its few houses and inhabitants, its desperate struggle to hold its place at all as a community, the narrow means of its citizens, the comparatively scant wardrobes of the wives and daughters, this restriction as to mask-wearing seems a grim jest. They were for sale in Salem and Boston, black velvet masks worth two shillings each; but these towns were more flourishing than Plymouth. And New York dames had them, and the planters' wives of Virginia and South Carolina.

I suppose Madam Symonds wore her mask when she mounted on a pillion behind some strong young lad, and rode out to Argilla Farm.

A few years later than the dates when Madam Symonds was ordering these fashionable articles of dress from England a rhyming catalogue of a lady's toilet was written by John Evelyn and entitled, *Mundus Muliebris or a Voyage to Mary-Land*; it might be a list of Madam Symonds's wardrobe. Some of the lines run : —

> " One gown of rich black silk, which odd is
> Without one coloured embroidered boddice.

Three manteaux, nor can Madam less
Provision have for due undress.
Of under-boddice three neat pair
Embroidered, and of shoes as fair ;
Short under petticoats, pure fine,
Some of Japan stuff, some of Chine,
With knee-high galoon bottomed ;
Another quilted white and red,
With a broad Flanders lace below.
Three night gowns of rich Indian stuff ;
Four cushion-cloths are scarce enough.
A manteau girdle, ruby buckle,
And brilliant diamond ring for knuckle.
Fans painted and perfumed three ;
Three muffs of ermine, sable, grey."

Other articles of personal and household comfort
were gathered in London shops by her dutiful son
and sent to Madam Symonds. The list is full of
interest, and helps to fill out the picture of daily
life. He despatched to her cloves, nutmegs, spices,
eringo roots, " coronation " and stock-gilly-flower
seed, " colly-flower seed," hearth brushes (these
came every year), silver whistles and several pomanders and pomander-beads, bouquet-glasses (which
could hardly have been the bosom bottles which
were worn later), necklaces, amber beads, many and
varied pins, needles, silk lacings, kid gloves, silver
ink-boxes, sealing-wax, gilt trunks, fancy boxes,
painted desks, tape, ferret, bobbin, bone lace, calico,
gimp, many yards of ducape, lustring, persian, and
other silk stuffs — all these items of transport show
the son's devoted selection of the articles his mother
wished. Gowns seem never to have been sent, but
manteaus, mantles, and " ferrandine " cloaks appear

frequently.   Of course there are some articles which
cannot be positively described to-day, such as the
" shape, with ruffles " and " double pleated drolls "
and " lace drolls " which appear several times on the
lists.   These " drolls " were, I believe, the " drowlas "
of Madame de Lange, in New Amsterdam.   " Men's
knives "   occasionally   were   sent,   and   " women's
knives " many times.   These latter had hafts of
ivory, agate, and " Ellotheropian."   This Ellotheropian or Alleteropeain or Illyteropian stone has been
ever a great puzzle to me until in another letter I
chanced to find the spelling Hellotyropian ; then I
knew the real word was the Heliotropium of the
ancients, our blood-stone.   It was a favorite stone
of the day not only for those fancy-handled knives,
but for seals, finger-rings and other forms of ornament.

A few books were on the list, — a Greek Lexicon
ordered as a gift for a student ; a very costly Bible,
bound in velvet, with silver clasps, the expense of
which was carefully detailed down to the Indian silk
for the inner-end leaves ; " *Dod on Commandments* —
my Ant Jane said you had a fancie for it, and I
have bound it in green plush for you."   Fancy any
one having a fancy for Dod on anything ! and fancy
Dod in green plush covers !

CHAPTER V

THE EVOLUTION OF COATS AND WAISTCOATS

This day the King began to put on his vest; and I did see several persons of the House of Lords and Commons too, great courtiers who are in it, being a long cassock close to the body, of long cloth, pinked with white silk under it, and a coat over it, and the legs ruffled with white ribbon like a pigeon's leg; and upon the whole I wish the King may keep it, for it is a very fine and handsome garment.

— "Diary," SAMUEL PEPYS, October 8, 1666.

Fashion then was counted a disease and horses died of it.

— "The Gulls Hornbook," ANDREW DEKKER, 1609.

CHAPTER V

OTH word and garment — coat — are of curious interest, one as a philological study, the other as an evolution. A singular transfer of meaning from cot or cote, a house and shelter, to the word coat, used for a garment, is duplicated in some degree, in chasuble, casule, and cassock; the words body, and bodice; and corse or corpse, and corselet and corset. The word coat, meaning a garment for men for covering the upper part of the body, has been in use for centuries; but of very changeable and confusing usage, for it also constantly meant petticoat. The garment itself was a puzzle, for many years; most bewildering of all the attire which was worn by the first colonists was the elusive, coatlike over-garment called in shipping-lists, tailors' orders, household inventories, and other legal and domestic records a doublet, a jerkin, a jacket, a cassock, a paltock, a coat, a horseman's coat, an upper-coat, and a buff-coat. All these garments resembled each other; all closed with a single row of buttons or points or hooks and eyes. There was not a double-breasted coat in the *Mayflower*, nor on any man in any of the colonies for many years;

they hadn't been invented.   Let me attempt to define these several coatlike garments.

In 1697 a jerkin was described by Randle Holme as "a kind of jacket or upper doublet, with four skirts or laps." These laps were made by slits up

A Plain Jerkin.

from the hem to the belt-line, and varied in number, but four on each side was a usual number, or there might be a slit up the back, and one on each hip, which would afford four laps in all. Mr. Knight, in his notes on Shakespere's use of the word, conjectures that the jerkin was generally worn over the doublet; but one guess is as good as another, and I guess it was not. I agree, however, with his surmise that the two garments were constantly confounded; in truth it is not a surmise, it is a fact. Shakespere expressed the situation when he said in *The Two Gentlemen of Verona*, " My jerkin is a doublet; " and I fancy there was slight difference in the garments, save that in the beginning the doublet was always of two thicknesses, as its name indicates ; and it was wadded.

As the jerkin was often minutely slashed, it could scarcely have been wadded ; though it may have had a lining for special display through the slashes.

A jerkin had no skirts in our modern sense of the word, — a piece set on at the waist-line, — nor could it on that account be what we term a coat, nor was it a coat, nor was it what the colonists deemed a coat.

The old Dutch word is *jurkken*, and it was often thus spelt, which has led some to deem it a Dutch name and article of dress. But then it was also spelt *irkin, ircken, jorken, jorgen, erkyn,* and *ergoin* — which are not Dutch nor any other tongue. Indeed, under the name *ergoin* I wonder that we recognize it or that it knew itself. A jerkin was often of leather like a buff-coat, but not always so.

Sir Richard Saltonstall wears a buff-coat, with handsome sword-belt, or trooping-belt, and rich gloves. His portrait faces page 18. As we look at his fine countenance we think of Hawthorne's words : —

" What dignitary is this crossing to greet the Governor. A stately personage in velvet cloak — with ample beard and a gold band across his breast. He has the authoritative port of one who has filled the highest civic position in the first of cities. Of all men in the world, we should least expect to meet the Lord Mayor of London — as Sir Richard Saltonstall has been once and again — in a forest-bordered settlement in the western wilderness."

A fine buff-coat and a buff-coat sleeve are given
in the chapter upon Armor.

All the early colonial inventories of wearing-ap-
parel contain doublets. Richard Sawyer died in
1648 in Windsor, Connecticut; he was a plain
average "Goodman Citizen." A part of his apparel was thus inventoried : —

		£	s.	d.
1 musck-colour'd cloth doublitt & breeches . .	1		
1 bucks leather doublitt		12	
1 calves leather doublitt		6	
1 liver-colour'd doublitt & jacket & breeches .		7	
1 haire-colour'd doublitt & jackett & breeches .		5	
1 paire canvas drawers		1	6
1 olde coate. 1 paire old gray breeches . .		5	
1 stuffe jackett		2	6

William Kempe of "Duxborrow," a settler of
importance, died in 1641. His wardrobe was
more varied, and ample and rich. He left two
buff-coats and leather doublets with silver buttons;
cloth doublets, three horsemen's coats, "frize jer-
kines," three cassocks, two cloaks.

Of course we turn to Stubbes to see what he can
say for or against doublets. His outcry here is
against their size; and those who know the "great
pease-cod-bellied doublets" of Elizabeth's day will
agree with him that they look as if a man were
wholly gone to "gourmandice and gluttonie."

Stubbes has a very good list of coats and jerkins
in which he gives incidentally an excellent description by which we may know a mandillion : —

A Doublet.

" Their coates and jerkins as they be diuers in colours so be they diuers in fashions; for some be made with collars, some without, some close to the body, some loose, which they call mandilians, couering the whole body down to the thigh, like bags or sacks, that were drawne ouer them, hiding the dimensions and lineaments of the body. Some are buttoned down the breast, some vnder the arme, and some down the backe, some with flaps over the brest, some without, some with great sleeves, some with small, some with none at all, some pleated and crested behind and curiously gathered and some not."

An old satirical print, dated 1644, gives drawings of men of all the new varieties of religious belief and practices which " pestered Christians " at the beginning of the century. With the exception of the Adamite, whose garb is that of Adam in the Garden of Eden, all ten wear doublets. These vary slightly, much less than in Stubbes's list of jerkins. One is open up the back with buttons and button-loops. Another has the " four laps on a side," showing it is a jerkin. Another is opened on the hips; one is slit at back and hips. All save one from neck to hem are buttoned in front with a single row of buttons, with no lapells, collar, or cuffs, and no " flaps," no ornaments or trimming. A linen shirt-cuff and a plain band finish sleeves and neck of all save the Arminian, who wears a small ruff. Not one of these doublets is a graceful or an elegant garment. All are shapeless and over-plain; and have none of the French smartness that came from the spreading coat-skirts of men's later wear. The welts or wings named in the early sumptuary laws were the pieces of cloth set at the shoulder over the arm-hole where body and sleeves meet. The welt was at first a sort of epaulet, but grew longer and often set out, thus deserving its title of wings.

A dress of the times is thus described : —

"His doublet was of a strange cut, the collar of it was up so high and sharp as it would cut his throat. His wings according to the fashion now were as little and diminutive as a Puritan's ruff."

A note to this says that "wings were lateral projections, extending from each shoulder" — a good round sentence that by itself really means nothing. Ben Jonson calls them "puff-wings."

There is one positive rule in the shape of doublets ; they were always welted at the arm-hole. Possibly the sleeves were sometimes sewn in, but even then there was always a cap, a welt or a hanging sleeve or some edging. In the illustrations of the *Roxburghe Ballads* there is not a doublet or jerkin on man, woman, or child but is thus welted. Some trimming around the arm-hole was a law. This lasted until the coat was wholly evolved. This had sleeves, and the shoulder-welt vanished.

These welts were often turreted or cut in squares. You will note this turreted shoulder in some form on nearly all the doublets given in the portraits displayed in this book — both on men and women. For doublets were also worn by women. Stubbes says, "Though this be a kind of attire proper only to a man, yet they blush not to wear it." The old

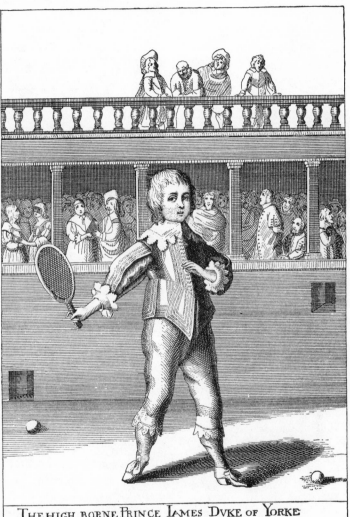

THE HIGH BORNE PRINCE IAMES DVKE OF YORKE
borne October = the 13.1633

print of the infamous Mrs. Turner given facing page
130 shows her in a doublet.

Another author complains : —

"If Men get up French standing collars Women will
have the French standing collar too : if Dublets with little
thick skirts, so short none are able to sit upon them, women's
foreparts are thick skirted too."

Children also had doublets and this same shoulder-
cap at the arm-hole; their little doublets were made
precisely like those of their parents. Look at the
childish portrait of Lady Arabella Stuart, the portrait with the doll.   Her fat little figure is squeezed
in a doublet which has turreted welts like those worn
by Anne Boleyn and by Pocahontas (facing page
122). Often a button was set between each square
of the welt, and the sleeve loops or points could be
tied to these buttons and thus hold up the detached
undersleeves. The portrait of Sir Richard Saltonstall vaguely shows these buttons.   Nearly all these
garments — jerkins, jackets, doublets, buff-coats, pal-
tocks, were sleeveless, especially when worn as the
uppermost or outer garment. Holinshed tells of
"doublets full of jagges and cuts and sleeves of
sundry colours."   These welts were "embroidered,
indented, waved, furred, chisel-punched, dagged,"
as well as turreted. On one sleeve the turreted
welt varied, the middle square or turret was long,
the others each two inches shorter. Thus the
sleeve-welt had a "crow-step" shape. A charming doublet sleeve of Elizabeth's day displayed a
short hanging sleeve that was scarce more than a

hanging welt.   This was edged around with crystal balls or buttons.   Other welts were scalloped, with an eyelet-hole in each scallop, like the edge of old ladies' flannel petticoats.   Othersome welts were a round stuffed roll.   This roll also had its day around the petticoat edge, as may be seen in the petticoat of the child Henry Gibbes.   This roll still appears on Japanese kimonos.

We are constantly finding complaints of the unsuitably ambitious attire of laboring folk in such sentences as this: —

> "The plowman, in times past content in russet, must now-a-daies have his doublett of the fashion with wide cuts; his fine garters of Granada, to meet his Sis on Sunday.   The fair one in russet frock and mockaldo sleeves now sells a cow against Easter to buy her silken gear."

Velvet jerkins and damask doublets were for men of dignity and estate.   Governor Winthrop had two tufted velvet jerkins.

Jerkins and doublets varied much in shape and detail: —

> "These doublets were this day short-waisted, anon, long-bellied; by-and-by-after great-buttoned, straight-after plain-laced, or else your buttons as strange for smallness as were before for bigness."

In Charles II's time at the May-pole dances still appear the old, welted doublets.   Jack may have worn Cicily's doublet, and Peg may have borrowed Will's for all the difference that can be seen.   The man's doublet did not ever have long, hanging

An Embroidered Jerkin.

sleeves, however, in the seventeenth century, while women wore such sleeves.

Sometimes the sleeves were very large, as in the Bowdoin portrait (facing page 198). The great puffs were held out by whalebones and rolls of cotton, and " tiring-sleeves" of wires, a fashion which has obtained for women at least seven times in the history of English costume. Gosson describes the vast sleeves of English doublets thus : —

" This Cloth of Price all cut in ragges,
    These monstrous bones that compass arms,
  These buttons, pinches, fringes, jagges,
    With them he (the Devil) weaveth woeful harms."

We have seen how bitterly the slashing of good
cloth exercised good men. The " cutting in rags "
was slashing.

A favorite pattern of slashing is in small, narrow
slits as shown in the portrait on page 225 of James
Douglas. These jerkins are of leather, and the slashes
are of course ornamental, and are also for health and
comfort, as those know who wear chamois jackets
with perforated holes throughout them, or slashes if
we choose to call them so. They permit a circula-
tion of the skin and a natural condition. These jerkins are slashed in curious little cuts, " carved of
very good intail," as was said of King Henry's jerkin, which means, in modern English, cut in very
good designs. And I presume, being of buff leather,
the slashes were simply cut, not overcast or embroidered as were some wool stuffs.

The guard was literally a guard to the seam, a
strip of galloon, silk, lace, velvet, put on over the
seam to protect and strengthen it.

The large openings or slashes were called panes.
Fynes Mayson says, " Lord Mountjoy wore jerkins
and round hose with laced panes of russet cloth."
The Swiss dress was painted by Coryat as doublet
and hose of panes intermingled of red and yellow,
trimmed with long puffs of blue and yellow rising up
between the panes. It was necessarily a costly dress.

Of course this is the same word with the same meaning as when used in the term a " pane of glass."

The word " pinches " refers to an elaborate pleating which was worn for years ; it lingered in America till 1750, and we have revived it in what we term " accordion pleating." The seventeenth-century pinching was usually applied to lawn or some washable stuff; and there must have been a pinching, a goffering machine by which the pinching was done to the washed garment by means of a heated iron.

John Lilburne.

Pinched sleeves, pinched partlets, pinched shirts, pinched wimples, pinched ruffs, are often referred to, all washable garments. The good wife of Bath wore a wimple which was " y-pinched full seemly." Henry VIII wore a pinched habit-shirt of finest lawn, and his fine, healthy skin glowed pink through the folds of the lawn after his hearty exercise at tennis and all kinds of athletic sports, for which he had thrown off his doublet. We are taught to deem him "a spot of grease and blood on England's page." There was more muscle than fat in him ; he could not be restrained from constant, violent, dangerous exercise ; this was one of the causes of the admiration of his subjects.

The pinched partlet made a fine undergarment for the slashed doublet.

So full, so close, were these " pinchings," that one author complained that men wearing them could not draw their bowstrings well. It was said that the " pinched partlet and puffed sleeves" of a courtier would easily make a lad a doublet and cloak.

In my chapter on Children's Dress I tell of the pinched shirt worn by Governor Bradford when an infant, and give an illustration of it.

Aglets or tags were a pretty fashion revived for women's wear three years ago. Under Stuart reign, these aglets were of gold or silver, and set with precious stones such as pear-shaped pearls. For ordinary wear they were of metal, silk, or leather. They secured from untwisting or ravelling the points which were worn for over a century ; these were ties or laces of ribbon, or woollen yarn or leather, decorated with tags or aglets at one end. Points were often home-woven, and were deemed a pretty gift to a friend. They were employed instead of buttons in securing clothes, and were used by the earliest settlers, chiefly, I think, as ornaments at the knee or for holding up the stockings in the place of garters. They were regarded as but foolish vanities, and were one of the articles of finery tabooed in early sumptuary laws. In 1651 the general court of Massachusetts expressed its " utter detestation and dislike that men of meane condition, education and calling should take upon them the garbe of

gentlemen by the wearinge of poynts at the knees."
Fashion was more powerful than law; the richly
trimmed, sashlike garters quickly displaced the
modest points.

The Earl of Southampton, friend of Shakespere
and of Virginia, as pictured on a later page, wears
a doublet with agletted points around his belt,
by which breeches and doublet are tied together.
This is a striking portrait. The face is very noble.
A similar belt was the favorite wear of Charles I.

Martin Frobisher, the hero of the Armada, wears
a jerkin fastened down the front with buttons and
aigletted points. (See page 164.) I suppose, when
the fronts of the jerkin were thoroughly joined, each
button had a point twisted or tied around it. Frobisher's lawn ruff is a modest and becoming one.
This portrait in the original is full length. The remainder of the costume is very plain; it has no
garters, no knee-points, no ribbons, no shoe-roses.
The foot-covering is Turkish slippers precisely like
the Oriental slippers which are imported to-day.

The Earl of Morton (page 225) wore a jerkin of
buff leather curiously pinked and slashed. Fulke
Greville's doublet (page 223) has a singular puff
around the waist, like a farthingale. Facing page
166 is shown a doublet of the commonest form;
this is worn by Edward Courtenay, Earl of Devon-
shire. The portrait is painted by Sir Antonio More
— the portrait of one artist by another, and a very
fine one, too.

Another garment, which is constantly named in
lists of clothing, was the cassock. Steevens says a

cassock "signifies a horseman's loose coat, and is used in that sense by the writers of the age of Shakespere." It was apparently a garment much like a doublet or jerkin, and the names were used interchangeably. I think the cassock was longer than the doublet, and without "laps." The straight, long coats shown on the gentlemen in the picture facing page 188 were cassocks. The name finally became applied only to the coat or gown of the clergy. In the will of Robert Saltonstall, made in 1650, he names a " Plush Cassock," but cloth cassocks were the commonest wear.

There were other names for the doublet which are now difficult to place precisely. In the reign of Henry VIII a law was passed as to men's wear of velvet in their sleeveless cotes, jackets, and jupes. This word jupe and its ally jupon were more frequently heard in women's lists ; but jump, a derivative, was man's wear. Randle Holme said : " A jump extendeth to the thighs ; is open and buttoned before, and may have a slit half way behind." It might be with or without sleeves — all this being likewise true of the doublet. From this jump descended the modern jumper and the eighteenth century jumps — what Dr. Johnson defined in one of his delightsome struggles with the names of women's attire, " Jumps : a kind of loose or limber stays worn by sickly ladies."

Coats were not furnished to the Massachusetts or Plymouth planters, but those of Piscataquay in New Hampshire had "lined coats," which were simply doublets like all the rest.

Colonel William Legge.

In 1633 we find that Governor Winthrop had several dozen scarlet coats sent from England to "the Bay." The consigner wrote, "I could not

find any Bridgwater cloth but Red; so all the coats
sent are red lined with blew, and lace suitable;
which red is the choise color of all." These coats
of double thickness were evidently doublets.

The word "coat" in the earliest lists must often
refer to a waistcoat. I infer this from the small cost
of the garments, the small amount of stuff it took to
make them, and because they were worn with "Vper
coats" — upper coats. Raccoon-skin and deerskin
coats were many; these were likewise waistcoats,
and the first lace coats were also waistcoats. Robert
Keayne of Boston had costly lace coats in 1640,
which he wore with doublets — these likewise were
waistcoats.

As years go on, the use of the word becomes constant. There were "moose-coats" of mooseskin.
Josselyn says mooseskin made excellent coats for
martial men. Then come papous coats and pappous coats. These I inferred — since they were
used in Indian trading — were for pappooses' wear,
pappoose being the Indian word for child. But
I had a painful shock in finding in the *Traders'
Table of Values* that "3 Pappous Skins equal 1
Beaver" — so I must not believe that pappoose
here means Indian baby. Match-coats were originally of skins dressed with the fur on, shaped in a
coat like the hunting-shirt. The "Duffield Match-
coat" was made of duffels, a woollen stuff, in the
same shape. Duffels was called match-cloth. The
word "coat" here is not really an English word; it
is matchigode, the Chippewa Indian name for this
garment.

We have in old-time letters and accounts occasional proof that the coat of the Puritan fathers was not at all like the shapely coat of our day. We have also many words to prove that the coat was a doublet which, as old Stubbes said, could be "pleated, or crested behind and curiously gathered."

The tailor of the Winthrop family was one John Smith; he made garments for them all, father, mother, children, and children's wives, and husband's sisters, nieces, cousins, and aunts. He was a good Puritan, and seems to have been much esteemed by Winthrop. One letter accompanying a coat runs: "Good Mr. Winthrop, I have, by Mr. Downing's direction sent you a coat, a sad foulding colour without lace. For the fittness I am a little vncerteyne, but if it be too bigg or too little it is esie to amend, vnder the arme

to take in or let out the lyning; the outside may
be let out in the gathering or taken in also without any prejudice." This instruction would appear
to prove not only that the coat was a doublet, "curiously gathered," but that the "fittness" was more
than "uncerteyne" of the coats of the Fathers.
Since even such wildly broad directions could not
"prejudice" the coat, we may assume that Governor
Winthrop was more easily suited as to the cut of
his apparel, than would have been Sir Walter
Raleigh or Sir Philip Sidney.

Though Puritan influence on dress simplified
much of the flippery and finery of the days of
Elizabeth and James, and the refining elegance of
Van Dyck gave additional simplicity as well as
beauty to women's attire, which it retained for many
years, still there lingered throughout the seventeenth century, ready to spring into fresh life at a
breath of encouragement, many grotesqueries of
fashion in men's dress which, in the picturesque
sneer of the day, were deemed meet only for "a
changeable-silk-gallant." At the restoration of
the crown, courtiers seemed to love to flaunt frivol-
ity in the faces of the Puritans.

One of these trumperies came through the excessive use of ribbons, a use which gave much
charm to women's dress, but which ever gave to
men's garments a finicky look. Beribboned doublets came in the butterfly period, between worm
and chrysalis, between doublet and coat; beribboned breeches were eagerly adopted.

On page 179 is the copy of an old print, which

shows the dress of an estimable and sensible gentleman, Sir Thomas Orchard, with ribbon-edged garments and much galloon or laces.   It is far too
much trimmed to be rich or elegant.   See also
The English Antick
on this page, from
a rare broadside.
His tall hat is be-
ribboned and be-
feathered; his face
is patched, ribbons
knot his love-locks,
his breeches are
edged with agletted
ribbons, and "on
either side are two
great bunches of
ribbons of several
colors." Similar
knots are at wrists
and belt. His boots
are fringed with
lace, and so wide
that he "straddled
as he went along
singing."

The English Antick.

Ribboned sleeves like those of Colonel Legge,
page 177, were a pretty fashion, but more suited to
women's wear than to men's.

George Fox, the founder of Quakerism, tells
us what he thought of such attire. He wrote
satirically : —

"If one have store of ribands hanging about his waist or his knees and in his hat; of divers colours red, white black or yellow, O! then he is a brave man. He hath ribands on his back, belly and knees, and his hair powdered, this is the array of the world. Are not these that have got ribands hanging about their arms, hands, back, waist, knees, hats, like fiddlers' boys? And further if one get a pair of breeches like a coat and hang them about with points, and tied up almost to the middle, a pair of double cuffs on his hands, and a feather in his cap, here is a gentleman!"

These beribboned garments were a French mode. The breeches were the "rhingraves" of the French court, which were breeches made wholly of loops of ribbons — like two ribboned petticoats. They caught the eye of seafaring men; we know that Jack ashore loves finery. We are told of sea-captains wearing beribboned breeches as they came into quiet little American ports, and of one English gallant landing from a ship in sober Boston, wearing breeches made wholly from waist to knee of over-lapping loops of gay varicolored ribbon. It is recorded that "the boys did wonder and call out thereat," and they "were chided therefor." It is easy to picture the scene: the staring boys, born in Boston, of Puritan parents, of dignified dress, and more familiar with fringes on the garments of savage Indians than on the breeches of English gentlemen; we can see the soberly reproving minister or schoolmaster looking with equal disapproval on the foppish visitor and the mannerless boys; and the gayly dressed ship's captain, armed with self-satisfaction and masculine vanity, swaggering along the narrow streets of the little town. It mattered not what he wore or what he did, a seafaring man was welcome. I wonder what the governor thought of those beribboned breeches! Perhaps he ordered a pair from London for himself, — of sad-colored ribbons, — offering the color as a compromise for the over-gayety of the ribbons. Randle Holme gave in 1658 three descriptions of the first petticoat-breeches, with drawings of each. One had the lining lower than the breeches, and tied in about the knees; ribbons extended halfway up the breeches, and ribbons hung out from the doublet all about the waist-band. The second had a single row of pointed ribbons hanging all around the lower edge of the breeches; these were worn with stirrup-hose two yards wide at the top, tied by points and eyelet-holes to the breeches. The third had stirrup-hose tied to the breeches, and another pair of hose over them turned down at the calf of the leg, and the ribbons edged the stirrup-hose. His drawings of them are foolish things — not even pretty. He says ribbons were worn first at the knees, then at the waist at the doublet edge, then around the neck, then on the wrists and sleeves. These knee-ribbons formed what Dryden called in 1674 "a dangling knee-fringe." It is difficult for me to think of Dryden living at that period of history. He seems to me infinitely modern in comparison with it. Evelyn describes the wearer of such a suit as "a fine silken thing"; and tells that the ribbons were of " well-chosen colours of red, orange, and blew, of well-gummed satin, which augured a happy fancy."

In 1672 a suit of men's clothes was made for the beautiful Duchess of Portsmouth to wear to a masquerade; this was with "Rhingrave breeches and cannons." The suit was of dove-colored silk brocade trimmed with scarlet and silver lace and ribbons.

The ten yards of brocade for this beautiful suit cost £14. The Rhingrave breeches were trimmed with thirty-six yards of figured scarlet ribbon and thirty-six yards of plain satin ribbon and thirty-six of scarlet taffeta ribbon; this made one hundred and eight yards of ribbon — a great amount — an unusable amount. I fear the tailor was not honest. There were also as trimmings twenty-two yards of scarlet and silver vellum lace for guards; six dozen scarlet and silver vellum buttons, smaller breast buttons, narrow laces for the waistcoat, and silver twist for buttonholes. The suit was lined with lutestring. There was a black beaver hat with scarlet and silver edging, and lace embroidered scarlet stockings, a rich belt and lace garters, and point lace ruffles for the neck, sleeves, and knees. This suit had an interlining of scarlet camlet; and lutestring drawers seamed with scarlet and silver lace. The total bill of £59 would be represented to-day by $1400, — a goodly sum, — but it was a goodly suit. There is a portrait of the Duchess of Richmond in a similar suit, now at Buckingham Palace. Portraits of the Duke of Bedford, and of George I, painted by Kneller, are almost equally beribboned. The one of the king is given facing this page to show his ribbons and also the extraordinary shoes, which were fashionable at this date.

"Indians gowns," or banyans, were for a century

George I.

worn in England and America, and are of enough importance to receive a separate chapter in this book. The graceful folds allured all men and all portrait painters, just as the fashionable new china allured all women. The banyan was not the only Oriental garment which had become of interest to Englishmen. John Evelyn described in his *Tyrannus or the Mode* the "comeliness and usefulnesse" of all Persian clothing; and he noted with justifiable gratification that the new attire which had recently been adopted by King Charles II was "a comely dress after ye Persian mode." He says modestly, "I do not impute to this my discourse the change which soone happen'd; but it was an identity I could not but take notice of."

Rugge in his *Diurnal* describes the novel dress which was assumed by King Charles and the whole court, due notice of a subject of so much importance having been given to the council the previous month ; and notice of the king's determination "never to change it," which he kept like many another of his promises and resolutions.

"It is a close coat of cloth pinkt with a white taffety under the cutts. This in length reached the calf of the leg; and upon that a sercoat cutt at the breast, which hung loose and shorter than the vest six inches. The breeches the Spanish cutt; and buskins some of cloth, some of leather but of the same colour as the vest or garment; of never the like garment since William the Conqueror."

Pepys we have seen further explained that it was all black and white, the black cassock being close to

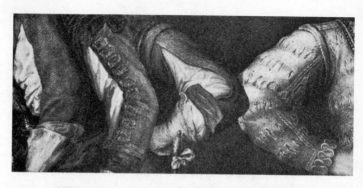

Three Cassock Sleeves and a Buff-coat Sleeve.

the body. "The legs ruffled with black ribands like
a pigeon's leg, and I wish the King may keep it
for it is a fine and handsome garment." The news
which came to the English court a month later that
the king of France had put all his footmen and servants in this same dress as a livery made Pepys
"mightie merry, it being an ingenious kind of
affront, and yet makes me angry," which is as curious a frame of mind as even curious Pepys could
record. Planché doubts this act of the king of
France; but in *The Character of a Trimmer* the story
is told *in extenso* — that the "vests were put on at
first by the King to make Englishmen look unlike
Frenchmen; but at the first laughing at it all ran
back to the dress of French gentlemen." The
king had already taken out the white linings as
"'tis like a magpie;" and was glad to quit it I do
not doubt. Dr. Holmes — and the rest of us —
have looked askance at the word "vest" as allied in
usage to that unutterable contraction, pants. But

here we find that vest is a more classic name than waistcoat for this dull garment — a garment with too little form or significance to be elegant or interesting or attractive.

Though this dress was adopted by the whole court, and though it was an age of portrait paint-

Henry Bennet, Earl of Arlington.

ing, — and surely no more delicate flattery to the king's taste could be given than to have one's portrait painted in the king's chosen vestments, — yet but one portrait remains which is stated to display this dress. This is the portrait of Henry Bennet, Earl of Arlington — it is shown on this page.   This

was painted by the king's own painter, Sir Peter
Lely. I must say that I cannot find much resemblance to Pepys's or Rugge's description, unless the
word "pinked" means cut out in an all-over pattern
like Italian cut-work ; then this inner vest might be
of "cloth pinkt with a white taffeta under the coat."
The surcoat is of black lined with white. Of course
the sash is present, but not in any way distinctive.
It was a characteristic act in the Earl to be painted
in this dress, for he was a courtier of courtiers,
perhaps the most rigid follower of court rules in
England. He was "by nature of a pleasant and
agreeable humour," but after a diplomatic journey
on the continent he assumed an absurd formality of
manner which was much ridiculed by his contemporaries. His letters show him to be exceeding nice
in his phraseology ; and he prided himself upon
being the best-bred man in court. He was a trimmer, "the chief trickster of the court," a member of
the Cabal, the first *a* in the word ; and he was heartily
hated as well as ridiculed. When a young man he
received a cut on the nose in a skirmish in Ireland ;
he never let his prowess be forgotten, but ever after
wore a black patch over the scar — it may be seen
in his portrait. When his fellow courtiers wished to
gibe at him, they stuck black patches on their noses
and with long white staves strutted around the court
in imitation of his pompous manner. He is a handsome fellow, but too fat — which was not a curse
of his day as of the present.

Of course the king changed his dress many times
after this solemn assumption of a lifelong garment,

Figures from Funeral Procession of the Duke of Albemarle, 1670.

It was a restless, uncertain, trying time in men's dress.   They had lost the doublet, and had not found the skirted coat, and stood like the Englishman of Andrew Borde — ready to take a covering from any nation of the earth.   I wonder the coat ever survived — that it did is proof of an inherent worth.   Knowing the nature of mankind and the modes, the surprise really is that the descendants of Charles and all English folk are not now wearing shawls or peplums or anything save a coat and waistcoat.

Some of the sturdy rich members of the governors' cabinets and the assemblies and some of our American officers who had been in his Majesty's army, or had served a term in the provincial militia, and had had a hot skirmish or two with marauding Indians on the Connecticut River frontier, and some very worthy American gentlemen who were not widely renowned either in military or diplomatic circles and had never worn armor save in the artist's studio, — these were all painted by Sir Godfrey Kneller and by Sir Peter Lely, and by lesser lights in art, dressed in a steel corselet of the artist, and wearing their own good Flanders necktie and their own full well-buckled wig.   There were some brave soldiers, too, who were thus painted, but there were far more in armor than had ever smelt smoke of powder.   It was a good comfortable fashion for the busy artist.   It must have been much easier when you had painted a certain corselet a hundred times to paint it again than to have to paint all kinds of new colors and stuffs. And the portrait in armor was almost always kitcat, and that disposed of the legs, ever a nuisance in portrait-painting.

While the virago-sleeves were growing more and more ornamental, and engageants were being more and more worn by women, men's sleeves assumed a most interesting form. The long coat, or cassock, had sleeves which were cut off at the elbow with great cuffs and were worn over enormous ruffled undersleeves; and they were even cut midway between shoulder and elbow, were slashed and pointed and beribboned to a wonderful degree. This lasted but a few years, the years when the cassock was shaping itself definitely into a skirted coat. Perhaps the height of ornamentation in sleeves was in the closing years of the reign of Charles II, though fancy sleeves lingered till the time of George I.

In an account of the funeral of George Monck, the Duke of Albemarle, in the year 1670, the dress is very carefully drawn of those who walked in the procession. (Some of them are given facing page 188.) It may be noted, first, that all the hats are lower crowned and straight crowned, not like a cone or a truncated cone, as crowns had been. The *Poor Men* are in robes with beards and flowing natural hair; they wear square bands, and carry staves. The *Clergymen* wear trailing surplices; but these are over a sort of cassock and breeches, and they all have high-heeled shoes with great roses. They also have their own hair. The *Doctors of Physic* are dressed like the *Gentlemen and Earls*, save that they wear a rich robe with bands at the upper arm, over the other fine dress. The gentlemen wear a cassock, or coat,

Earl of Southampton.

which reaches to the knee; the pockets are nearly as low as the knee. These cassocks have lapels from neck to hem, with a long row of gold buttons which are wholly for ornament, the cassock never being fastened with the buttons. The sleeves reach only to the elbow and turn back in a spreading cuff; and from the elbow hang heavy ruffles and under-sleeves, some of rich lace, others of embroidery. The gentlemen and earls wear great wigs.

This coat was called a surcoat or tunic. The under-coat, or waistcoat, was also called a vest, as by Charles the king.

From this vest, or surcoat, was developed a coat, with skirts, such as had become, ere the year 1700, the universal wear of English and American men. Its first form was adopted about at the close of the reign of Charles II. By 1688 Quaker teachers warned their younger sort against " cross-pockets on men's coats, side slopes, over-full skirted coats.

In an old play a man threatens a country lad, " I'll make your buttons fly." The lad replies, " All my buttons is loops." Some garments, especially leather ones, like doublets, which were cumbersome to button, were secured by loops. For instance, in spatterdashes, a row of holes was set on one side, and of loops on the other. To fasten them, one must begin at the lower loop, pass this through the first hole, then put the second loop through that first loop and the second hole, and so on till the last loop was fastened to the breeches by buckle and strap or large single button. From these loops were developed frogs and loops.

Major John Pyncheon had, in 1703, a "light coulour'd cape-coat with Frogs on it." In the *New England Weekly Journal* of 1736 "New Fashion'd Frogs" are named; and later, "Spangled Scalloped & Brocaded Frogs."

Though these jerkins and mandillions and doublets which were furnished to the Bay colonists were fastened with hooks and eyes, buttons were worn also, as old portraits and old letters prove. John Eliot ordered for traffic with the Indians, in 1651, three gross of pewter buttons; and Robert Keayne, of Boston, writing in 1653, said bitterly that a "haynous offence" of his had been selling buttons at too large profit — that they were gold buttons and he had sold them for two shillings ninepence a dozen in Boston, when they had cost but two shillings a dozen in London (which does not seem, in the light of our modern profits on imported goods, a very "haynous" offence). He also added with acerbity that "they were never payd for by those that complayned."

Buttonholes were a matter of ornament more than of use; in fact, they were never used for closing the garment after coats came to be worn. They were carefully cut and "laid around" in gay colors, embroidered with silver and gold thread, bound with vellum, with kid, with velvet. We find in old-time letters directions about modish buttonholes, and drawings even, in order that the shape may be exactly as wished. An English contemporary of John Winthrop's has tasselled buttonholes on his doublet.

Various are the reasons given for the placing of the two buttons on the back of a man's coat. One is that they are a survival of buttons which were used on the eighteenth-century riding-coat. The coat-tails were thus buttoned up when the wearer was on horseback. Another is that they were used for looping back the skirts of the coats; it is said that loops of cord were placed at the corners of the said skirts.

A curious anecdote about these two buttons on the back of the coat is that a tribe of North American Indians, deep believers in the value of symbolism, refused to heed a missionary because he could not explain to them the significance of these two buttons.

CHAPTER VI

RUFFS AND BANDS

" *Fashion has brought in deep ruffs and shallow ruffs, thick ruffs and thin ruffs, double ruffs and no ruffs. When the Judge of the quick and the dead shall appear he will not know those who have so defaced the fashion he hath created.*"

— Sermon, John King, Bishop of London, 1590.

" *Now up aloft I mount unto the Ruffe*
Which into foolish Mortals pride doth puffe ;
Yet Ruffe's antiquitie is here but small —
Within these eighty Years not one at all
For the 8th Henry, as I understand
Was the first King that ever wore a Band
And but a Falling Band, plaine with a Hem
All other people know no use of them."

— " The Prayse of Clean Linnen," John Taylor, the " Water Poet," 1640.

A Bowdoin Portrait.

CHAPTER VI

RUFFS AND BANDS

E have in this poem of the old " Water Poet " a definite statement of the date of the introduction of ruffs for English wear. We are afforded in the portraiture given in this book ample proof of the fall of the ruff.

Like many of the most striking fashions of olden times, the ruff was Spanish. French gentlemen had worn frills or ruffs about 1540; soon after, these appeared in England; by the date of Elizabeth's accession the ruff had become the most imposing article of English men's and women's dress. It was worn exclusively by fine folk; for it was too frail and too costly for the common wear of the common people, though lawn ruffs were seen on many of low degree. A ruff such as was worn by a courtier contained eighteen or nineteen yards of fine linen lawn. A quarter of a yard wide was the fashionable width in England. Ruffs were carefully pleated in triple box-plaits as shown in the Bowdoin portrait facing page 198. Then they were bound with a firm neck-binding.

This carefully made ruff was starched with good English or Dutch starch; fluted with " setting

sticks" of wood or bone, to hold each pleat up;
then fixed with struts — also of wood — placed in a
manner to hold the pleats firmly apart; and finally
"seared" or goffered with "poking sticks" of iron
or steel, which, duly heated, dried the stiffening
starch. To "do up" a formal ruff was a wearisome,
difficult, and costly process. Women of skill acquired
considerable fortunes as "gofferers."

Stubbes tells us further of the rich decoration of
ruffs with gold, silver, and silk lace, with needlework,
with openwork, and with purled lace. This was in
Elizabeth's day. John Winthrop's ruff (on page
10) is edged with lace; in general a plain ruff was
worn by plain gentlemen; one may be seen on
Martin Frobisher (page 164). Rich lace was for the
court. Their great cost, their inconvenience, their
artificiality, their size, were sure to make ruffs a
"reason of offence" to reformers. Stubbes gave
voice to their complaints in these words: —

"They haue great and monstrous ruffes, made either of
cambrike, holland, lawne, or els of some other the finest
cloth that can be got for money, whereof some be a
quarter of a yarde deepe, yea, some more, very few lesse,
so that they stande a full quarter of a yearde (and more)
from their necks hanging ouer their shoulder points in
steade of a vaile."

Still more violent does he grow over starch: —

"The one arch or piller whereby his (the Devil's) kyng-
dome of great ruffes is vnderpropped, is a certaine kind of
liquid matter, whiche they call starch, wherein the deuill
hath willed them to washe and dive their ruffes well, whiche,

beeying drie, will then stande stiff and inflexible about their necks.

"The other piller is a certaine device made of wiers, crested for the purpose; whipped ouer either with gold thred, siluer, or silke, and this he calleth a supportasse or vnderpropper; this is to bee applied round about their neckes vnder the ruffe, vpon the out side of the bande, to beare vp the whole frame and bodie of the ruffe, from fallying and hangying doune."

Starch was of various colors. We read of "blue-starch-women," and of what must have been especially ugly, "goose-green starch." Yellow starch was most worn. It was introduced from France by the notorious Mrs. Turner. (See facing page 130.)

Wither wrote thus of the varying modes of dressing the neck: —

> "Some are graced by their Tyres
> As their Quoyfs, their Hats, their Wyres,
> One a Ruff cloth best become ;
> Falling bands allureth some ;
> And their favours oft we see
> Changéd as their dressings be."

The transformation of ruff to band can be seen in the painting of King Charles I. The first Van Dyck portrait of him shows him in a moderate ruff turned over to lie down like a collar; the lace edge formed itself by the pleats into points which developed into the lace points characteristic of Van Dyck's later pictures and called by his name.

Evelyn, describing a medal of King Charles I struck in 1633, says, "The King wears a falling band, a new mode which has succeeded the cumber-

some ruff; but neither do the bishops nor the Judges
give it up so soon." Few of the early colonial portraits show ruffs, though the name appears in many
inventories, but " playne bands " are more frequently

William Pyncheon.

named than ruffs. Thus in an Inventory of William
Swift, Plymouth, 1642, he had " 2 Ruff Bands and
4 Playne Bands." The " playne band " of the Puritans is shown in this portrait of William Pyncheon,
which is dated 1657.

The first change from the full pleated ruff of the sixteenth century came in the adoption of a richly laced collar, unpleated, which still stood up behind the ears at the back of the head. Often it was wired in place with a supportasse. This was worn by both men and women. You may see one facing page 122, on the neck of Pocahontas, her portrait painted in 1616. This collar, called a standing-band, when turned down was known as a falling-band or a rebato.

The rich lace falling-band continued to be worn until the great flowing wig, with long, heavy curls, covered the entire shoulders and hid any band ; the floating ends in front were the only part visible. In time they too vanished. Pepys wrote in 1662, " Put on my new lace band and so neat ; am re-solved my great expense shall be lace bands, and it will set off anything else the more."

I scarcely need to point out the falling-band in its various shapes as worn in America ; they can be found readily in the early pages of this book. It was a fashion much discussed and at first much dis-liked ; but the ruff had seen its last day — for men's wear, when the old fellows who had worn it in the early years of the seventeenth century dropped off as the century waned. The old Bowdoin gentleman must have been one of the last to wear this cumber-some though stately adjunct of dress — save as it was displaced on some formal state occasion or as part of a uniform or livery.

There is a constant tendency in all times and among all English-speaking folk to shorten names

and titles for colloquial purposes; and soon the
falling-band became the fall.   In the *Wits' Recrea-*
tion are two epigrams which show the thought of the
times : —

> " WHY WOMEN WEARE A FALL
>
> " A Question 'tis why Women wear a fall ?
> And truth it is to Pride they're given all.
> And *Pride,* the proverb says, *will have a fall.*"

> " ON A LITTLE DIMINUTIVE BAND
>
> " What is the reason of God-dam-me's band,
> Inch deep ? and that his fashion doth not alter,
> God-dam-me saves a labor, understand
> In pulling it off, where he puts on the Halter."

" God-dam-me " was one of the pleasant epithets
which, by scores, were applied to the Puritans.

Reverend Jonathan Edwards.

The bands worn by the
learned professions, two
strips of lawn with squared
ends, were at first the elon-
gated ends of the shirt collar of Jonathan Edwards.
We have them still, to re-
mind us of old fashions ;
and we have another word
and thing, band-box, which
must have been a stern necessity in those days of
starch, and ruff, and band.
It was by no means a convention of dress that
" God-dam-me " should wear a small band.   Neither

Cromwell nor his followers clung long to plain bands ;
nor did they all assume them. It would be wholly
impossible to generalize or to determine the standing of individuals, either in politics or religion, by
their neckwear. I have before me a little group of
prints of men of Cromwell's day, gathered for extra
illustration of a history of Cromwell's time. Let
us glance at their bands.

First comes Cromwell himself from the Cooper
portrait at Cambridge ; this portrait has a plain linen
turnover collar, or band, but two to three inches
wide. Then his father is shown in a very broad,
square, plain linen collar extending in front expanse
from shoulder seam to shoulder seam. Sir Harry
Vane and Hampden, both Puritans, have narrow
collars like Cromwell's ; Pym, an equally precise
sectarian, has a broader one like the father's, but
apparently of some solid and rich embroidery like
cut-work. Edward Hyde, the Earl of Clarendon,
in narrow band, Lucius Cary, Lord Falkland, in
band and band-strings, were members of the Long
Parliament, but passed in time to the Royal Camp.
Other portraits of both noblemen are in richly laced
bands. The Earl of Bristol, who was in the same
standing, has the widest of lace, Vandyked collars.
John Selden wears the plain band ; but here is
Strafford, the very impersonation of all that was
hated by Puritans, and yet he wears the simplest of
puritanical bands. William Lenthal, Speaker of the
House of Commons, is in a beautiful Cavalier collar
with straight lace edges. There are a score more,
equally indifferent to rule.

There is no doubt, however, that the Puritan regarded his plain band — if he wore it — with jealous
care. Poor Mary Downing, niece of Governor
Winthrop, paid dearly for her careless " searing," or
ironing, of her brother's bands. Her stepmother's
severity at her offence brought forth this plaintive
letter : —

" Father, I trust that I have not provoked you to har-
bour soe ill an opinion of mee as my mothers lres do
signifie and give me to understand; the ill opinion and
hard pswasion which shee beares of mee, that is to say, that
I should abuse yor goodness, and bee prodigall of yor purse,
neglectful of my brothers bands, and of my slatterishnes
and lasines; for my brothers bands I will not excuse myselfe, but I thinke not worthy soe sharpe a reproofe; for
the rest I must needs excuse, and cleare myselfe if I may
bee believed. I doe not know myselfe guilty of any of
them; for myne owne part I doe not desire to be myne
owne judge, but am willinge to bee judged by them with
whom I live, and see my course, whether I bee addicted to
such things or noe."

Ruffs and bands were not the only neckwear of
the colonists. Very soon there was a tendency to
ornament the band-strings with tassels of silk, with
little tufts of ribbon, with tiny rosettes, with jewels
even ; and soon a graceful frill of lace hung where
the band was tied together. This may be termed
the beginning of the necktie or cravat; but the
article itself enjoyed many names, and many forms,
which in general extended both to men's and
women's wear.

Captain George Curwen.

Let us turn to the old inventories for the various names of this neckwear.

A Maryland gentleman left by will, with other attire, in 1642, "Nine laced stripps, two plain stripps, nine quoifes, one call, eight crosse-cloths, a paire holland sleeves, a paire women's cuffs, nine plaine neck-cloths, five laced neck-cloths, two plaine gorgetts, seven laced gorgetts, three old clouts, five plaine neckhandkerchiefs, two plain shadowes."

John Taylor, the "Water Poet," wrote a poem entitled *The Needles Excellency*. I quote from the twelfth edition, dated 1640. In the list of garments which we owe to the needle he names: —

> "Shadows, Shapparoones, Cauls, Bands, Ruffs, Kuffs,
> Kerchiefs, Quoyfes, Chin-clouts, Marry-muffes,
> Cross-cloths, Aprons, Hand-kerchiefs, or Falls."

His list runs like that of the Maryland planter. The strip was something like the whisk; indeed, the names seem interchangeable. Bishop Hall in his *Satires* writes: —

> "When a plum'd fan may hide thy chalked face
> And lawny strips thy naked bosom grace."

Dr. Smith wrote in 1658 in *Penelope and Ulysses*: —

> "A stomacher upon her breast so bare
> For strips and gorget were not then the wear."

The gorget was the frill in front; the strip the lace cape or whisk. It will be noted that nine gorgets are named with these strips.

The gorget when worn by women was enriched with lace and needlework.

"These Holland smocks as white as snow
    And gorgets brave with drawn-work wrought
  A tempting ware they are you know."

Thus runs a poem published in 1596.

Mary Verney writes in 1642 her desire for " gorgetts and eyther cutt or painted callico to wear
under them or what is most in fashion."

The shadow has been a great stumbling-block to
antiquaries.   Purchas's *Pilgrimage* is responsible for
what is to me a very confusing reference.   It says
of a certain savage race : —

"They have a skin of leather hanging about their necks
whenever they sit bare-headed and bare-footed, with their
right arms bare; and a broad Sombrero or Shadow in their
hands to defend them in Summer from the Sunne, in Winter from the Rain."

This would make a shadow a sort of hand-screen
or sunshade; but all other references seem as if a
shadow were a cap.   As early as 1580, Richard
Fenner's *Wardship Roll* has "Item a Caul and
Shadoe 4 shillings."   I think a shadow was a great
cap like a cornet.   Cross-cloths were a form of
head-dress.   I have seen old portraits with a cap or
head-dress formed of crossed bands which I have
supposed were cross-cloths.

Cross-cloths also bore a double meaning; for
certainly neck-cloths or neckerchiefs were sometimes called cross-cloths or cross-clothes.   Another
name is the picardill or piccadilly, a French title
for a gorget.   Fitzgerald, in 1617, wrote of "a

spruse coxcomb" that he glanced at his pocket
looking-glass to see : —

> " How his Band jumpeth with his Peccadilly
> Whether his Band-strings ballance equally."

Another satirical author could write in 1638 that
" pickadillies are now out of request."

The portrait of Captain Curwen of Salem (facing page 204) is unlike many of his times.   Over
his doublet he
wears a hand-
some embroid-
ered shoulder
sash called a
trooping-scarf;
and his broad
lace tie is very
unusual for the
year 1660.   I
know few like
it upon Amer-
ican gentlemen
in portraits;
and I fancy it

is a gorget, or
a piccadilly. It

Lace Gorget and Cane of Captain George
Curwen.

is pleasant to know that this handsome piece of
lace has been preserved.   It is here shown with his
cane.

A little negative proof may be given as to one
word and article.   The gorget is said to be an
adaptation of the wimple.   Our writers of historical

tales are very fond of attiring their heroines in
wimples and kirtles. Both have a picturesque, an
antique, sound — the wimple is Biblical and Shake-
sperian, and therefore ever satisfying to the ear,
and to the sight in manuscript. But I have never
seen the word wimple in an inventory, list, invoice,
letter, or book of colonial times, and but once the
word kirtle. Likewise are these modern authors a
bit vague as to the manner of garment a wimple is.
One fair maid is described as having her fair form
wrapped in a warm wimple. She might as well be
described as wrapped in a warm cravat. For a
wimple was simply a small kerchief or covering for
the neck, worn in the thirteenth and fourteenth
centuries.

Another quaint term, already obsolete when the
Mayflower sailed, was partlet. A partlet was an
inner kerchief, worn with an open-necked bodice or
doublet. Its trim plaited edge or ruffle seems to
have given rise to the popular name, " Dame Partlet," for a hen. It appeared in the reign of Henry
VIII ; the courtiers imitating the king threw open
their garments at the throat, and further opened
them with slashes ; hence the use of the partlet,
which was a trim form of underhabit or gorget,
worn well up to the throat. An old dictionary explains that the partlet can be " set on or taken off
by itself without taking off the bodice, as can be
pickadillies now-a-days, or men's bands." It adds
that women's neckerchiefs have been called partlets.

In October, 1662, Samuel Pepys wrote in his
Diary, " Made myself fine with Captain Ferrers lace

band; being loathe to wear my own new scallop; it is so fine." This is one of his several references to this new fashion of band which both he and his wife adopted. He paid £3 for his scallop, and 45*s*. for one for his wife. He was so satisfied with his elegance in this new scallop, that like many another lover of dress he determined his chief extravagance should be for lace. The fashion of scallop-wearing came to America. For several years the word was used in inventories, then it became as obsolete as a caul, a shadow, a cornet.

The word "cravat" is not very ancient. Its derivation is said to be from the Cravates or Croats in the French military service, who adopted such neckwear in 1636. An early use of the word is by Blount in 1656, who called a cravat "a new fashioned Gorget which Women wear."

The cravat is a distinct companion of the wig, and was worn whenever and wherever wigs were donned.

Evelyn gave the year 1666 as the one when vest, cravat, garters, and buckles came to be the fashion. We could add likewise wigs. Of course all these had been known before that year, but had not been general wear.

An early example of a cravat is shown in the portrait of old William Stoughton in my later chapter on Cloaks. His cravat is a distinctly new mode of neck-dressing, but is found on all American portraits shortly after that date. One is shown with great exactness in the portrait on page 210, which is asserted to be that of "the handsomest man in the Plantations," William Coddington, Governor of Rhode Island and Providence Plantations.

He was a precise man, and wearisome in his precision — a bore, even, I fear. His beauty went for little in his relation of man to man, and, above

Governor Coddington.

all, of colonist to colonist; and poor Governor Winthrop must have been sorely tormented with his frequent letters, which might have been written from Mars for all the signs they bore of news of things of this earth. His dress is very neat and rich — a characteristic dress, I think. It has slightly wrought buttonholes, plain sleeve ruffles and gloves. His full curled peruke has a mass of long curls hanging in front of the right shoulder, while the curls on the left side are six or eight inches shorter. This was the most elegant London fashion, and extreme fashion too. His neck-scarf or cravat was

a characteristic one. It consisted of a long scarf
of soft, fine, sheer, white linen over two yards long,
passed twice or thrice close around the throat and
simply lapped under the chin, not knotted. The
upper end hung from
twelve to sixteen inches
long. The other and
longer end was carried
down to a low waist-
line and tucked in be-
tween the buttons of
the waistcoat. Often
the free end of this
scarf was trimmed with
lace or cut-work ; in-
deed, the whole scarf
might be of embroid-
ery or lace, but the
simpler lawn or mull
appears to have been

Thomas Fayerweather.

in better taste. This tie is seen in this portrait of
Thomas Fayerweather, by Smybert, and in modified forms on many other pages.

We now find constant references to the Steinkirk,
a new cravat. As we see it frequently stated that
the Steinkirk was a black tie, I may state here that
all the Steinkirks I have seen have been white. I
know no portraits with black neck-cloths. I find
no allusions in old-time literature or letters to black
Steinkirks.

A Steinkirk was a white cravat, not knotted, but
fastened so loosely as to seem folded rather than

tied, twisted sometimes twice or thrice, with one or
both ends passed through a buttonhole of the coat.
Ladies wore them, as well as men, arranged with
equal appearance of careless negligence; and the
soft diagonal folds of linen and lace made a pretty
finish at the throat, as pretty as any high neck-
dressing could be. These cravats were called Steinkirks after the battle of Steinkirk, when some of
the French princes, not having time to perform an
elaborate toilet before going into action, hurriedly
twisted their lace cravats about their necks and
pulled them through a buttonhole, simply to fix
them safely in place. The fashionable world eagerly
followed their example. It is curious that the
Steinkirk should have been popular in England,
where the name might rather have been a bitter
avoidance.

The battle of Steinkirk took place in 1694. An
early English allusion to the neckwear thus named
is in *The Relapse*, which was acted in 1697. In it
the Semstress says, " I hope your Lordship is
pleased with your Steenkirk." His Lordship answers with eloquence, " In love with it, stap my
vitals ! Bring your bill, you shall be paid to-
morrow ! "

The Steinkirk, both for men's and women's wear,
came to America very promptly, and was soon widely
worn. The dashing, handsome figure of young
King Carter gives an illustration of the pretty studied
negligence of the Steinkirk. I have seen a Steinkirk tie on at least twenty portraits of American
gentlemen, magistrates, and officers; some of them

"King" Carter in Youth, by Sir Godfrey Kneller.

were the royal governors, but many were American born and bred, who never visited Europe, but turned eagerly to English fashions.

Certain old families have preserved among their ancient treasures a very long oval brooch with a bar across it from end to end — the longest way of the brooch. These are set sometimes with topaz or moonstone, garnet, marcasite, heliotropium, or paste jewels. Many wonder for what purpose these were used. They were to hold the lace Steinkirk in place, when it was not pulled through the button-hole. The bar made it seem like a tongueless buckle — or perhaps it was like a long, narrow buckle to which a brooch pin had been affixed to keep it firmly in place.

The cravat, tied and twisted in Steinkirk form, or more simply folded, long held its place in fashion-able dress.

> " The stock with buckle made of paste
>   Has put the cravat out of date,"

wrote Whyte in 1742.

With this quotation we will turn from neckwear until a later period.

CHAPTER VII

CAPS AND BEAVERS IN COLONIAL DAYS

" *So many poynted cappes*
Lased with double flaps
And soe gay felted cappes
Saw I never.

So propre cappes
So lyttle hattes
And so false hartes
Saw I never."

— "The Maner of the World Nowe-a-dayes," JOHN SKELTON, 1548.

" *The Turk in linen wraps his head*
The Persian his in lawn, too,
The Russ with sables furs his cap
And change will not be drawn to.

" *The Spaniard's constant to his block*
The Frenchman inconstant ever;
But of all felts that may be felt
Give me the English beaver.

" *The German loves his coney-wool*
The Irishman his shag, too,
The Welsh his Monmouth loves to wear
And of the same will brag, too."

— " A Challenge for Beauty," THOMAS HAYWARD.

CHAPTER VII

CAPS AND BEAVERS IN COLONIAL DAYS

NY student of English history and letters would know that caps would positively be part of the outfit of every emigrating Englishman. A cap was, for centuries, both the enforced and desired headwear of English folk of quiet lives.

Belgic Britons, Welshmen, Irish, Anglo-Saxons, Danes, and Normans all had worn caps, as well as ancient Greeks and Romans. These English caps had been of divers colors and manifold forms, some being grotesque indeed. When we reach the reign of Henry VIII we are made familiar in the paintings of Holbein with a certain flat-cap which sometimes had a small jewel or feather

City Flat-cap worn by " Bilious " Bale.

or a double fold, but never varied greatly. This was known as the city flat-cap.

It is shown also in the Holbein portrait of Adam Winthrop, grandfather of Governor John Winthrop; he was a man of dignity, Master of the Cloth Workers' Guild.

The muffin-cap of the boys of Christ's Hospital is a form of this cap.

This was at first and ever a Londoner's cap. A poet wrote in 1630 : —

> " Flat caps as proper are to city gowns
>   As to armour, helmets, or to kings, their crowns."

Winthrop also wears the city gown.

This flat-cap was often of gay colors, scarlet being a favorite hue.

> " Behold the bonnet upon my head
>   A staryng colour of scarlet red
>   I promise you a fyne thred
>   And a soft wool
>   It cost a noble."

These lines were written for the character " Pride," in the *Interlude of Nature*, before the year 1500.

A statute was passed in 1571, " If any person above six years of age (except maidens, ladies, gentlemen, nobles, knights, gentlemen of twenty marks by year in lands, and their heirs, and such as have born office of worship) have not worn upon the Sunday or holyday (except it be in the time of his travell out of the city, town or hamlet where he dwelleth) one cap of wool, knit, thicked and dressed in England, and only dressed and furnished by some of the trade of cappers, shall be fined £3 4d. for each day's transgression." The caps thus worn were called Statute caps.

This was, of course, to encourage wool-workers in the pride of the nation. Winthrop, master of a guild whose existence depended on wool, would, of course, wear a woollen cap had he not been a Londoner. It was a plain head-covering, but it was also the one worn by King Edward VI.

There was a formal coif or cap worn by men of dignity ; always worn, I think, by judges and elderly lawyers, ere the assumption of the formal wig. This coif may be seen on the head of the venerable Dr. Dee, and also on the head of Lord Burleigh, and of Thomas Cecil, surmounted with the citizen's flat-cap. One of these caps in heavy black lustring lingered by chance in my home — worn by some forgotten ancestor. It had a curious loop, as may be seen on Dr. Dee. This was not a narrow string for tying the coif on the head; it was a loop. And if there was any need of fastening the cap on the head, a narrow ribbon or ferret, a lacing, was put through both loops.

In the inventory of the apparel of the first settlers which I have given in the early pages of this book, we find that each colonist to the Massachusetts Bay settlement had one Monmouth cap and five red milled caps. All the lists of necessary clothing for the planters have as an item, caps ; but a well-made, well-lined hat was also supplied.

Monmouth caps were in general wear in England. Thomas Fuller said, " Caps were the most ancient, general, warm, and profitable coverings of men's heads in this Island." In making them thousands of people were employed, especially before the invention of fulling-mills, when caps were wrought, beaten, and thickened by the hands and feet of men. Cap-making afforded occupation to fifteen different callings: carders, spinners, knitters, parters of wool, forcers, thickers, dressers, walkers, dyers, battellers, shearers, pressers, edgers, liners, and band-makers.

King James I of England.

The Monmouth caps were worth two shillings each, which were furnished to the Massachusetts colonists. These were much affected by seafaring men. We read, in *A Satyr on Sea Officers*, "With Monmouth cap and cutlass at my side, striding at least a yard at every stride." "The Ballad of the Caps," 1656, gives a wonderful list of caps. Among them are: —

> The Monmouth Cap, the Saylors thrum,
> And that wherein the tradesmen come,
> The Physick, Lawe, the Cap divine,
> And that which crowns the Muses nine,

The Cap that Fools do countenance,
The goodly Cap of Maintenance,
    And any Cap what e're it be,
    Is still the sign of some degree.

"The sickly Cap both plaine and wrought,
The Fuddling-cap however bought,
The quilted, furred, the velvet, satin,
For which so many pates learn Latin,
The Crewel Cap, the Fustian pate,
The Perriwig, the Cap of Late,
    And any Cap what e'er it be
    Is still the sign of some degree."

                — "Ballad of the Caps," 1656.

We seldom have in manuscript or print, in America, titles or names given to caps or hats, but one occasionally seen is the term " montero-cap," spelled also mountero, montiro, montearo ; and Washington Irving tells of "the cedar bird with a little monteiro-cap of feathers."   Montero-caps were frequently recommended to emigrants, and useful dress they were, being a horseman's or huntsman's cap with a simple round crown, and a flap which went around the sides and back of the cap and which could be worn turned up or brought down over the back of the neck, the ears and temples, thus making a most protecting head-covering.   They were, in general, dark colored, of substantial woollen stuff, but Sterne writes in *Tristram Shandy* of a montero-cap which he describes as of superfine Spanish cloth, dyed scarlet in the grain, mounted all round with fur, except four inches in front, which was faced with light blue lightly embroidered.   It is a montero-cap which is seen on the head of Bamfylde Moore Carew, the " King of the Mumpers," a most genial English rogue, sneak-thief, and cheat of the eighteenth century, who spent some of his ill-filled years in the American colonies, whither he was brought after being trepanned, and where he had to bear the ignominy of wearing an iron collar welded around his neck.

A montero-cap seems to have been the favorite dress of rogues. In Head's *English Rogue* we read, " Beware of him that rides in a montero-cap and of him that whispers oft." The picaro Guzman wore one ; and as montero is the Spanish word for huntsman, Head may have obtained the word from that special scamp, Guzman, whose life was published in 1633. It is a very ancient name, being given in Cotgrave as a hood, or as the horseman's helmet. It is worn still by Arctic travellers and Alpine climbers. Sets of knitted montero-caps were presented by the Empress Eugenie to the Arctic expedition of 1875, and the Jackies dubbed them " Eugenie Wigs."

Another and widely different class of men wore likewise the montero-cap, the English and American Quakers. Thomas Ellwood, in the early days of his Quaker belief, suffered much for his hat, both from his fellow Quakers and his father, a Church of England man. The Quakers thought his " large Mountier cap of black velvet, the skirt of which being turned up in Folds looked somewhat above the common Garb of a Quaker." A young priest at another time snatched this montero-cap off because he wore it in the presence of magistrates, and then Ellwood's father fell upon it in this wise : —

" He could not contain himself but running upon me with both hands, first violently snatcht off my Hat and threw it away and then giving me some buffets in the head said Sirrah get you up to your chamber. I had now lost one hat and had but one more. The next Time my Father saw it on my head he tore it violently from me and laid it up with the other, I know not where. Wherefore I put my Mountier Cap which was all I had left to wear on my head, and but a little while I had that, for when my Father came where I was, I lost that also."

Fulke Greville (Lord Brooke).

Finally the father refused to let him wear his " Hive," as he called the hat, at the table while eating, and thereafter Ellwood ate with his father's servants.

The vogue of beaver hats was an important factor in the settlement of America.

The first Spanish, Dutch, English, and French colonists all came to America to seek for gold and furs. The Spaniards found gold, the Dutch and French found furs, but the English who found fish found the greatest wealth of all, for food is ever more than raiment.

Of the furs the most important and most valuable was beaver. The English sent some beaver back to Europe; the very first ship to return from Plymouth carried back two hogsheads. Winslow sent twenty hogsheads as early as 1634, and Bradford shows that the trade was deemed important. But the wild creatures speedily retreated. Johnson declares that as early as 1645 the beaver trade had left the frontier post of Springfield, on the Connecticut River.

From the earliest days both the French and English crown had treated the fishing and fur industries with unusual discretion, giving a monopoly to the fur trade and leaving the fisheries free, so the latter constantly increased, while in New England the fur trade passed over to the Dutch, distinctly to the advantage of the English, for the lazy trader at a post was neither a good savage nor a good citizen, while the hardy fishermen and bold sailors of New England brought wealth to every town. For some years the Dutch appeared to have the best of it, for they received ten to fifteen thousand beaver skins annually from New England; and they had trading-posts on Narragansett and Buzzards Bay. Still the trade drew the Dutch away from agriculture, and the real success of New Netherland did not come with furs, but with corn.

The fur trade was certainly an interesting factor in the growth of the Dutch settlement. Fort Orange, or Albany, called the *Fuyck*, was the natural topographical *fuyck* or trap-net to catch this trade, and in the very first season of its settlement fifteen hundred beaver and five hundred otter skins were despatched to Holland. In 1657 Johannes Dyckman asserted that 40,900 beaver and otter skins were sent that year from Fort Orange to Fort Amsterdam (New York City). As these skins were valued at from eight to ten guilders apiece

James Douglas (Earl of Morton).

(about $3.50 and with a purchasing value equal to $20 to-day), it can readily be seen what a source of wealth seemed opened. The authorities at Fort Orange, the patroons of Renssalaerwyck and Beverwyck, were not to be permitted to absorb all this wondrous gain in undisturbed peace. The increment of the India Company was diverted and hindered in various ways. Unscrupulous and crafty citizens of Fort Orange (independent *handælers* or handlers) and their thrifty, penny-turning *vrouw's* decoyed the Indian trappers and hunters into their peaceful, honest kitchens under pretence of kindly Christian welcome to the peltry-bearing braves; and they filled the guileless savages with Dutch schnapps, or Barbadoes "kill-devil," until the befuddled or half-crazed Indians parted with their precious stores of hard-trapped skins and threw off their well-perspired and greased beaver coats and exchanged them for such valuable Dutch wares as knives, scissors, beads, and jews'-harps, or even a few pints of quickly vanishing rum, instead of solid Dutch guilders or substantial Dutch blankets. And even before these strategic Dutch citizens could corral and fleece them, the incoming fur-bearers had to run as insinuating a gantlet of *boschloopers*, bush-runners, drummers, or "broakers," who sallied out on the narrow Indian paths to buy the coveted furs even before they were brought into Fort Orange. Much legislation ensued. Scout-buying was prohibited. Citizens were forbidden "to addresse to speak to the wilden of trading," or to entice them to "traffique," or to harbor them over night. Indian houses to lodge the trappers were built just outside the gate, where the dickering would be public. These were built by rates collected from all "Christian dealers" in furs.

But Indian paths were many, and the water-ways were unpatrolled, and kitchen doors could be slyly opened in the dusk; so the government, in spite of laws and shelter-houses, did not get all the beaver skins. Too many were eager for the lucrative and irregular trade; agricultural pursuits were alarmingly neglected; other communities became rivals, and the beavers soon were exterminated from the valley of the Hudson, and by 1660 the Fort Orange trade was sadly diminished. The governor of Canada had an itching palm, and lured the Indians — and beaver skins — to Montreal. Thus "impaired by French wiles," scarce nine thousand peltries came in 1687 to Fort Orange. With a few fluttering rallies until Revolutionary times the fur trade of Albany became extinct; it passed from both Dutch and French, and was dominated by the Hudson Bay Fur Company.

So clear a description of the fur of the beaver and the use of the pelt was given by Adriaen van der Donck, who lived at Fort Orange from the year 1641 to 1646, and traded for years with the Indians, that it is well to give his exact words: —

"The beaver's skin is rough but thickly set with fine fur of an ash-gray color inclining to blue. The outward points also incline to a russet or brown color. From the fur of the beaver the best hats are made that are worn. They are called beavers or castoreums from the material of which they are made, and they are known by this name over all Europe. Outside of the coat of fur many shining hairs appear called wind-hairs, which are more properly winter-hairs, for they fall out in summer and appear again in winter. The outer coat is of a chestnut-brown color, the browner the color the better is the fur. Sometimes it will be a little reddish.

"When hats are made of the fur, the rough hairs are pulled out for they are useless. The skins are usually first sent to Russia, where they are highly valued for their outside shining hair, and on this their greatest recommendation depends with the Russians. The skins are used there for mantle-linings and are also cut into strips for borders, as we cut rabbit-skins. Therefore we call the same peltries. Whoever has there the most and costliest fur-trimmings is deemed a person of very high rank, as with us the finest stuffs and gold and silver embroideries are regarded as the appendages of the great. After the hairs have fallen out, or are worn, and the peltries become old and dirty and apparently useless, we get the article back, and convert the fur into hats, before which it cannot be well used for this purpose, for unless the beaver has been worn, and is greasy and dirty, it will not felt properly, hence these old peltries are the most valuable. The coats which the Indians make of beaver-skins and which they have worn for a long time around their bodies until the skins have become foul with perspiration and grease are afterwards used by the hatters and make the best hats."

One notion about beaver must be told. Its great popularity for many years arose, it is conjectured, from its original use as a cap for curative purposes. Such a beaver cap would "unfeignedly" recover to a man his hearing, and stimulate his memory to a wonder, especially if the "oil of castor" was rubbed in his hair.

The beaver hat was for centuries a choice and costly article of dress; it went through many bizarre forms. On the head of Henry IV of France and Navarre, as made known in his portrait, is a hat which effectually destroys all possibility of dignity.

Elihu Yale.

It is a bell-crowned stove-pipe, of the precise shape worn later by coachmen and by dandies about the years 1820 to 1830.   It is worn very much over one royal ear, like the hat of a well-set-up, self-important coachman of the palmy days of English coaching, and gives an air of absurd modernity and cockney importance to the picture of a king of great dignity. The hat worn by James I, ere he was King of England, is shown on page 220.   It is funnier than any seen for years in a comic opera.   The hat worn by Francis Bacon is a plain felt, greatly in contrast with his rich laced triple ruff and cuffs and embroidered garments.   That of Thomas Cecil on page 230 varies slightly.

Two very singular shapings of the plain hat may be seen, one on page 223 on the head of Fulke Greville, where the round-topped, high crown is most disproportionate to the narrow brim.   The second, on page 225, shows an extreme sugar-loaf, almost a pointed crown.

A good hat was very expensive, and important enough to be left among bequests in a will.   They were borrowed and hired for many years, and even down to the time of Queen Anne we find the rent of a *subscription hat* to be £2 6s. per annum !   The hiring out of a hat does not seem strange when hiring out clothes was a regular business with tailors. The wife of a person of low estate hired a gown of Queen Elizabeth's to be married in.   Tailor Thomas Gylles complained of the Yeoman of the queen's wardrobe for suffering this.   He writes, " The copper cloth of gold gowns which were made last, and another, were sent into the country for the marriage of Lord Montague." The bequest of half-worn garments was highly regarded. On the very day of Darnley's funeral, Mary Queen of Scots gave his clothes to Bothwell, who sent them to his tailor to be refitted. The tailor, bold with the riot and disorder of the time, returned them with the impudent message that " the duds of dead men were given to the hangman."

Thomas Cecil.

The duds of men who were hanged were given to the hangman almost as long as hangings took place. A poor New England girl, hanged for the murder of her child, went to the scaffold in her meanest attire, and taunted the executioner that he would get but a poor suit of clothes from her. The last woman hanged in Massachusetts wore a white satin gown, which I expect the sheriff's daughter much revelled in the following winter at dancing-parties.

Old Philip Stubbes has given us a wonderful description of English head-gear: —

"Hats of Sundrie Fations"

"Sometymes they vse them sharpe on the Croune, pearking vp like the Spire, or Shaft of a Steeple, standyng a quarter of a yarde aboue the Croune of their heades, some more, some lesse, as please the phantasies of their inconstant mindes.   Othersome be flat and broad on the Crowne, like the battlemetes of a house.   An other sorte haue rounde Crownes, sometymes with one kinde of Band, sometymes with another, now black, now white, now russet, now red, now grene, now yellowe, now this, now that, never content with one colour or fashion two daies to an ende.   And thus in vanitie they spend the Lorde his treasure, consuming their golden yeres and siluer daies in wickednesse and sinne. And as the fashions bee rare and strange, so is the stuffe whereof their hattes be made divers also; for some are of Silke, some of Veluet, some of Taffatie, some of Sarcenet, some of Wooll, and, whiche is more curious, some of a certaine kinde of fine Haire; these they call Bever hattes, or xx. xxx. or xl. shillinges price, fetched from beyonde the seas, from whence a great sorte of other vanities doe come besides.   And so common a thing it is, that euery seruyngman, countrieman, and other, euen all indefferently, dooe weare of these hattes.   For he is of no account or estimation amongst men if he haue not a Veluet or Taffatie hatte, and that must be Pincked, and Cunnyngly Carved of the beste fashion.   And good profitable hattes be these, for the longer you weare them the fewer holes they haue.   Besides this, of late there is a new fashion of wearyng their hattes sprong vp amongst them, which they father vpon a Frenchman, namely, to weare them with bandes, but how vnsemely (I will not saie how hassie) a fashion that is let the wise judge; notwithstanding, howeuer it be, if it please them, it shall not displease me.

"And another sort (as phantasticall as the rest) are

content with no kinde of hat without a greate Bunche of
Feathers of diuers and sondrie Colours, peakyng on top of
their heades, not vnlike (I dare not saie) Cockescombes, but
as sternes of pride, and ensignes of vanity. And yet, notwithstanding these Flutterying Sailes, and Feathered Flagges
of defiaunce of Vertue (for so they be) are so advanced that
euery child hath them in his Hat or Cap; many get good
liuing by dying and selling of them, and not a few proue
the selues more than Fooles in wearyng of them."

Notwithstanding this list of Stubbes, it is very
curious to note that in general the shape of the
real beaver hat remained the same as long as it was
worn uncocked.

The hat was worn much more constantly within-
doors than in the present day. Pepys states that they

Cornelius Steinwyck.

were worn in church; even
the preacher wore his hat.
Hats were removed in the
presence of royalty. An
hereditary honor and priv-
ilege granted to one of my
ancestors was that he might
wear his hat before the king.

It is somewhat difficult
to find out the exact date
when the wearing of hats
by men within-doors ceased
to be fashionable and became distinctly low bred.
We can turn to contemporary art. In 1707 at a
grand banquet given in France to the Spanish Em-
bassy, a ceremonious state affair with the women in
magnificent full-dress, the men seated at the table

and in the presence of royalty wore their cocked hats — so much for courtly France.

This wearing of the hat in church, at table, and elsewhere that seems now strange to us, was largely as an emblem of dignity and authority. Miss Moore in the *Caldwell Papers* writes of her grandfather : —

" I' my grandfather's time, as I have heard him tell, ilka maister of a family had his ain seat in his ain house ; aye, and sat there with his hat on, afore the best in the land ; and had his ain dish, and was aye helpit first and keepit up his authority as a man should so. Parents were parents then ; and bairns dared not set up their gabs afore them as they do now."

That the covering of the head in church still has a significance on important occasions, is shown by a rubric from the " Form and Order " for the Coronation of King Edward VII and Queen Alexandra ; this provides that the king remains uncovered during the saying of the Litany and the beginning of the Communion Service, but when the sermon begun that he should put on his " Cap of crimson velvet turned up with Ermine, and so continue," to the end of the discourse.

Hatbands were just as important for men's hats as women's — especially during the years of the reign of James I. Endymion Porter had his wife's diamond necklace to wear on his hat in Spain. It probably looked like paste beside the gorgeousness of the Duke of Buckingham, who had " the Mirror of France," a great diamond, the finest in England, " to wear alone in your hat with a little blacke

feather," so the king wrote him.   A more curious
hat ornament was a glove.

This handsome hat is from a portrait of George,
Earl of Cumberland.   It has a woman's glove as a

favor.   This is said to have
been a gift of Queen Elizabeth after his prowess in a
tournament.   He always
wore this glove on state occasions.   Gloves were worn
on a hat in three meanings :
as a memorial of a dead
friend, as a favor of a mistress, or as a mark of chal-

Hat with a Glove as a Favor.

lenge.   A pretty laced or tasselled handkerchief was
also a favor and was worn like a cockade.

An excellent representation of the Cavalier hat
may be seen on the figure of Oliver Cromwell (page
35), which shows him dismissing Parliament.   Cornelius Steinwyck's flat-leafed hat has no feather.

The steeple-crowned hat of both men and women
was in vogue in the second half of the seventeenth
century in both England and America, at the time
when the witchcraft tragedies came to a culmination.
The long scarlet cloak was worn at the same date.
It is evident that the conventional witch of to-day,
an old woman in scarlet cloak and steeple-crowned
hat, is a relic of that day.   Through the striking
circumstances and the striking dress was struck off a
figurative type which is for all time.

William Kempe of "Duxburrow" in 1641 left
hats, hat-boxes, rich hatbands, bone laces, leather hat-

cases; also ten "capps." Hats were also made of cloth. In the tailor's bill of work done for Jonathan Corwin of Salem, in 1679, we read: "To making a Broadcloth Hatt 14*s*. To making 2 hatts & 2 jackets for your two sonnes 19*s*." In 1672 an association of Massachusetts hatters asked privileges and protection from the colonial government to aid and encourage American manufacture, but they were refused until they made better hats. Shortly after, however, the exportation of raccoon fur to England was forbidden, or taxed, as it was found to be useful in the home manufacture of hats.

The eighteenth century saw many and varied forms of the cocked hat; the nineteenth returned to a straight crown and brim. The description of these will be given in the due course of the narrative of this book.

CHAPTER VIII

THE VENERABLE HOOD

"*Paul saith, that a woman ought to have a* Power *on her head.* This Power *that some of them have is disguised gear and strange fashions. They must wear French Hoods — and I cannot tell you — I — what to call it. And when they make them ready and come to the Covering of their Head they will say,* 'Give me my French Hood, and Give me my Bonnet or my Cap.' *Now here is a* Vengeance-Devil; *we must have our* Power *from Turkey of Velvet, and gay it must be; far-fetched and dear-bought; and when it cometh it is a* False Sign."

— Sermon, Archbishop Latimer, 1549.

"*Hoods are the most ancient covering for the head and far more elegant and useful than the more modern fashion of hats, which present a useless elevation, and leave the neck and ears completely exposed.*"

— " Glossary of Ecclesiastical Ornament and Costume," Pugin, 1868.

CHAPTER VIII

THE VENERABLE HOOD

E are told by the great Viollet le Duc that the faces of fifteenth-century women were of a uniform type. Certainly a uniform head-dress tends to establish a seeming resemblance of the wearers; the strange, steeple head-dress of that century might well have that effect; and the "French hood" worn so many years by English, French, and American women has somewhat the same effect on women's countenances; it gives a uniformity of severity. It is difficult for a face to be pretty and gay under this gloomy hood. This French hood is plainly a development of the head-rail, which was simply an unshaped oblong strip of linen or stuff thrown over the head, and with the ends twisted lightly round the neck or tied loosely under the chin with whatever grace or elegance the individual wearer possessed.

Varying slightly from reign to reign, yet never greatly changed, this sombre plain French hood was worn literally for centuries. It was deemed so grave and dignified a head-covering that, in the reign of Edward III, women of ill carriage were forbidden the wearing of it.

In the year 1472 " Raye Hoods," that is, striped hoods, were enjoined in several English towns as the distinctive wear of women of ill character.   And in France this black hood was under restriction ; only

Gulielma Penn.

ladies of the French court were permitted to wear velvet hoods, and only women of station and dignity, black hoods.

This black hood was dignified in allegorical literature as " the venerable hood," and was ever chosen by limners to cover the head of any woman of age or dignity who was to be depicted.

In the *Ladies' Dictionary* a hood is defined thus: "A Dutch attire covering the head, face and all the body." And the long cloak with this draped hood, which must have been much like the Shaker cloak of to-day, seems to have been deemed a Dutch garment. It was warm and comfortable enough to be adopted readily by the English Pilgrims in Holland. It had come to England, however, in an earlier century. Of Ellinor Rummin, the alewife, Skelton wrote about the year 1500: —

> "A Hake of Lincoln greene
> It had been hers I weene
> More than fortye yeare
> And soe it doth appeare
> And the greene bare threds
> Looked like sere wedes
> Withered like hay
> The wool worn awaye
> And yet I dare saye
> She thinketh herself gaye
> Upon a holy day."

It is impossible to know how old this hood is. When I have fancied I had the earliest reference that could be found, I would soon come to another a few years earlier. We know positively from the *Lisle Papers* that it was worn in England by the name "French hood" in 1540. Anne Basset, daughter of Lady Lisle, had come into the household of the queen of Henry VIII, who at that time was Anne of Cleves. The "French Apparell" which the maid of honor fetched from Calais was not pleasing to the queen, who promptly ordered the young girl to wear "a velvet bonnet with a frontlet and edge of pearls." These bonnets are familiar to us on the head of Anne's predecessor, Anne Boleyn. They were worn even by young children. One is shown on page 108. The young lady borrowed a bonnet; and a factor named Husee — the biggest gossip of his day — promptly chronicles to her mother, " I saw her (Anne Basset) yesterday in her velvet bonnet that my Lady Sussex had tired her in, and thought it became her nothing so well as the French hood, — but the Queen's pleasure must be done ! "

Hannah Callowhill Penn.

Doubtless some of the Pilgrim Mothers wore bonnets like this one of Anne Basset's, especially if the wearer were a widow, when there was also an under frontlet which was either plain, plaited, or folded, but which came in a distinct point in the middle of the forehead.

This cap, or bandeau, with point on the forehead, is precisely the widow's cap worn by Catherine de Medicis. She was very severe in dress, but she introduced the wearing of neck-ruffs. She also wore hoods, the favorite head-covering of all Frenchwomen at that time. This form of head-

gear was sometimes called a widow's peak, on account of a similar peak of black silk or white being
often worn by widows, apparently of all European
nations. Magdalen Beeckman, an American woman
of Dutch descent (facing page 104), wears one. The
name is still applied to a pointed growth of hair on
the forehead. It has also been known as a head-
dress of Mary Queen of Scots, because some of her
portraits display this pointed outline of head-gear.
It continued until the time of Charles II. It is
often found on church brasses, and was plainly a
head-gear of dignity. A modified form is shown in
the portrait of Lady Mary Armine.

Stubbes in his *Anatomie of Abuses* gives a notion
of the importance of the French hood when he
speaks of the straining of all classes for rich attire :
that " every artificer's wife " will not go without her
hat of velvet every day ; " every merchant's wife
and meane gentlewoman " must be in her " French
hood " ; and " every poor man's daughter " in her
" taffatie hat or of wool at least." We have seen
what a fierce controversy burned over Madam
Johnson's " schowish " velvet hood.

An excellent account of this black hood as worn
by the Puritans is given in rhyme in " Hudibras
Redivivus," a long poem utterly worthless save for
the truthful descriptions of dress ; it runs : —

> " The black silk Hood, with formal pride
> First roll'd, beneath the chin was tied
> So close, so very trim and neat,
> So round, so formal, so complete,
> That not one jag of wicked lace

Or rag of linnen white had place
Betwixt the black bag and the face,
Which peep'd from out the sable hood
Like Luna from a sullen cloud."

It was doubtless selected by the women followers of Fox on account of its ancient record of sobriety and sanctity.

" Are the pinch'd cap and formal hood the emblems of sanctity ?   Does your virtue consist in your dress, Mrs. Prim ? "

writes Mrs. Centlivre in *A Bold Stroke for a Wife.*

The black hood was worn long by Quaker women ere they adopted the beaver hat of the eighteenth century, and the poke-bonnet of the nineteenth century.   On page 242 is given a portrait of Hannah Callowhill Penn, a Quaker, the second wife of William Penn.   She was a sensible woman brought up in a home where British mercantile thrift vied with Quaker belief in adherence to sober attire, and her portrait plainly shows her character.   Penn's young and pretty wife of his youth wears a fashionable pocket-hoop and rich brocade dress ; but she wears likewise the simple black hood (page 240).

The dominance of this black French hood came not, however, through its wear by sober-faced, discreet English Puritans and Quakers, but through a French influence, a court influence, the earnestness of its adoption by Madame de Maintenon, wife of King Louis XIV of France.   The whole dress of this strange ascetic would by preference have been that of a penitent ; but the king had a dislike of anything like mourning, so she wore dresses of some dark color other than black, generally a dull brown. The conventual aspect of her attire was added to by this large black hood, which was her constant wear, and is seen in her portraits. The life at court became melancholy, dejected, filled with icy reserve. And Madame, whether she rode "shut up in a close chair," says Duclos, "to avoid the least breath of air, while the King walked by her side, taking off his hat each time he stopped to speak to her"; or when she attended services in

Madame de Miramion.

the chapel, sitting in a closed gallery; or even in her own sombre apartments, bending in silence over ecclesiastic needlework, — everywhere, her narrow, yellow, livid face was shadowed and buried in this black hood.

Her strange power over the king was in force in 1681, and, until his death in 1715, this sable hood, so unlike the French taste, covered the heads of French women of all ages and ranks. The genial, almost quizzical countenance of that noble and charitable woman, Madame de Miramion, wears a like hood.

This French hood is prominent everywhere in book

illustrations of the eighteenth century and even of earlier years. The loosely tied corners and the sides appear under the straw hats upon many of the figures in Tempest's *Cryes of London*, 1698, such as the Milk woman, the "Newes" woman, etc., which

The Strawberry Girl.

publication, I may say in passing, is a wonderful source for the student of everyday costume. I give the Strawberry Girl on this page to show the ordinary form of the French hood on plain folk. *Misson's Memories*, published also in 1698, gives the milkmaids on Mayday in like hoods. The early editions of Hudibras show these hoods, and in Hogarth's works they may be seen; not always of black, of course, in later years, but ever of the same shape.

The hood worn by the Normans was called a chaperon. It was a sort of pointed bag with an oval opening for the face; sometimes the point was of great length, and was twisted, folded, knotted. In the Bodleian Library is a drawing of eleven figures

of young lads and girls playing *Hoodman-blind*
or *Blindman's-buff*. The latter name came from
the buffet or blow which the players gave with
their twisted chaperon hoods. The blind man
simply put his hood on "hind side afore," and
was effectually blinded.
These figures are of
the fifteenth century.

Black Silk Hood.

The wild latitude of
spelling often makes it
difficult to define an
article of dress. I have
before me a letter of
the year 1704, written
in Boston, asking that
a riding-hood be sent
from England of any
color save yellow ; and
one sentence of the in-
structions reads thus,
" If 'tis velvet let it
be a shabbaroon ; if of
cloth, a French hood."
I abandoned " shabba-
roon " as a wholly lost
word; until Mrs. Gum-
mere announced that the word was chaperon, from
the Norman hood just described. This chaperon is
specifically the hood worn by the Knights of the
Garter when in full dress ; in general it applies to
any ample hood which completely covers head and
face save for eye-holes. Another hood was the sortie.

The term "coif," spelt in various ways, quoif, quoiffe, coiffer, ciffer, quoiffer, has been held to ap-

Quilted Hood.

ply to the French hood; but it certainly did not in America, for I find often in inventories side by side items of black silk hoods and another of quoifs, which I believe were the white undercaps worn with the French hood; just as a coif was the close undercap for men's wear.

Through the two centuries following the assumption of the French hood came a troop of hoods, though sometimes under other names. In 1664 Pepys tells of his wife's yellow bird's-eye hood, "very fine, to church, as the fashion now is." Planché says hoods were not displaced by caps and bonnets till George II's time.

In the list of the "wedding apparell" of Madam Phillips, of Boston, are velvet hoods, love-hoods, and "sneal hoods"; hoods of Persian, of lustring, of gauze; frequently scarlet hoods are named. In 1712 Richard Hall sent, from Barbadoes to Boston, a trunk of his deceased wife's finery to be sold, among which was "one black Flowered Gauze Hoode," and he added rather spitefully that he "could send better but it would be too rich for Boston." He was a grandson of Madam Symonds of Ipswich. Furbelowed gauze hoods were then owned by Boston women, and must have been pretty things. Their delicacy has kept them from being preserved as have been velvet and Persian hoods.

For the years 1673 to 1721 we have a personal record of domestic life in Boston, a diary which is the sole storehouse to which we can turn for intimate knowledge of daily deeds in that little town. A scant record it is, as to wearing apparel; for the diary-writer, Samuel Sewall, sometime business man, friend, neighbor, councillor, judge, — and always Puritan, — had not a regard of dress as had his English contemporary, the gay Samuel Pepys, or even that sober English gentleman, John Evelyn. In Pepys's pages we have frequent and light-giving entries as to dress, interested and interesting entries. In Judge Sewall's diary, any references to dress are wholly accidental and not related as matters of any moment, save one important exception, his attitude toward wigs and wig-wearing. I could wish Sewall had had a keener eye for dress, for he wrote in strong, well-ordered English; and when he was deeply moved he wrote with much color in his pen. The most spirited episodes in the book are the judge's remarkable and varied courtships after he was left a widower at the age of sixty-five, and again when sixty-eight. While thus courting he makes almost his sole reference to women's dress, — that Madam Mico when he called came to him in a splendid dress, and that Madam Winthrop's dress, *after she had refused him*, was "not so clean as sometime it had been." But an article of his own dress, nevertheless, formed an important factor in his unsuccessful courtship of Madam Winthrop — his hood. When all the other widowers of the community, dignified magistrates, parsons, and men of professions, all bourgeoned out in stately full-bottomed wigs, what woman would want to have a lover who came a-courting in a hood? A detachable hood with a cloak, I doubt not he wore, like the one owned by Judge Curwen, his associate in that terrible tale of Salem's bigotry, cruelty, and credulity, the Witchcraft Trial. I cannot fancy Judge Sewall in a scarlet cloak and hood — a sad-colored one seems more in keeping with his temperament.

Perhaps our old friend, the judge, wore his hood under his hat, as did the sober citizens in *Piers Plowman ;* and as did judges in England.

It is certain that many men wore hoods; and they wore occasionally a garment which was really woman's wear, namely, a "riding hood"; which was also called a Dutch hood, and was like Elinor Rummin's hake. This riding-hood was really more of a cloak than a head-covering, as it often had arm-holes. It might well be classed with cloaks. I may say here that it is not possible, either by years or by topics, to isolate completely each chapter of this book from the other. Its very arrangement, being both by chronology and subject, gives me considerable liberty, which I now take in this chapter, by retaining the riding-hood among hoods, simply because of its name.

On May 6, 1717, the *Boston News Letter* gave a description of a gayly attired Indian runaway; she wore off a " red Camblet Ryding Hood fac'd with blue." Another servant absconded with an orange-colored riding-hood with arm-holes. I have an ancient pattern of a riding-hood; it was found in the bottom of an old hair-covered trunk. It was marked " London Ryding Hood." With it were rolled several packages of bits of woollen stuff, one of scarlet broadcloth, one of blue camlet, plainly labelled " Cuttings from Ap-

Pink Silk Hood.

phia's ryding hood " and " Pieces from Mary's ryding hood," showing that they had been placed there with the pattern when the hood was cut. It is a cape, cut in a deep point in front and back; the extreme length of the points from the collar being about twenty-six inches. The hood is precisely like the one on Judge Curwen's cloak, like the hoods of

Pug Hood.

Shaker cloaks. As bits of silk are rolled with the wool pieces, I infer that these riding-hoods were silk lined.

A most romantic name was given to the riding-hood after the battle of Preston in 1715. The Earl of Nithsdale, after the defeat of the Jacobites, was imprisoned in the Tower of London under sentence of death. From thence he made his escape through his wife's coolness and ingenuity. She visited him dressed in a large riding-hood which could be drawn closely over her face. He escaped in her dress and hood, fled to the continent, and lived thirty years in safety in France. After that dashing rescue, these hoods were known as Nithsdales. The head-covering portion still resembled the French hood, but the shoulder-covering portion was circular and ruffled — according to Hogarth. In Durfey's *Wit and Mirth*, 1719, is a spirited song commemorating this " sacred wife," who —

> " by her Wits immortal pains
> With her quick head has saved his brains."

One verse runs thus : —

> " Let Traitors against Kings conspire
> Let secret spies great Statesmen hire,
> Nought shall be by detection got
> If Woman may have leave to plot.
> There's nothing clos'd with Bars or Locks
> Can hinder Night-rayls, Pinners, Smocks ;
> For they will everywhere make good
> As now they've done the Riding-hood."

In 1737 " pug hoods " were in fashion. We have no proof of their shape, though I am told they were the close, plain, silk hood sometimes worn under other hoods. One is shown on page 252. Pumpkin hoods of thickly wadded wool were prodigiously hot head-coverings; they were crudely pumpkin shaped. Knitted hoods, under such names as "comforters," "fascinators," "rigolettes," "nubias," "opera hoods," "molly hoods," are of nineteenth-century invention.

CHAPTER IX

CLOAKS AND THEIR COUSINS

" *Within my memory the Ladies covered their lovely Necks with a Cloak, this was exchanged for the Manteel; this again was succeeded by the Pelorine; the Pelorine by the Neckatee; the Neckatee by the Capuchin, which hath now stood its ground for a long time.*" — "Covent Garden Journal," May 1, 1752.

" *Mary Wallace and Clemintina Ferguson Just arrived from the Kingdom of Ireland intend to follow the business of Mantua making and have furnished themselves from London in patterns of the following kinds of wear, and have fixed a correspondence so to have from thence the earliest Fashions in Miniature. They are at Peter Clarke's within two doors of William Walton's, Esq., in the Fly. Ladies and Gentlemen that employ them may depend on being expeditiously and reasonably served in making the following Articles, that is to say — Sacks, Negligees, Negligee-night-gowns, plain-night-gowns, pattanlears, shepherdesses, Roman cloaks, Cardinals, Capuchins, Dauphinesses, Shades lorrains, Bonnets and Hives.*"

— " New York Mercury," May, 1757.

CHAPTER IX

UNDER the general heading of cloaks I intend to write of the various capelike shoulder-coverings, for both men and women, which were worn in the two centuries of costume whereof this book treats. Often it is impossible to determine whether a garment should be classed as a hood or a cloak, for so many cloaks were made with head-coverings. Both capuchins and cardinals, garments of popularity for over a century, had hoods, and were worn as head-gear.

There is shown facing page 258 a full, long cloak of rich scarlet broadcloth, which is the oldest cloak I know. It has an interesting and romantic history. No relic in Salem is more noteworthy than this. It has survived since witchcraft days; and with right care, care such as it receives from its present owner, will last a thousand years. It was worn by Judge Curwen, one of the judges in those dark hours for Salem; and is still owned by Miss Bessie Curwen, his descendant. It will be noted that it bears a close resemblance to the Shaker cloaks of to-day, though the hood is handsomer. This hood also is detached from the cape. The presiding

justice in the Salem witchcraft trials was William
Stoughton, a severe Puritan.   In later years Judge
Sewall, his fellow-judge, in an agony of contrition,
remorse, self-reproach, self-abnegation, and exceeding sorrow at those judicial murders, stood in Boston
meeting-house, at a Sabbath service while his pastor
read aloud his confession of his cruel error, his expression of his remorse therefor.   A striking figure
is he in our history.   No thoughtful person can regard without emotions of tenderest sympathy and
admiration that benignant white-haired head, with
black skullcap, bowed in public disgrace, which was
really his honor.   But Judge Stoughton never expressed, in public or private, remorse or even regret.
I doubt if he ever felt either.   He plainly deemed his
action right.   I wish he could tell us what he thinks
of it now.   In his portrait facing page 260 he wears
a skullcap, as does Judge Sewall in his portrait, and
a cloak with a cape like that of his third associate,
Judge Curwen.   Judge Sewall had both cloak and
hood.   Possibly all judges wore them.   Judge
Stoughton's cloak has a rich collar and a curious clasp.
   Stubbes of course told of the fashion of cloak-
wearing : —

   " They have clokes also in nothing discrepant from the
rest ; of dyverse and sundry colours, white red tawnie
black, green yellow russet purple violet and an infinyte of
other colours.   Some of cloth silk velvet taffetie and such
like ; some of the Spanish French or Dutch fashion.   Some
short, scarcely reaching to the gyrdlestead or waist, some to
the knee, and othersome trayling upon the ground almost
like gownes than clokes.   These clokes must be garded

Scarlet Broadcloth Hooded Cloak.

laced & thorouly full, and sometimes so lined as the inner side standeth almost in as much as the outside. Some have sleeves, othersome have none. Some have hoodes to pull over the head, some have none. Some are hanged with points and tassels of gold silver silk, some without all this. But howsoever it bee, the day hath bene when one might have bought him two Clokes for lesse than now he can have one of these Clokes made for. They have such store of workmanship bestowed upon them."

It is such descriptions as this that make me regard in admiration this ancient Puritan. Would that I had the power of his pen! Fashion-plates, forsooth! The *Journal of the Modes!* — pray, what need have we of any pictures or any mantua-maker's words when we can have such a description as this. Why! the man had a perfect genius for millinery! Had he lived three centuries later, we might have had Master Stubbes in full control (openly or secretly, according to his environment) of some dress-making or tailoring establishment *pour les dames.*

The lining of these cloaks was often very gay in color and costly; "standing in as much as the outside." We find a son of Governor Winthrop writing in 1606 : —

"I desire you to bring me a very good camlet cloake lyned with what you like except blew. It may be purple or red or striped with those or other colors if so worn suitable and fashionable. . . . I would make a hard shift rather than not have the cloak."

Similar cloaks of scarlet, and of blue lined with scarlet, formed part of the uniform of soldiers for

many years and for many nations. They were certainly the wear of thrifty comfortable English gentlemen. Did not John Gilpin wear one on his famous
ride?

> " There was all that he might be
> Equipped from head to toe,
> His long red cloak well-brushed and neat
> He manfully did throw."

Scarlet was a most popular color for all articles of
dress in the early years of the eighteenth century.
Like the good woman in the Book of Proverbs, both
English and American housewife " clothed her household in scarlet." Women as well as men wore these
scarlet cloaks. It is curious to learn from Mrs.
Gummere that even Quakers wore scarlet. When
Margaret Fell married George Fox, greatest of
Quakers, he bought her a scarlet mantle. And in
1678 he sent her scarlet cloth for another mantle.
There was good reason in the wear of scarlet; it both
was warm and looked warm; and the color was a
lasting one. It did not fade like many of the home-
made dyes.

A very interesting study is that of color in wearing apparel. Beginning with the few crude dyes of
mediæval days, we could trace the history of dyeing,
and the use and invention of new colors and tints.
The names of these colors are delightful; the older
quaint titles seem wonderfully significant. We read
of such tints as billymot, phillymurt, or philomot
(feuille-mort), murry, blemmish, gridolin (gris-de-lin
or flax blossom), puce colour, foulding colour,
Kendal green, Lincoln green, treen-colour, watchet

Judge Stoughton.

blue, barry, milly, tuly, stammel red, Bristol red, zaffer-blue, which was either sapphire-blue or zaffre-blue, and a score of fanciful names whose signification and identification were lost with the death of the century. Historical events were commemorated in new hues; we have the political, diplomatic, and military history of various countries hinted to us. Great discoveries and inventions give names to colors. The materials and methods of dyeing, especially domestic dyes, are most interesting. An allied topic is the significance of colors, the limitation of their use. For instance, the study of blue would fill a chapter. The dress of 'prentices and serving-men in Elizabeth's day was always blue ; blue cloaks in winter, blue coats in summer. Blue was not precisely a livery ; it was their color, the badge of their condition in life, as black is now a parson's. Different articles of dress clung to certain colors. Green stockings had their time and season of clothing the sturdy legs of English dames as inevitably as green stalks filled the fields. Think of the years of domination of the green apron ; of the black hood — it is curious indeed.

In such exhaustive books upon special topics as the *History of the Twelve Great Livery Companies of London* we find wonderfully interesting and significant proof of the power of color; also in many the restrictive sumptuary laws of the Crown.

It would appear that this long, scarlet cloak never was out of wear for men and women until the nineteenth century. It was, at times, not the height of the fashion, but still was worn. Various ancient citizens of Boston, of Salem, are recalled through letter or traditions as clinging long to this comfortable cloak. Samuel Adams carried a scarlet cloak with him when he went to Washington.

I shall tell in a later chapter of my own great-great-grandmother's wear of a scarlet cloak until the opening years of the nineteenth century. During and after the Revolution these cloaks remained in high favor for women. French officers, writing home to France glowing accounts of the fair Americans, noted often that the ladies wore scarlet cloaks, and Madame Riedesel asserted that all gentlewomen in Canada never left the house save in a scarlet silk or cloth cloak.

"A woman's long scarlet cloak, almost new with a double cape," had been one of the articles feloniously taken from the house of Benjamin Franklin, printer, in Philadelphia, in 1750. Debby Franklin's dress, if we can judge from what was stolen, was a gay revel of color. Among the articles was one gown having a pattern of "large red roses and other large yellow flowers with blue in some of the flowers with many green leaves."

In the *Life of Jonathan Trumbull* we read that when a collection was taken in the Lebanon church for the benefit of the soldiers of the Continental army, when money, jewels, clothing, and food were gathered in a great heap near the pulpit, Madam Faith Trumbull rose up, threw from her shoulders her splendid scarlet cloth cloak, a gift from Count Rochambeau, advanced to the altar and laid the cloak with other offerings of patriotism and generosity.   It was used, we are told, to trim the uniforms of the Continental officers and soldiers.

One of the first entries in regard to dress made by Philip Fithian in 1773, when he went to Virginia as a school-teacher, was that "almost every Lady wears a Red Cloak; and when they ride out they tye a Red Handkerchief over their Head & Face; so when I first came to Virginia, I was distrest whenever I saw a Lady, for I thought she had the Tooth-Ach!"   When the young tutor left his charge a year later, he wrote a long letter of introduction, instruction, and advice to his successor; and so much impression had this riding-dress still upon him that he recounted at length the "Masked Ladies," as he calls them, explaining that the whole neck and face was covered, save a narrow slit for the eyes,

Woman's Cloak.   From Hogarth.

as if they had "the Mumps or Tooth-Ach."   It is possible that the insect torments encountered by the fair riders may have been the reason for this cloaking and masking.   Not only mosquitoes and flies and fleas were abundant, but Fithian tells of the irritating illness and high fever of the fairest of his little flock from being bitten with ticks, " which cover her like a distinct smallpox."

In seventeenth-century inventories an occasional item is a rocket. I think no better description of a rocket can be given than that of Celia Fiennes : —

"You meete all sorts of countrywomen wrapped up in the mantles called West Country Rockets, a large mantle doubled together, of a sort of serge, some are linsey-woolsey and a deep fringe or fag at the lower end; these hang down, some to their feet, some only just below the waist; in the summer they are all in white garments of this sort, in the winter they are in red ones."

This would seem much like a blanket shawl, but the word was also applied to the scarlet round cloak.

Another much-used name and cloaklike garment was the roquelaure. A very good contemporary definition may be copied from *A Treatise on the Modes*, 1715; it says it is "a short abridgement or compendium of a coat which is dedicated to the Duke of Roquelaure." It was simply a shorter cloak than had been worn, and it was hoodless; for the great curled wigs with heavy locks well over the shoulders made hoods superfluous, and even impossible, for men's wear. It was very speedily taken into favor by women; and soon the advertisements of lost articles show that it was worn by women universally as by men. In the *Boston News Letter*, in 1730, a citizen advertises that he has lost his " Blue Cloak or Roculo with brass buttons." This was the first of an ingenious series of misspellings which produced at times a word almost unrelated to the original French word. Rocklow, rockolet, roquelo, rochelo, roquello, and even rotkello have I found. Ashton says that scarlet cloth was the favorite fabric for roquelaures in England; and he deems the scarlet roclows and rocliers with gold loops and buttons "exceeding magnifical." I note in the American advertisements that the lost roquelaures are of very bright colors; some were of silk, some of camlet; generally they are simply 'cloth.' Many of the American roquelaures had double capes. I think those handsome, gay cloaks must have given a very bright, cheerful aspect to the town streets of the middle of the eighteenth century.

Sir William Pepperell, who was ever a little shaky in his spelling, but possibly no more so than his neighbors, sent in 1737 from Piscataqua to one Hooper in England for "A Handsom Rockolet for my daughter of about 15 yrs. old, or what is ye Most Newest Fashion for one of her age to ware at meeting in ye Wint^r Season."

The capuchin was a hooded cloak named from the hooded garment worn by the Capuchin monks. The date 1752 given by Fairholt as an early date of its wear is far wrong. Fielding used the word in *Tom Jones* in 1749; other English publications, in 1709; and I find it in the *Letters of Madame de Sévigné* as early as 1686. The cardinal, worn at the same date, was originally of scarlet cloth, and I find was generally of some wool stuff. At one time I felt sure that cardinal was always the name for the woollen cloak, and capuchin of the silken one; but now I am a bit uncertain whether this is a rule. Judging from references in literature and advertisements, the capuchin was a richer garment than the cardinal.   Capuchins were frequently trimmed liberally with lace, ribbons, and robings; were made of silk with gauze ruffles, or of figured velvet.   One is here shown which is taken from one of Hogarth's prints.

A Capuchin.   From Hogarth.

This notice is from the *Boston Evening Post* of January 13, 1772:—

"Taken from Concert Hall on Thursday Evening a handsom Crimson Satin Capuchin trimmed with a rich white Blond Lace with a narrow Blond Lace on the upper edge Lined with White Sarsnet."

In 1752 capuchins and cardinals were much worn, especially purple ones. The *Connoisseur* says all colors were neglected for purple. "In purple we glowed from hat to shoe. In such request were ribbons and silks of that famous color that neither milliner mercer nor dyer could meet the demand."

The names "cardinal" and "capuchin" had been

derived from monkish wear, and the cape, called a
pelerine, had an allied derivation; it is said to be
derived from *pèlerin* — meaning a pilgrim. It was
a small cape with longer ends hanging in front;
and was invented as a light, easily adjustable covering for the ladies' necks, which had been left so
widely and coldly bare by the low-cut French bodices. It is said that the garment was invented in
France in 1671. I do not find the word in use in
America till 1730. Then mantua-makers advertised
that they would make them. Various materials were
used, from soft silk and thin cloth to rich velvet;
but silk pelerines were more common.

In 1743, in the *Boston News Letter*, Henrietta
Maria East advertised that "Ladies may have their
Pellerines made" at her mantua-making shop. In
1749 "pellerines" were advertised for sale in the
Boston Gazette and a black velvet "pellerine" was
lost.

In the quotation heading this chapter, manteel,
pelerine, and neckatee precede the capuchin; but
in fact the capuchin is as old as the pelerine. Beyond the fact that all mantua-makers made neckatees, and that they were a small cape, this garment
cannot be described. It required much less stuff
than either capuchin or cardinal. The "manteel"
was, of course, as old as the cloak. Elijah "took
his mantle and wrapped it together, and smote the
waters." In the Middle Ages the mantle was a
great piece of cloth in any cloaklike shape, of
which the upper corners were fastened at the neck.
Often one of the front edges was thrown over one

shoulder. In the varied forms of spelling and wearing, as manto, manteau, mantoon, mantelet, and man-
tilla the foundation is the same. We have noted
the richness and
elegance of Madam
Symonds's mantua.
We could not for-
get the word and its
signification while
we have so impor-
tant a use of it in
mantua-maker.

Dauphiness was
the name of a cer-
tain style of man-
tle, which was most
popular about
1750. Harriot
Paine had "Dauph-
iness Mantles" for
sale in Boston in
1755. A rude draw-
ing in an old letter
indicates that the
"Dauphiness" had
a deep point at the
back, and was cut
up high at the arm-
hole. It was of thin

Lady Caroline Montagu.

silk, and was trimmed all around the lower edge with
a deep, full frill of the silk, which at the arm-hole
fell over the arm like a short sleeve.

Many were the names of those pretty little cloaks and capes which were worn with the sacque-shaped gowns. The duchess was one; we revived the name for a similar mantle in 1870. The pelisse was in France the cloak with arm-holes, shown, on page 268, upon one of Sir Joshua Reynolds's engaging children. The pelisse in America sometimes had sleeves, I am sure; and was hardly a cloak. It is difficult to classify some forms which seem almost jackets. A general distinction may be made not to include sleeved garments with the cloaks; but several of the manteaus had loose, large, flowing sleeves, and some like Madam Symonds's had detached sleeves. It is also difficult to know whether some of the negligees were cloaks or sacque-like gowns. And there is the other extreme; some of the smaller, circular neck-coverings like the vandykes are not cloaks. They are scarcely capes; they are merely collars; but there are still others which are a bit bigger and are certainly capes. And are there not also capes, like the neckatee, which may be termed cloaks? Material, too, is bewildering; a light gauze thing of ribbons and furbelows like the Unella is not really a cloak, yet it takes a cloaklike form. There are no cut and dried rules as to size, form, or weight of these cloaks, capes, collars, and hoods, so I have formed my own classes and assignments.

CHAPTER X

THE DRESS OF OLD-TIME CHILDREN

" *Rise up to thy Elders, put off thy Hat, make a Leg.*"

— "Janua Linguarum," COMENIUS, 1664.

" *Little ones are taught to be proud of their clothes before they can put them on.*"

— " Essay on Human Understanding," LOCKE, 1687.

" *When thou thyself, a watery, pulpy, slobbery Freshman and newcomer on this Planet, sattest mewling in thy nurse's arms; sucking thy coral, and looking forth into the world in the blankest manner, what hadst thou been without thy blankets and bibs and other nameless hulls?* "

— " Sartor Resartus," THOMAS CARLYLE, 1836.

CHAPTER X

THE DRESS OF OLD-TIME CHILDREN

WHEN we reflect that in any community the number of "the younger sort" is far larger than of grown folk, when we know, too, what large families our ancestors had, in all the colonies, we must deem any picture of social life, any history of costume, incomplete unless the dress of children is shown. French and English books upon costume are curiously silent regarding such dress. It might be alleged as a reason for this singular silence that the dress of young children was for centuries precisely that of their elders, and needed no specification. But infants' dress certainly was widely different, and full of historic interest, as well as quaint prettiness; and there were certain details of the dress of older children that were most curious and were wholly unlike the contemporary garb of their elders; sometimes these details were survivals of ancient modes for grown folk, sometimes their name was a survival while their form had changed.

For the dress of children of the early years of colonial life — the seventeenth century — I have an unusual group of five portraits. One is the little Padishal child, shown with her mother in the frontispiece, one is Robert Gibbes (shown facing page 316). The third child is said to be John Quincy — his picture is opposite this page. The two portraits of Margaret and Henry Gibbes are owned in Virginia; but are too dimly photographed for reproduction. The portrait of Robert Gibbes is owned by inheritance by Miss Sarah B. Hager, of Kendal Green, Massachusetts. It is well preserved, having hung for over a hundred years on the same wall in the old house. He was four years old when this portrait was painted. It is marked 1670. John Quincy's portrait is marked also plainly as one and a half years old, and with a date which is a bit dimmed; it is either 1670 or 1690. If it is 1690, the picture can be that of John Quincy, though he would scarcely be as large as is the portrayed figure. If the date is 1670, it cannot be John Quincy, for he was born in 1689. The picture has the same checker-board floor as the three other Gibbes portraits, four rows of squares wide; and the child's toes are set at the same row as are the toes of the shoes in the picture of Robert Gibbes.

The portraits of Henry and Margaret Gibbes are also marked plainly 1670. There was a fourth Gibbes child, who would have been just the age of the subject of the Quincy portrait; and it is natural that there should be a suspicion that this fourth portrait is of the fourth Gibbes child, not of John Quincy.

Margaret Gibbes was born in 1663. Henry Gibbes was born in 1667. He became a Congregational minister. His daughter married Nathaniel

John Quincy.

Appleton, and through Nathaniel, John, Dr. John S., and John, the portrait, with that of Margaret, came to the present owner, General John W. S. Appleton, of Charlestown, West Virginia.

The dress of these five children is of the same rich materials that would be worn by their mothers. The Padishal child wears black velvet like her mother's gown; but her frock is brightened with scarlet points of color. The linings of the velvet hanging sleeves, the ribbon knots of the white virago-sleeve, the shoe-tip, the curious cap-tassel, are of bright scarlet. We have noted the dominance of scarlet in old English costumes. It was evidently the only color favored for children. The lace cap, the rich lace stomacher, the lace-edged apron, all are of Flemish lace. Margaret Gibbes wears a frock of similar shape, and equally rich and dark in color; it is a heavy brocade of blue and red, with a bit of yellow. Her fine apron, stomacher, and full sleeves are rich in needlework. Robert Gibbes's "coat," as a boy's dress at that age then was called, is a striking costume. The inmost sleeves are of white lawn, over them are sleeves made of strips of galloon of a pattern in yellow, white, scarlet, and black, with a rolled cuff of red velvet. There is a similar roll around the hem of the coat. Still further sleeves are hanging sleeves of velvet trimmed with the galloon.

It will be noted that his hanging sleeve is cut square and trimmed squarely across the end. It is similar to the sleeves worn at the same time by citizens of London in their formal "liveryman's" dress, which had bands like pockets, that sometimes really were pockets.

His plain, white, hemstitched band would indicate that he was a boy, did not the swing of his petticoats plainly serve to show it, as do also his brothers' "coats." That child knew well what it was to tread and trip on those hated petticoats as he went upstairs. I know how he begged for breeches. The apron of John Quincy varies slightly in shape from that of the other boy, but the general dress is like, save his pretty, gay, scarlet hood, worn over a white lace cap. One unique detail of these Gibbes portraits, and the Quincy portrait, is the shoes. In all four, the shoes are of buff leather, with absolutely square toes, with a thick, scarlet sole to which the buff-leather upper seems tacked with a row either of long, thick, white stitches or of heavy metal-headed nails; these white dots are very ornamental. One pair of the shoes has great scarlet roses on the instep. The square toe was distinctly a Cavalier fashion. It is in Miss Campion's portrait, facing this page, and in the print of the Prince of Orange on page 282, and is found in many portraits of the day. But these American shoes are in the minor details entirely unlike any English shoes I have seen in any collection elsewhere, and are most interesting. They were doubtless English in make.

The portrait of John Quincy resembles much in its dress that of Oliver Cromwell when two years old, the picture now at Chequers Court. Cromwell's linen collar is rounded, and a curious ornament is worn in front, as a little girl would wear a

1661
Aes̅ 2 Men̅ 2

Miss Campion, 1667.

locket.   The whole throat and a little of the upper
neck is bare.   Dark hair, slightly curled, comes out
from the close cap in front of the ears.   This picture of Cromwell distinctly resembles his mother's
portrait.

The quaint tassel or rosette or feather on the cap
of the Padishal child was a fashion of the day.   It is
seen in many Dutch portraits of children.   In a curious old satirical print of Oliver Cromwell preaching
are the figures of two little children drawn standing
by their mother's side.   One child's back is turned
for our sight, and shows us what might well be the
back of the gown of the Padishal child.   The cap
has the same ornament on the crown, and the hanging sleeves — of similar form — have, at intervals of
a few inches apart from shoulder to heel, an outside
embellishment of knots of ribbon.   There is also a
band or strip of embroidery or passementerie up the
back of the gown from skirt-hem to lace collar, with
a row of buttons on the strip.   This proves that
the dress was fastened in the back, as the stiff, un-
broken, white stomacher also indicates.   The other
child is evidently a boy.   His gown is long and fur-
edged.   His cap is round like a Scotch bonnet, and
has also a tuft or rosette at the crown.   On either
side hang long strings or ribbon bands reaching from
the cap edge to the knee.

These portraits of these little American children
display nothing of that God-given attribute which
we call genius, but they do possess a certain welcome
trait, which is truthfulness; a hard attention to detail, which confers on them a quality of exactness of

likeness of which we are very sensible. We have for comparison a series of portraits of the same dates, but of English children, the children of the royal and court families. I give on page 126 a part of the portrait group of the family of the Duke of Buckingham; namely, the Duchess of Buckingham and her two children, an infant son and a daughter, Mary. She was a wonderful child, known in the court as "Pretty Moll," having the beauty of her father, the "handsomest-bodied" man in court, his vivacity, his vigor, and his love of dancing, all of which made him the prime favorite both of James and his son, Charles.

A letter exists written by the duchess to her husband while he was gone to Spain with his thirty suits of richly embroidered garments of which I have written in my first chapter. The duchess writes of "Pretty Moll," who was not a year old : —

"She is very well, I thank God; and when she is set to her feet and held by her sleeves she will not go softly but stamp, and set one foot before another very fast, and I think she will run before she can go. She loves dancing extremely; and when the Saraband is played, she will get her thumb and finger together offering to snap; and then when "Tom Duff" is sung, she will shake her apron; and when she hears the tune of the clapping dance my Lady Frances Herbert taught the Prince, she will clap both her hands together, and on her breast, and she can tell the tunes as well as any of us can; and as they change tunes she will change her dancing. I would you were here but to see her, for you would take much delight in her now she is so full of pretty play and tricks. Everybody says she grows each day more like you."

Can you not see the engaging little creature, clapping her hands and trying to step out in a dance? No imaginary description could equal in charm this bit of real life, this word-picture painted in bright and living colors by a mother's love. I give another merry picture of her childhood and widowhood in a later chapter. Many portraits of " Pretty Moll "

Infant's Cap.

were painted by Van Dyck, more than of any woman in England save the queen. One shows her in the few months that she was the child-wife of the eldest son of the Earl of Pembroke. She is in the centre of the great family group. She was married thrice; her favorite choice of character in which to be painted was Saint Agnes, who died rather than be married at all.

Both mother and child in this picture wear a lace cap of unusual shape, rather broader where turned over at the ear than at the top. It is seen on a few other portraits of that date, and seems to have come to England with the queen of James I. It disappeared before the graceful modes of hair-dressing introduced by Queen Henrietta Maria.

The genius of Van Dyck has preserved for us a wonderful portraiture of children of this period, the children of King Charles I. The earliest group shows the king and queen with two children; one a baby in arms with long clothes and close cap — this might have been painted yesterday. The little prince standing at his father's knee is in a dark green frock, much like John Quincy's, and apparently no richer. A painting at Windsor shows king and queen with the two princes, Charles and James; another, also at Windsor, gives the mother with the two sons. One at Turin gives the two princes with their sister. At Windsor, and in *replica* at Berlin, is the famous masterpiece with the five children, dated 1637.

This exquisite group shows Charles, the Prince of Wales (aged seven), with his arm on the head of a great dog; he is in the full garb of a grown man, a Cavalier. His suit is red satin; the shoes are white, with red roses. Mary, demure as in all her portraits, is aged six; she wears virago-sleeves made like those of Margaret Gibbes, with hanging sleeves over them, a lace stomacher, and cap, with tufts of scarlet, and hair curled lightly on the forehead, and pulled out at the side in ringlets, like that of her mother, Henrietta Maria. The Duke of York, aged two, wears a red dress spotted with yellow, with sleeves precisely like those of Robert Gibbes; white lace-edged apron, stomacher, and cap; his hair is in curls. The Princess Elizabeth was aged about two; she is in blue. Her cap is of wrought and tucked lawn, and she wears either a pearl ear-ring or a pearl pendant at the corner of the cap just at the ear, and a string of pearls around her neck. She has a gentle, serious face, one with a premonitory tinge of sad-

Eleanor Foster.   1755.

ness.   She was the favorite daughter of the king,
and wrote the inexpressibly touching account of his
last days in prison.   She was but thirteen, and he
said to her the day before his execution, " Sweetheart, you will forget all this."   " Not while I
live," she answered, with many tears, and promised
to write it down.   She lived but a short time, for
she was broken-hearted ; she was found dead, with
her head lying on the religious book she had been
reading — in which attitude she is carved on her
tomb.   The baby is Princess Anne, a fat little thing
not a year old ; she is naked, save for a close cap and
a little drapery.   She died when three and a half
years old ; died with these words on her lips,
" Lighten Thou mine eyes, O Lord, that I sleep
not the sleep of Death."   It was not Puritan children only at that time who were filled with deep
religious thought, and gave expression to that
thought even in infancy ; children of the Church
of England and of the Roman Catholic Church
were all widely imbued with religious feeling, and
Biblical words were the familiar speech of the day,
of both young and old.   It rouses in me strange
emotions when I gaze at this portrait and remember
all that came into the lives of these royal children.
They had been happier had they been born, like the
little Gibbes children, in America, and of untitled
parents.

At Amsterdam may be seen the portrait of
Princess Mary painted with her cousin, William
of Orange, who became her child-husband.   She
had the happiest life of any of the five — if she ever

could be happy after her father's tragic death. In this later portrait she is a little older and sadder and stiffer. Her waist is more pinched, her shoulders

THE PORTRAICTVRE OF THE MOST ILLVSTRIOVS &
Noble William of Nassau Prince of Orange, &c born 1627
& married 13 May 1641

narrower, her face more demure. His likeness is here given. The only marked difference in the dress of these children from the dress of the Gibbes children is in the lace; the royal family wear laces with deeply pointed edges, the point known as a Vandyke. The American children wear straight-edged laces, as was the general manner of laces of that day. An old print of the Duke of York when about seven years old is given (facing page 168). He carries in his hand a quaint racket.

The costume worn by these children is like that of plebeian English children of the same date. A manuscript drawing of a child of the people in the reign of Charles I shows a precisely similar dress, save that the child is in leading-strings held by the mother; and in the belt to which the leading-strings are attached is thrust a " muckinder " or handkerchief.

These leading-strings are seldom used now, but they were for centuries a factor in a child's progress. They were a favorite gift to children ; and might be a simple flat strip of strong stuff, or might be richly worked like the leading-strings which Mary, Queen of Scots embroidered for her little baby, James. These are three bands of Spanish pink satin ribbon, each about four or five feet long and over an inch wide. The three are sewed with minute over-and-over stitches into a flat band about four inches wide, and are embroidered with initials, emblems of the crown, a verse of a psalm, and a charming flower and grape design. The gold has tarnished into brown, and the flower colors are fled ; but it is still a beautiful piece of work, speaking with no uncertain voice of a tender, loving mother and a womanly queen. There were crewel-worked leading-strings in America. One is prettily lined with strips of

handsome brocade that had been the mother's wedding petticoat; it is not an ill rival of the princely
leading-strings.

Another little English girl, who was not a princess,
but who lived in the years when ran and played our
little American children, was Miss Campion, who
"minded her horn-book" — minded it so well that
she has been duly honored as the only English child
ever painted with horn-book in hand.   Her petticoat and stomacher, her apron, and cap and hanging
sleeves and square-toed shoes are just like Margaret
Gibbes's — bought in the same London shops, very
likely.

Not only did all these little English and American
children dress alike, but so did French children, and
so did Spanish children — only little Spanish girls
had to wear hoops.   Hoops were invented in Spain;
and proud was the Spanish queen of them.

Velasquez, contemporary with Van Dyck, painted
the Infanta Maria Theresa; the portrait is now in
the Prado at Madrid.   She carries a handkerchief
as big as a tablecloth; but above her enormous
hoop appears not only the familiar virago-sleeve,
but the straight whisk or collar, just like that of
English children and dames.   This child and the
Princess Marguerite, by Velasquez, have the hair
parted on one side with the top lock turned aside
and tied with a knot of ribbon precisely as we tie
our little daughters' hair to-day; and as the bride
of Charles II wore her hair when he married her.
French children had not assumed hoops.   I have
an old French portrait before me of a little demoi-

selle, aged five, in a scarlet cloth gown with edgings
of a narrow gray gimp or silver lace. All the sleeves,
the slashes, the long, hanging sleeves are thus edged.
She wears a long, narrow, white lawn apron, and her
stiff bodice has a stomacher of lawn. There is a
straight white collar tied with tiny bows in front and
white cuffs ; a scarlet close cap edged with silver lace
completes an exquisite costume, which is in shape
like that of Margaret Gibbes. The garments of all
these children, royal and subject, are too long, of
course, for comfort in walking ; too stiff, likewise,
for comfort in wearing ; too richly laced to be suitable for everyday wear ; too costly, save for folk of
wealth ; yet nevertheless so quaint, so becoming, so
handsome, so rich, that we reluctantly turn away
from them.

The dress of all young children in families of
estate was cumbersome to a degree. There exists
to-day a warrant for the purchase of clothing of
Mary Tudor, sister of Henry VIII, when she was
a sportive, wilful, naughty little child of four. She
wore such unwieldy and ugly guise as this : kirtles
of tawny damask and black satin ; gowns of green
and crimson striped velvet edged with purple tinsel,
which must have been hideous. All were lined with
heavy black buckram. Indeed, the inner portions,
the linings of old-time garments, even of royalty,
were far from elegant. I have seen garments worn
by grown princesses of the eighteenth century,
whereof the rich brocade bodies were lined with
common, heavy fabric, usually a stiff linen ; and
the sewing was done with thread as coarse as shoe-

thread, often homespun.   This, too, when the sleeve
and neck-ruffles would be of needlework so exquisite
that it could not be rivalled in execution to-day.

Many of the older portraits of children show
hanging sleeves.   The rich claret velvet dresses of
the Van Cortlandt twins, aged four, had hanging
sleeves.   This dress is given in my book, *Child Life
in Colonial Days*, as is that of Katherine Ten Broeck,
another child of Dutch birth living in New York,
who also wore heavy hanging sleeves.

The use of the word hanging sleeves in common speech and in literature is most interesting.   It
had a figurative meaning; it symbolized youth and
innocence.   This meaning was acquired, of course,
from the wear for centuries of hanging sleeves by
little children, both boys and girls.   It had a second,
a derivative signification, being constantly employed
as a figure of speech to indicate second childhood; it
was used with a wistful tender meaning as an emblem
of the helplessness of feeble old age.   The following example shows such an employment of the term.

In 1720, Judge Samuel Sewall, of Boston, then
about seventy-five years of age, wrote to another
old gentleman, whose widowed sister he desired to
marry, in these words : —

"I remember when I was going from school at New-
bury to have sometime met your sisters Martha and Mary
in Hanging Sleeves, coming home from their school in
Chandlers Lane, and have had the pleasure of speaking to
them.   And I could find it in my heart now to speak
to Mrs. Martha again, now I myself am reduc'd to Hanging Sleeves."

William Byrd, of Westover, in Virginia, in one of his engaging and sprightly letters written in 1732, pictures the time of the patriarchs when "a man was reckoned at Years of Discretion at 100; Boys went into Breeches at about 40; Girles continued in Hanging Sleeves till 50, and plaid with their Babys till Threescore."

When Benjamin Franklin was seven years old, he wrote a poem which was sent to his uncle, a bright old Quaker. This uncle responded in clever lines which begin thus : —

> "'Tis time for me to throw aside my pen
> When Hanging-Sleeves read, write and rhyme like men.
> This forward Spring foretells a plenteous crop
> For if the bud bear grain, what will the top?"

A curious use of the long hanging sleeve was as a pocket; that is, it would seem curious to us were it not for our acquaintance with the capacity of the sleeves of our unwelcome friend, Ah Sing. The pocketing sleeve of the time of Henry III still exists in the heraldic charge known as the manche, borne by the Hastings and Norton family. This is also called maunch, émanche, and mancheron. The word "manchette," an ornamented cuff, retains the meaning of the word, as does manacle ; all are from *manus*.

Hanging sleeves had a time of short popularity for grown folk while Anne Boleyn was queen of England ; for the little finger of her left hand had a double tip, and the long, graceful sleeves effectually concealed the deformity.

In my book entitled *Child Life in Colonial Days* I have given over thirty portraits of American children. These show the changes of fashions, the wear of children at various periods and ages. Childish dress ever reflected the dress of their elders, and often closely imitated it. Two very charming costumes are worn by two little children of the province of South Carolina. The little girl is but two years old. She is Ellinor Cordes, and was painted about 1740. She is a lovely little child of French features and French daintiness of dress, albeit a bright yellow brocaded satin would seem rather gorgeous attire for a girl of her years. The boy is her kinsman, Daniel Ravenel, and was then about five years old. He wore what might be termed a frock with spreading petticoats, which touched the ground; there is a decided boyishness in the tight-fitting, trim waistcoat with its silver buttons and lace, and the befrogged coat with broad cuffs and wrist ruffles, and turned-over revers, and narrow linen inner collar. It is an exceptionally pleasing boy's dress, for a little boy.

A somewhat similar but more feminine coat is worn by Thomas Aston Coffin; it opens in front over a white satin petticoat, and it has a low-cut neck and sleeves shortened to the elbow, and worn over full white undersleeves. Other portraits by Copley show the same dress of white satin, which boys wore till six years of age.

Copley's portrait of his own children is given on a later page. This family group always startles all who have seen it only in photographs; for its colors

Mrs. Theodore Sedgwick and Daughter.

are so unexpected, so frankly crude and vivid. The individuals are all charming. The oldest child, the daughter, Elizabeth, stands in the foreground in a delightful white frock of striped gauze. This is worn over a pink slip, and the pink tints show in the thinner folds of whiteness; a fine piece of texture-painting. The gauze sash is tied in a vast knot, and lies out in a train; this is a more vivid pink, inclining to the tint of the old-rose damask furniture-covering. She wears a pretty little net and muslin cap with a cap-pin like a tiny rose. This single figure is not excelled, I think, by any child's portrait in foreign galleries, nor is it often equalled. Nor can the exquisite expression of childish love and confidence seen on the face of the boy,

Infant Child of Francis Hopkinson, "the Signer." Painted by Francis Hopkinson.

John Singleton Copley, Junior, who later became Lord Lyndhurst, find a rival in painting. It is an unspeakably touching portrait to all who have seen upturned close to their own eyes the trusting and loving face of a beautiful son as he clung with strong boyish arms and affection to his mother's neck.

This little American boy, who became Lord Chancellor of England, wears a nankeen suit with a lilac-tinted sash. It is his beaver hat with gold hatband and blue feather that lies on the ground at the feet of the grandfather, Richard Clarke. The baby, held by the grandfather, wears a coral and bells on a lilac sash-ribbon ; such a coral as we see in many portraits of infants. Another child in white-embroidered robe and dark yellow sash completes this beautiful family picture. Its great fault to me is the blue of Mrs. Copley's gown, which is as vivid as a peacock's breast. This painting is deemed Copley's masterpiece ; but an equal interest is that it is such an absolute and open expression of Copley's lovable character and upright life. In it we can read his affectionate nature, his love of his sweet wife, his happy home-relations, and his pride in his beautiful children.

There is ample proof, not only in the inventories which chance to be preserved, but in portraits of the times, that children's dress in the eighteenth century was often costly. Of course the children of wealthy parents only would have their portraits painted ; but their dress was as rich as the dress of the children of the nobility in England at the same time. You can see this in the colored reproduction of the portraits of Hon. James Bowdoin and his sister, Augusta, afterwards Lady Temple. That they were good likenesses is proved by the fact that the faces are strongly like those of the same persons in more mature years. You find little Augusta changed but slightly in matronhood in the fine pastel by Copley. In this portrait of the two Bowdoin children, the entire dress is given. Seldom are the shoes shown. These are interesting, for the boy's square-toed black shoes with buckles are wholly unlike his sister's blue morocco slippers with turned-up peaks and gilt ornaments from toe to instep, making a foot-gear much like certain Turk-

ish slippers seen to-day. Her hair has the bedizenment of beads and feathers, which were worn by young girls for as many years as their mothers wore the same. The young lad's dress is precisely like his father's. There is much charm in these straight little figures. They have the aristocratic bearing which is a family trait of all of that kin. I should not deem Lady Temple ever a beauty, though she was called so by

Mary Seton, 1763.

Manasseh Cutler, a minister who completely yielded to her charms when she was a grandmother and forty-four. This portrait of brother and sister is, I believe, by Blackburn. The dress is similar and the date the same as the portrait of the Misses Royall (one of whom became Lady Pepperell), which is by Blackburn.

The portrait of a charming little American child

is shown on page 291. This child, in feature, figure, and attitude, and even in the companionship of the kitten, is a curious replica of a famous English portrait of "Miss Trimmer."

I have written at length in Chapter IV of a grandmother in the Hall family and of the Hall family connection. Let me tell of another grandmother, Madam Lydia Coleman, the daughter of the old Indian fighter, Captain Joshua Scottow. She, like Madam Symonds and Madam Stoddard, had had several husbands — Colonel Benjamin Gibbs, Attorney-General Anthony Checkley, and William Coleman. The Hall children were her grandchildren; and came to Boston for schooling at one time. Many letters exist of Hon. Hugh Hall to and from his grandmother, Madam Coleman. She writes thus: —

"As for Richard since I told him I would write to his Father he is more orderly, & he is very hungry, and has grown so much yt all his Clothes is too Little for him. He loves his book and his play too. I hired him to get a Chapter of ye Proverbs & give him a penny every Sabbath day, & promised him 5 shillings when he can say them all by heart. I would do my duty by his soul as well as his body. . . . He has grown a good boy and minds his School and Lattin and Dancing. He is a brisk Child & grows very Cute and wont wear his new silk coat yt was made for him. He wont wear it every day so yt I don't know what to do with it. It wont make him a jackitt. I would have him a good husbander but he is but a child. For shoes, gloves, hankers & stockins, they ask very deare, 8 shillings for a paire & Richard takes no care of them.

Richard wears out nigh 12 paire of shoes a year. He
brought 12 hankers with him and they have all been lost
long ago; and I have bought him 3 or 4 more at a time.
His way is to tie knottys at one end & beat ye Boys with
them and then to lose them & he cares not a bit what I
will say to him."

Madam Coleman, after this handful, was given
charge of his sister Sarah. When Missy arrived from
the Barbadoes, she was eight years old. She brought
with her a maid. The grandmother wrote back
cheerfully to the parents that the child was well and
brisk, as indeed she was. All the very young gentlemen and young ladies of Boston Brahmin blood paid
her visits, and she gave a feast at a child's dancing-
party with the sweetmeats left over from her sea-
store. Her stay in her grandmother's household
was surprisingly brief. She left unbidden with her
maid, and went to a Mr. Binning's to board; she
sent home word to the Barbadoes that her grandmother made her drink water with her meals. Her
brother wrote to Madam Coleman: —

" We were all persuaded of your tender and hearty affection to my Sister when we recommended her to your pa-
rental care. We are sorry to hear of her Independence in
removing from under the Benign Influences of your Wing
& am surprised she dare do it without our leave or consent or that Mr. Binning receive her at his house before
he knew how we were affected to it. We shall now desire
Mr. Binning to resign her with her waiting maid to you and
in our Letter to him have strictly ordered her to Return
to your House."

But no brother could control this spirited young damsel.   Three months later a letter from Madam Coleman read thus : —

"Sally wont go to school nor to church and wants a nue muff and a great many other things she don't need.   I tell her fine things are cheaper in Barbadoes.   She is well and brisk, says her Brother has nothing to do with her as long as her father is alive."

Hugh Hall wrote in return, saying his daughter ought to have one room to sleep in, and her maid another, that it was not befitting children of their station to drink water, they should have wine and beer.   We cannot wonder that they dressed like their elders since they were treated like their elders in other respects.

The dress of very young girls was often extraordinarily rich.   We find this order sent to London in 1739, for finery for Mary Cabell, daughter of Dr. William Cabell of Virginia, when she was but thirteen years old : —

" 1 Prayer Book (almost every such inventory had this
        item).
    1 Red Silk Petticoat.
    1 Very good broad Silver laced hat and hat-band.
    1 Pair Stays 17 inches round the waist.
    2 Pair fine Shoes.
  12 Pair fine Stockings.
    1 Hoop Petticoat.
    1 Pair Ear rings.
    1 Pair Clasps.
    3 Pair Silver Buttons set with Stones.

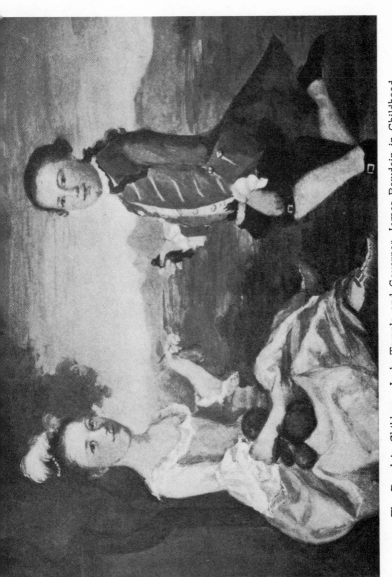

The Bowdoin Children. Lady Temple and Governor James Bowdoin in Childhood.

1 Suit of Headclothes.
4 Fine Handkerchiefs and Ruffles suitable.
A Very handsome Knot and Girdle.
A Fine Cloak and Short Apron."

I never read such a list as this without picturing the delight of little Mary Cabell when she opened the box containing all these pretty garments.

The order given by Colonel John Lewis for his young ward of eleven years old — another Virginia child — reads thus : —

"A cap, ruffle, and tucker, the lace 5*s.* per yard.
  1 pair White Stays.
  8 pair White kid gloves.
  2 pair Colour'd kid gloves.
  2 pair worsted hose.
  3 pair thread hose.
  1 pair silk shoes laced.
  1 pair morocco shoes.
  4 pair plain Spanish shoes.
  2 pair calf shoes.
  1 Mask.
  1 Fan.
  1 Necklace.
  1 Girdle and Buckle.
  1 Piece fashionable Calico.
  4 yards Ribbon for Knots.
  1 Hoop Coat.
  1 Hat.
  1½ Yard of Cambric.
A Mantua and Coat of Slite Lustring."

Orders for purchases were regularly despatched to a London agent by George Washington after his marriage. In 1761 he orders a full list of garments for both his stepchildren. "Miss Custis" was only six years old. These are some of the items : —

"1 Coat made of Fashionable Silk.
A Fashionable Cap or fillet with Bib apron.
Ruffles and Tuckers, to be laced.
4 Fashionable Dresses made of Long Lawn.
2 Fine Cambrick Frocks.
A Satin Capuchin, hat, and neckatees.
A Persian Quilted Coat.
1 p. Pack Thread Stays.
4 p. Callimanco Shoes.
6 p. Leather Shoes.
2 p. Satin Shoes with flat ties.
6 p. Fine Cotton Stockings.
4 p. White Worsted Stockings.
12 p. Mitts.
6 p. White Kid Gloves.
1 p. Silver Shoe Buckles.
1 p. Neat Sleeve Buttons.
6 Handsome Egrettes Different Sorts.
6 Yards Ribbon for Egrettes.
12 Yards Coarse Green Callimanco."

A Virginia gentleman, Colonel William Fleming, kept for several years a close account of the money he spent for his little daughters, who were young misses of ten and eleven in the year 1787. The most expensive single items are bonnets, each at £4 10s.; an umbrella, £2 8s. Cloth cloaks and saddles and bridles for riding were costly items. Tamboured muslin was at that time 18s. a yard; durant, 3s. 6d.; lutestring, 12s.; calico, 6s. 3d. Scarlet cloaks for each girl cost £2 14s. each.   Other dress materials besides those named above were cambric, linen, cotton, osnaburgs, negro cotton, bookmuslin, ermin, nankeen, persian, Turkey cotton, shalloon, and swanskin.   There were many yards of taste and ribbon, black lace, and edgings, and gauze — gauze — gauze.   A curious item several times appearing is a " paper bonnet," not bonnet-paper, which latter was a constant purchase on women's lists.   There were pen-knives, " scanes of silk," crooked combs, morocco shoes, " nitting pins," constant " sticks of pomatum," fans, " chanes," a shawl, a tamboured coat, gloves, stockings, trunks, bands and clasps, tooth-brushes, silk gloves, necklaces, " fingered gloves," silk stockings, handkerchiefs, china teacups and saucers and silver spoons.   All these show a very generous outfit.

In the year 1770 a delightful, engaging little child came to Boston from Nova Scotia to live for a time with her aunt, a Boston gentlewoman, and to attend Boston schools.   For the amusement of her parents so far away, and for practice in penmanship, she kept during the years 1771 and part of 1772 a diary. She was but ten years old when she began, but her intelligence and originality make this diary a valuable record of domestic life in Boston at that date. I have had the pleasure of publishing her diary with notes under the title, *Diary of Anna Green Winslow, a Boston School Girl, in the Year 1771*.   I lived so much with her while transcribing her words that she seems almost like a child of my own.   Like other unusual children she died young — when but nineteen. She was not so gifted and wonderful and rare a creature as that star among children, Marjorie Fleming, yet she was in many ways equally interesting; she was a frank, homely little flower of New England life destined never to grow old or weary, or tired or sad, but to live forever in eternal, happy childhood, through the magic living words in the hundred pages of her time-stained diary.

She was of what Dr. Holmes called Boston Brahmin blood, was related to many of the wealthiest and best families of Boston and vicinity, and knew the best society. Dress was to her a matter of distinct importance, and her clothes were carefully fashionable. Her distress over wearing "an old red Domino" was genuine. We have in her words many references to her garments, and we find her dress very handsome. This is what she wore at a child's party: —

"I was dressed in my yellow coat, black bib & apron, black feathers on my head, my past comb & all my past garnet, marquesett & jet pins, together with my silver plume — my loket, rings, black collar round my neck, black mitts & yards of blue ribbin (black & blue is high tast), striped tucker & ruffels (not my best) & my silk shoes completed my dress."

A few days later she writes: —

"I wore my black bib & apron, my pompedore shoes, the cap my Aunt Storer since presented me with (blue ribbins on it) & a very handsome locket in the shape of a hart she gave me, the past Pin my Hon'd Papa presented me with in my cap. My new cloak & bonnet, my pompedore gloves, &c.   And I would tell you that *for the first time they all on lik'd my dress very much*.   My cloak & bonnett are really very handsome & so they had need be.   For they cost an amasing sight of money, not quite £45, tho' Aunt Suky said that she suppos'd Aunt Deming would be frighted out of her Wits at the money it cost.   I have got *one* covering by the cost that is genteel & I like it much myself."

As this was in the times of depreciated values, £45 was not so large a sum to expend for a girl's outdoor garments as at first sight appears.

She gives a very exact account of her successions of head-gear, some being borrowed finery.   She apparently managed to rise entirely above the hated "black hatt" and red domino, which she patronizingly said would be "Decent for Common Occations."   She writes : —

"Last Thursday I purchased with my aunt Deming's leave a very beautiful white feather hat, that is the outside, which is a bit of white hollowed with the feathers sew'd on in a most curious manner; white and unsully'd as the falling snow.   As I am, as we say, a Daughter of Liberty I chuse to were as much of our own manufactory as pocible. . . .   My Aunt says if I behave myself very well indeed, not else, she will give me a garland of flowers to orniment it, tho' she has layd aside the biziness of flower-making."

The dress described and portrayed of these children all seems very mature; but children were quickly grown up in colonial days.   Cotton Mather wrote, " New English youth are very sharp and early ripe in their capacities."   They married early; though

none of the "child-marriages" of England disfigure
the pages of our history. Sturdy Endicott would
not permit the marriage of his ward, Rebecca
Cooper, an " inheritrice," — though Governor Winthrop wished her for his nephew, — because the girl
was but fifteen. I am surprised at this, for marriages at fifteen were
common enough. My
far-away grandmother,
Mary Burnet, married
William Browne, when
she was fourteen; an-
other grandmother,
Mary Philips, married
her cousin at thirteen,
and there is every evi-
dence that the match
was arranged with little
heed of the girl's wishes.
It was the happiest of
marriages. Boys be-
came men by law when
sixteen. Winthrop
named his son as execu-
tor of his will when the

Miss Lydia Robinson, aged 12 Years,
Daughter of Colonel James Rob-
inson.   Marked " Corné pinxt,
Sept. 1805."

boy was fourteen — but there were few boys like
that boy. We find that the Virginia tutor who
taught in the Carter family just previous to the war
of the Revolution deemed a young lady of thirteen
no longer a child.

" Miss Betsy Lee is about thirteen, a tall, slim, genteel
girl. She is very far from Miss Hale's taciturnity, yet is

by no means disagreeably Forward. She dances extremely well, and is just beginning to play the Spinet. She is dressed in a neat Shell Callico Gown, has very light Hair done up with a Feather, and her whole carriage is Inoffensive, Easy and Graceful."

The christening of an infant was not only a sacrament of the church, and thus of highest importance, but it was also of secular note. It was a time of great rejoicing, of good wishes, of gift-making. In mediæval times, the child was arrayed by the priest in a white robe which had been anointed with sacred oil, and called a chrismale, or a chrisom. If the child died within a month, it was buried in this robe and called a chrisom-child. The robe was also called a christening palm or pall. When the custom of redressing the child in a robe at the altar had passed away, the christening palm still was used and was thrown over the child when it was brought out to receive visitors. This robe was also termed a bearing-cloth, a christening sheet, and a cade-cloth.

This fine coverlet of state, what we would now call a christening blanket, was usually made of silk; often it was richly embroidered, sometimes with a text of Scripture. It was generally lace-bordered, or edged with a narrow, home-woven silk fringe. The christening-blanket of Governor Bradford of the Plymouth Colony still is owned by a descendant; it is whole of fabric and unfaded of dye. It is rich crimson silk, soft of texture, like heavy sarcenet silk, and is powdered at regular distances about six inches apart with conventional sprays of flowers, embroidered chiefly in pink and yellow, in minute silk cross-stitch. Another beautiful silk christening blanket was quilted in an intricate flower pattern in almost imperceptible stitches. Another of yellow satin has a design in white floss that gives it the appearance of being trimmed with white silk lace. Best of all was to embroider the cloth with designs and initials and emblems and biblical references. A coat-of-arms or crest was very elegant. The words, " God Bless the Babe," were not left wholly to the pincushions which every babe had given him or her, but appeared on the christening blanket. A curious design shown me was called *The Tree of Knowledge*. The figure of a child in cap, apron, bib, and hanging sleeves stands pointing to a tree upon which grew books as though they were apples. The open pages of each book-apple is printed with a title, as, *The New England Primer*, *Lilly's Grammar*, *Janeway's Holy Children*, *The Prodigal Daughter*.

An inventory of the christening garments of a child in the seventeenth century reads thus: —

" 1. A lined white figured satin cap.

2. A lined white satin cap embroidered in sprays with gold coloured silk.

3. A white satin palm embroidered in sprays of yellow silk to match. This is 44 inches by 34 inches in size.

4. A palm of rich ' still yellow ' silk lined with white satin. This is 54 inches by 48 inches in size.

5. A pair of deep cuffs of white satin, lace trimmed and embroidered.

6. A pair of linen mittens trimmed with narrow lace, the back of the fingers outlined with yellow silk figures."

Knitted Flaxen Mittens.

The satin cuffs were for the wear of the older person who carried the child. The infant was placed upon the larger palm or cloth, and the smaller one thrown over him, over his petticoats. The inner cap was very tight to the head. The outer was embroidered; often it turned back in a band.

There was a significance in the use of yellow; it is the altar color for certain church festivals, and was proper for the pledging of the child.

All these formalities of christening in the Church of England were not abandoned by the Separatists. New England children were just as carefully christened and dressed for christening as any child in the Church of England. In the reign of James I tiny shirts with little bands or sleeves or cuffs wrought in

silk or in coventry-blue thread were added to the
gift of spoons from the sponsors. I have one of
these little coventry-blue embroidered things with
quaint little sleeves; too faded, I regret, to reveal
any pattern to the camera.

The christening shirts and mittens given by the
sponsors are said to be a relic of the ancient custom
of presenting white clothes to the neophytes when
converted to Christianity. These "Christening
Sets" are preserved in many families.

Of the dress of infants of colonial times we can
judge from the articles of clothing which have been
preserved till this day. These are of course the
better garments worn by babies, not their everyday
dress; their simpler attire has not survived, but
their christening robes, their finer shirts and petticoats and caps remain.

Linen formed the chilling substructure of their
dress, thin linen, low-necked, short-sleeved shirts;
and linen remained the underwear of infants until
thirty years ago. I do not wonder that these little
linen shirts were worn for centuries. They are infinitely daintier than the finest silk or woollen underwear that have succeeded them; they are edged with
narrowest thread lace, and hemstitched with tiny rows
of stitches or corded with tiny cords, and sometimes
embroidered by hand in minute designs. They were
worn by all babies from the time of James I, never
varying one stitch in shape; but I fear this pretty
garment of which our infants were bereft a few years
ago will never crowd out the warm, present-day silk
wear. This wholly infantile article of childish dress

Mrs. Elizabeth Lux Russell and Daughter.

had tiny little revers or collarettes or laps made to turn over outside the robe or slip like a minute bib, and these laps were beautifully oversewn where the corners joined the shirt, to prevent tearing down at this seam. These tiny shirts were the dearest little garments ever made or dreamed of. When a baby had on a fresh, corded slip, low of neck, with short, puffed sleeve, and the tiny hemstitched laps were turned down outside the neck of the slip, and the little sleeves were caught up by fine strings of gold-clasped pink coral, the baby's dimpled shoulders and round head rose up out of the little shirt-laps like some darling flower.

I have seen an infant's shirt and a cap embroidered on the laps with the coat-of-arms of the Lux and Johnson families and the motto, " God Bless the Babe ; " these delicate garments, the work of fairies, were worn in infancy by the Revolutionary soldier, Governor Johnson of Virginia.

In the Essex Institute in Salem, Massachusetts, are the baptismal shirt and mittens of the Pilgrim father, William Bradford, second governor of the Plymouth colony, who was born in 1590. They are shown on page 306. All are of firm, close-woven, homespun linen, but the little mittens have been worn at the ends by the active friction of baby hands, and are patched with red and yellow figured "chiney" or calico. A similar colored material frills the sleeves and neck. This may have been part of their ornamentation when first made, but it looks extraneous.

The sleeves of this shirt are plaited or goffered in a way that seems wholly lost ; this is what I have

already described — *pinching*. I have seen the sleeve
of a child's dress thus pinched which had been worn
by a little girl aged three. The wrist-cuff measured
about five inches around, and was stoutly corded.
Upon ripping the sleeve apart, it was found that the
strip of fine mull which was thus pinched into the
sleeve was two yards in length. The cuff flared

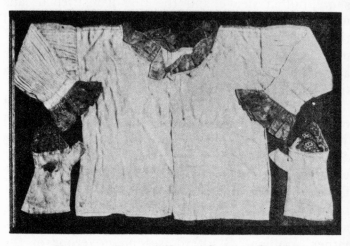

Christening Shirt and Mitts of Governor Bradford.

slightly, else even this length of sheer lawn could
not have been confined at the wrist. In the so-called
" Museum," gloomily scattered around the famous
old South Church edifice in Boston, are fine examples
of this pinched work.

Many of the finest existing specimens of old guipure, Flanders, and needlepoint laces in England and
America are preserved on the ancient shirts, mitts,
caps, and bearing-cloths of infants. Often there is

a little padded bib of guipure lace accompanied with
tiny mittens like these.

This pair was wrought and worn in the sixteenth
century, and the stitches and work are those of the
Flanders point
laces. I have
seen tiny mitts
knitted of silk,
of fine linen
thread, also
made of linen,
hem-stitched,
or worked in
drawn-work, or
embroidered,
and one pair of
mittens, and the

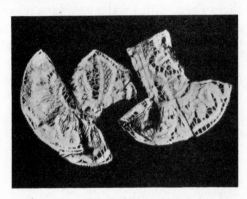

Flanders Lace Mitts.

cap that matched was of tatting-work done in the
finest of thread. No needlepoint could be more
beautiful. Some are shown on page 303.

Mitts of yellow nankeen or silk, made with long
wrists or arms, were also worn by babies, and must
have proved specially irritating to tiny little hands
and arms. These had the seams sewed over and
over with colored silks in a curiously intricate netted
stitch.

I have an infant's cap with two squares of lace
set in the crown, one over each ear. The lace is
of a curious design; a conventionalized vase or urn
on a standard. I recognize it as the lace and pattern
known as " pot-lace," made for centuries at Antwerp,
and worn there by old women on their caps with a

devotion to a single pattern that is unparalleled. It was the "flower-pot" symbol of the Annunciation. The earliest representation of the Angel Gabriel in the Annunciation showed him with lilies in his hand ; then these lilies were set in a vase. In years the angel has disappeared and then the lilies, and the lily-pot only remains. It is a whimsical fancy that this symbol of Romanism should have been carefully transferred to adorn the pate of a child of the Puritans. The place of the medallion, set over each ear, is so unusual that I think it must have had some significance. I wonder whether they were ever set thus in caps of heavy silk or linen to let the child hear more readily, as he certainly would through the thin lace net.

The word "beguine" meant a nun; and thus derivatively a nun's close cap. This was altered in spelling to biggin, and for a time a nun's plain linen cap was thus called. By Shakespere's day biggin had become wholly a term for a child's cap. It was a plain phrase and a plain cap of linen. Shakespere calls them "homely biggens."

I have seen it stated that the biggin was a night-cap. When Queen Elizabeth lost her mother, Anne Boleyn, she was but three years old, a neglected little creature. A lady of the court wrote that the child had "no manner of linen, nor forsmocks, nor kerchiefs, nor rails, nor body-stitches, nor handkerchiefs, nor sleeves, nor mufflers, nor biggins."

In 1636 Mary Dudley, the daughter of Governor John Winthrop, had a little baby. She did not live in Boston town, therefore her mother had to purchase supplies for her; and many letters crossed, telling of wants, and their relief. " Holland for biggins " was eagerly sought. At that date all babies wore caps. I mean English and French, Dutch and Spanish, all mothers deemed it unwise and almost improper for a young baby ever to be seen bareheaded. With the imperfect heating and many draughts in all the houses, this mode of dress may have been wholly wise and indeed necessary. Every child's head was covered, as the pictures of children in this book show, until he or she was several years old. The finest needlework and lace stitches were lavished on these tiny infants' caps, which were not, when thus adorned and ornamented, called biggins.

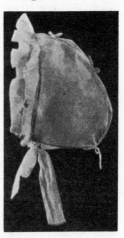

Infant's Adjustable Cap.

A favorite trimming for nightcaps and infants' caps is a sort of quilting in a leaf and vine pattern, done with a white cord inserted between outer and inner pieces of linen — a cord stuffing, as it were. It does not seem oversuited for caps to be worn in bed or by little infants, as the stiff cords must prove a disagreeable cushion. This work was done as early as the seventeenth century; but nearly all the pieces preserved were made in the early years of the nineteenth century in the revival of needlework then so universal.

Often a velvet cap was worn outside the biggin or lace cap.

I have never seen a woollen petticoat that was worn by an infant of pre-Revolutionary days. I think infants had no woollen petticoats; their shirts, petticoats, and gowns were of linen or some cotton stuff like dimity. Warmth of clothing was given by tiny shawls pinned round the shoulders and heavier blankets and quilts and shawls in which baby and petticoats were wholly enveloped.

The baby dresses of olden times are either rather shapeless sacques drawn in at the neck with narrow cotton ferret or linen bobbin, or little straight-waisted gowns of state. All were exquisitely made by hand, and usually of fine stuff. Many are trimmed with fine cording.

It is astounding to note the infinite number of stitches put in garments. An infant's slips quilted with a single tiny backstitch in a regular design of interlaced squares, stars, and rounds. By counting the number of rounds and the stitches in each, and so on, it has been found that there are 397,000 stitches in that dress. Think of the time spent even by the quickest sewer over such a piece of work.

Within a few years we have shortened the long clothes worn by youngest infants; twenty-five years ago the handsome dress of an infant, such as the christening-robe, was so long that when the child was held on the arm of its standing nurse or mother, the edge of the robe barely escaped touching the ground. Two hundred years ago, a baby's dress was

much shorter.   In the family group of Charles I and
Henrietta Maria and their children, in the Copley
family picture, and in the picture of the Cadwalader
family, we find the little baby in scarce " three-quar-
ters length " of robe.   With this exception it is
astonishing to find how little infants' dress has
changed during the two centuries.   In 1889, at the
Stuart Exhibition, some of the infant dresses of
Charles I were shown.   They had been preserved in
the family of Sir Thomas Coventry, Lord Keeper.
And Charles II's baby linen was on view in the New
Gallery in 1901.   Both sets had the dainty little
shirts, slips, bibs, mitts, and all the babies' dress of
fifty years ago, and the changes since then have
been few.   The " barrow-coat," a square of flannel
wrapped around an infant's body below the arms
with the part below the feet turned up and pinned,
was part of the old swaddling-clothes ; and within
ten years it has been largely abandoned for a flannel
petticoat on a band or waist.   The bands, or binders,
have always been the same as to-day, and the bibs.
The lace cuffs and lace mittens were left off before
the caps.   The shirt is the most important change.
   Nowadays a little infant wears long clothes till
three, four, or even eight months old ; then he is
put in short dresses about as long as he is.   In
colonial days when a boy was taken from his swaddling-clothes, he was dressed in a short frock with
petticoats and was " coated " or sometimes " short-
coated."   When he left off coats, he donned breeches.
In families of sentiment and affection, the " coating "
of a boy was made a little festival.   So was also the

assumption of breeches an important event — as it really is, as we all know who have boys.

One of the most charming of all grandmothers' letters was written by a doting English grandmother to her son, Lord Chief Justice North, telling of the " leaving off of coats " of his motherless little son, Francis Guilford, then six years old. The letter is dated October 10, 1679 : —

" DEAR SON : You cannot beleeve the great concerne that was in the whole family here last Wednesday, it being the day that the taylor was to helpe to dress little ffrank in his breeches in order to the making an everyday suit by it. Never had any bride that was to be drest upon her weding night more handes about her, some the legs, some the armes, the taylor butt'ning, and others putting on the sword, and so many lookers on that had I not a ffinger amongst I could not have seen him.   When he was quite drest he acted his part as well as any of them for he desired he might goe downe to inquire for the little gentleman that was there the day before in a black coat, and speak to the man to tell the gentleman when he came from school that there was a gallant with very fine clothes and a sword to have waited upon him and would come again upon Sunday next.   But this was not all, there was great contrivings while he was dressing who should have the first salute; but he sayd if old Joan had been here, she should, but he gave it to me to quiett them all.   They were very. fitt, everything, and he looks taller and prettyer than in his coats.   Little Charles rejoyced as much as he did for he jumpt all the while about him and took notice of everything.   I went to Bury, and bot everything for another suitt which will be finisht on Saturday so the coats are to be quite left off on Sunday. I consider it is not yett terme time and since you could not

have the pleasure of the first sight, I resolved you should
have a full relation from

> " Yo*r* most Aff*nate* Mother
>> " A. North.

" When he was drest he asked Buckle whether muffs
were out of fashion because they had not sent him one."

This affectionate letter, written to a great and
busy statesman, the Lord Keeper of the Seals, shows
how pure and delightful domestic life in England
could be; it shows how beautiful it was after Puritanism perfected the English home.

In an old family letter dated 1780 I find this
sentence : —

" Mary is most wise with her child, and hath no new-
fangledness. She has little David in what she wore herself,
a pudding and pinner."

For a time these words " pudding and pinner "
were a puzzle; and long after pinner was defined
we could not even guess at a pudding. But now
I know two uses of the word " pudding " which are
in no dictionary. One is the stuffing of a man's
great neck-cloth in front, under the chin. The other
is a thick roll or cushion stuffed with wool or some
soft filling and furnished with strings. This pudding was tied round the head of a little child while
it was learning to walk. The head was thus pro-
tected from serious bruises or injury. Nollekens
noted with satisfaction such a pudding on the head
of an infant, and said: " That is right. I always
wore a pudding, and all children should." I saw
one upon a child's head last summer in a New Eng-

land town; I asked the mother what it was, and she answered, "A pudding-cap"; that it made children soft (idiotic) to bump the head frequently.

The word "pinner" has two meanings. The earlier use was precisely that of pinafore, or pincurtle, or pincloth — a child's apron. Thus we read in the Harvard College records, of the expenses of the year 1677, of "Linnen Cloth for Table Pinners," which makes us suspect that Harvard students of that day had to wear bibs at commons.

All children wore aprons, which might be called pinners; these were aprons with pinned-up bibs; or they might be tiers, which were sleeved aprons covering the whole waist, sleeves, and skirt, an outer slip, buttoned in the back.

A severe and ancient moralist looked forth from her window in Worcester, one day last spring, at a band of New England children running to their morning school. She gazed over her glasses reprovingly, and turned to me with bitterness: "There they go! *Such* mothers as they must have! Not a pinner nor a sleeved tier among 'em."

The sleeved tier occupied a singular place in childish opinion in my youth; and I find the same feeling anent it had existed for many generations. It was hated by all children, regarded as something to be escaped from at the earliest possible date. You had to wear sleeved tiers as you had to have the mumps. It was a thing to endure with what childish patience and fortitude you could command for a short time; but thoughtful, tender parents would not make you suffer it long.

There were aprons, and aprons. Pinners and tiers were for use, but there were elegant aprons for ornament. Did not Queen Anne wear one? Even babies wore them. The little Padishal child has one richly laced. I have seen a beautiful apron for a little child of three. It was edged with a straight insertion of Venetian point like that pictured on page 64. It had been made in 1690. Tender affection for a beloved and beautiful little child preserved it in one trunk in the same attic for sixty-five years; and a beautiful sympathy for that mother's long sorrow kept the apron untouched by young lace-lovers. This lace has white horsehair woven into the edge.

We find George Washington ordering for his little stepdaughter (a well-dressed child if ever there was one), when she was six years old, "A fashionable cap or fillet with bib apron." And a few years later he orders, "Tuckers, Bibs, and Aprons if Fashionable." Boys wore aprons as long as they wore - coats; aprons with stomachers or bibs of drawn-work and lace, or of stiffly starched lawn; aprons just like those of their sisters. It was hard to bear. Hoop-coat, masks, packthread stays — these seem strange dress for growing girls.

George Washington sent abroad for masks for his wife and his little stepdaughter, "Miss Custis," when the little girl was six years old; and "children's masks" are often named in bills of sale. Loo-masks were small half-masks, and were also imported in all sizes.

The face of Mrs. Madison, familiarly known as "Dolly Madison," wife of President James Madison, long retained the beauty of youth. Much of this was surely due to a faithful mother, who, when little Dolly Payne was sent to school, sewed a sun-bonnet on the child's head every morning, placed on her arms and hands long gloves, and made her wear

a mask to keep every ray of sun-light from her face. When masks were so universally worn by women, it is not strange, after all, that children wore them.

I read with horror an advertisement of John McQueen, a New York stay-maker in 1767, that he has children's packthread stays, children's bone stays, and "neat polished steel collars for young Misses so much worn at the boarding schools in London."

Rev. J. P. Dabney
when a Child.

Poor little "young Misses"!

There were also "turned stays, jumps, gazzets, costrells and caushets" (which were perhaps corsets) to make children appear straight. Costrells and gazzets we know not to-day. Jumps were feeble stays.

> "Now a shape in neat stays
> Now a slattern in jumps."

Jumps were allied to jimps, and perhaps to jupe; and I think jumper is a cousin of a word. One pair of stays I have seen is labelled as having been made for a boy of five. One of the worst instruments of torture I ever beheld was a pair of child's stays worn in 1760. They were made, not of little strips

Robert Gibbes.

of wood, but of a large piece of board, front and back, tightly sewed into a buckram jacket and reën-forced across at right angles and diagonally over the hips (though really there were no hip-places) with bars of whalebone and steel.   The tin corsets I have heard of would not have been half as ill to wear.   It is true, too, that needles were placed in the front of the stays, that the stay-wearer who " poked her head " would be well pricked.   The daughter of General Nathanael Greene, the Revolutionary patriot, told her grandchildren that she sat many hours every day in her girlhood, with her feet in stocks and strapped to a backboard.   A friend has a chair of ordinary size, save that the seat is about four inches wide from the front edge of seat to the back.   And the back is well worn at certain points where a heavy leather strap strapped up the young girl who was tortured in it for six years of her life.   The result of back board, stocks, steel collar, wooden stays, is shown in such figures as have Dorothy Q. and her sister Elizabeth. Elizabeth Storer, on page 98 of my *Child Life in Colonial Days*, is an extreme example, straight-backed indeed, but narrow-chested to match.

Dr. Holmes wrote in jest, but he wrote in truth, too : —

> " They braced My Aunt against a board
>   To make her straight and tall,
> They laced her up, they starved her down,
>   To make her light and small.
> They pinched her feet, they singed her hair,
>   They screwed it up with pins,
> Oh, never mortal suffered more
>   In penance for her sins."

Nankeen was the favorite wear for boys, even before the Revolution. The little figure of the boy who became Lord Lyndhurst, shown in the Copley family portrait, is dressed in nankeen; he is the

Nankeen Breeches with Silver Buttons.

engaging, loving child looking up in his mother's face. Nankeen was worn summer and winter by men, and women, and children. If it were deemed too thin and too damp a wear for delicate children in extreme winters, then a yellow color in wool was preferred for children's dress. I have seen a little pair of breeches of yellow flannel made precisely like these nankeen breeches on this page. They were worn in 1768.

Carlyle in his *Sartor Resartus* gives this account of the childhood of the professor and philosopher of his book : —

" My first short clothes were of yellow serge ; or rather, I should say, my first short cloth ; for the vesture was one and indivisible, reaching from neck to ankle ; a single body with four limbs ; of which fashion how little could I then divine the architectural, much less the moral significance."

It is a curious coincidence that a great philosopher of our own world wore a precisely similar dress in his youth. Madam Mary Bradford writes in a private letter, at the age of one hundred and three, of her life in 1805 in the household of Rev. Joseph Emerson. Ralph Waldo Emerson was then a little child of two years, and he and his brother William till several years old were dressed wholly in yellow flannel, by night and by day. When they put on trousers, which was at about the age of seven, they

Ralph Izard when a Little Boy.   1750.

wore complete home-made suits of nankeen. The picture amuses me of the philosophical child, Ralph Waldo, walking soberly around in ugly yellow flannel, contentedly sucking his thumb; for Mrs. Bradford records that he was the hardest child to break of sucking his thumb whom she ever had seen during her long life. I cannot help wondering whether in their soul-to-soul talks Emerson ever told Carlyle of the yellow woollen dress of his childhood, and thus gave him the thought of the child's dress for his philosopher.

Fortunately for the children who were our grandparents, French fashions were not absorbingly the rage in America until after some amelioration of dress had come to French children. Mercier wrote at length at the close of the eighteenth century of the abominable artificiality and restraint in dress of French children; their great wigs, full-skirted coats, immense ruffles, swords on thigh, and hat in hand. He contrasts them disparagingly with English boys. The English boy was certainly more robust, but I find no difference in dress. Wigs, swords, ruffles, may be seen at that time both in English and American portraits. But an amelioration of dress did come to both English and American boys through the introduction of pantaloons, and a change to little girls' dress through the invention of pantalets, but the changes came first to France, in spite of Mercier's animadversions. These changes will be left until the later pages of this book; for during nearly all the two hundred years of which I write children's dress varied little. It followed the changes of the parent's dress, and adopted some modes to a degree but never to an extreme.

CHAPTER XI

PERUKES AND PERIWIGS

"*As to a Periwigg, my best and Greatest Friend begun to find me with Hair before I was Born, and has continued to do so ever since, and I could not find it in my Heart to go to another.*"

— "Diary," JUDGE SAMUEL SEWALL, 1718.

A phrensy or a periwigmanee
That over-runs his pericranie.

—JOHN BYRON, 1730 (circa).

CHAPTER XI

TO-DAY, when every man, save a football player or some eccentric reformer or religious fanatic, displays in youth a close-cropped head, and when even hoary age is seldom graced with flowing, silvery locks, when women's hair is dressed in simplicity, we can scarcely realize the important and formal part the hair played in the dress of the eighteenth century.

In the great eagerness shown from earliest colonial days to acquire and reproduce in the New World every change of mode in the Old, to purchase rich dress, and to assume novel dress, no article was sought for more speedily and more anxiously than the wig. It has proved an interesting study to compare the introduction of wigs in England with the wear of the same form of head-gear in America. Wigs were not in general use in England when Plymouth and Boston were settled; though in Elizabeth's day a "peryuke" had been bought for the court fool. They were not in universal wear till the close of the seventeenth century.

The "Wig Mania" arose in France in the reign of Louis XV. In 1656 the king had forty court perruquiers, who were termed and deemed artists, and had their academy. The wigs they produced were superb. It is told that one cost £200, a sum equal in purchasing power to-day to $5000. The French statesman and financier, Colbert, aghast at the vast sums spent for foreign hair, endeavored to

introduce a sort of cap to supplant the wig, but fashions are not made that way.

For information of English manners and customs in that day, I turn (and never in vain) to those fascinating volumes, the *Verney Memoirs*. From them I learn this of early wig-wearing by Englishmen; that Sir Ralph Verney, though in straitened

Governor and Reverend
Gurdon Saltonstall.

circumstances during his enforced residence abroad, felt himself compelled to follow the French mode, which at that period, 1646, had not reached England. That exemplary gentleman paid twelve livres for a wig, when he was sadly short of money for household necessaries. It was an elaborate wig, curled in great rings, with two locks tied with black ribbon, and made without any parting at the back. This wig was powdered.

Sir Ralph wrote to his wife that a good hair-powder was very difficult to get and costly, even in France. It was an appreciable addition to the weight of the

wig and to the expense, large quantities being used,
sometimes as much as two pounds at a time.   It
added not only to the expense, but to the discom-
fort, inconvenience, and untidiness of wig-wearing.

Pomatum made of fat, and that sometimes rancid,
was used to make the powder stick; and noxious
substances were introduced into the powder, as a certain kind is mentioned which must not be used alone,
for it would produce headache.

Charles II was the earliest king represented on the
Great Seal wearing a large periwig.   Dr. Doran as-
sures us that the king did not bring the fashion to
Whitehall.   " He forbade,"
we are told, " the members
of the Universities to wear
periwigs, smoke tobacco, or
read their sermons.   The
members did all three, and
Charles soon found himself
doing the first two."

Pepys's *Diary* contains
much interesting information
concerning the wigs of this
reign.   On 2d of November,
1663, he writes: " I heard
the Duke say that he was

Mayor Rip Van Dam.

going to wear a periwig, and says the King also will.
I never till this day observed that the King is mighty
gray."   It was doubtless this change in the color of
his Majesty's hair that induced him to assume the
head-dress he had previously so strongly condemned.

The wig he adopted was very voluminous, richly

curled, and black. He was very dark. "Odds fish! but I'm an ugly black fellow!" he said of himself when he looked at his portrait. Loyal colonists quickly followed royal example and complexion. We have very good specimens of this curly black wig in many American portraits.

As might be expected, and as befitted one who delighted to be in fashion, Pepys adopted this wig. He took time to consider the matter, and had consultations with Mr. Jervas, his old barber, about the affair. Referring to one of his visits to his hairdresser, Pepys says : —

" I did try two or three borders and periwigs, meaning to wear one, and yet I have no stomach for it ; but that the pains of keeping my hair clean is great. He trimmed me, and at last I parted, but my mind was almost altered from my first purpose, from the trouble which I foresee in wearing them also."

Weeks passed before he could make up his mind to wear a wig. Mrs. Pepys was taken to the periwig-maker's shop to see one, and expressed her satisfaction with it. We read in April, 1665, of the wig being back at Jervas's under repair. Later, under date of September 3d, he writes : —

" Lord's day. Up ; and put on my coloured silk suit, very fine, and my new periwig, bought a good while since, but durst not wear, because the plague was in Westminster when I bought it ; and it is a wonder what will be in fashion, after the plague is done, as to periwigs, for nobody will dare to buy any hair, for fear of the infection, that it had been cut off the heads of people dead of the plague."

In 1670, only five years after this entry of Pepys, we find Governor Barefoot of New Hampshire wearing a periwig; and in 1675 the court of Massachusetts, in view of the distresses of the Indian wars, denounced the "manifest pride openly appearing amongst us in that long hair, like women's hair is worn by some men, either their own hair, or others' hair made into periwigs."

In 1676 Wait Winthrop sent a wig (price £3) to his brother in New London. Mr. Sergeant had brought it from England for his own use; but was willing to sell it to oblige a friend, who was, I am confident, very devoted to wig-wearing. The largest wig that I recall upon

Abraham De Peyster.

any colonist's head is in the portrait of Governor Fitz-John Winthrop. He is painted in armor; and a great wig never seems so absurd as when worn with armor. Horace Walpole said, "Perukes of outrageous length flowing over suits of armour compose wonderful habits." An edge of Winthrop's own dark hair seems to show under the wig front. I do not know the precise date of this portrait. It was, of course, painted in England. He served in the

Parliamentary army with General Monck; returned
to New England in 1663, and was commander of the
New England forces.   He spent 1693 to 1697 in
England as commissioner.   Sir Peter Lely and Sir
Godfrey Kneller both
were painting in Eng-
land in those years, and
both were constant in
painting men with armor
and perukes. This por-
trait seems like Knel-
ler's work.

Another portrait
attired also in armor
and peruke is of Sir
Nathaniel Johnson, who
was appointed governor
of South Carolina by
the Lords Proprietors
in 1702.   The portrait
was painted in 1705.

Governor De Bienville.

It is one of the few of that date which show a faint
mustache; he likewise wears a seal ring with coat-
of-arms on the little finger of his left hand, which
was unusual at that day.   De Bienville, the governor of Louisiana, is likewise in wig and armor.
In 1682 Thomas Richbell died in Boston, leaving
a very rich and costly wardrobe.   He had eight
wigs.   Of these, three were small periwigs worth
but a pound apiece.   In New York, in Virginia,
in all the colonies, these wigs were worn, and were
just as large and costly, as elaborately curled,

as heavily powdered, as at the English and French courts.

Archbishop Tillotson is usually regarded as the first amongst the English clergy to adopt the wig. He said in one of his sermons : —

"I can remember since the wearing of hair below the ears was looked upon as a sin of the first magnitude, and when ministers generally, whatever their text was, did either find or make occasion to reprove the great sin of long hair; and if they saw any one in the congregation guilty in that kind, they would point him out particularly, and let fly at him with great zeal."

Dr. Tillotson died on November 24, 1694.

Long before that American preachers had felt it necessary to "let fly" also; to denounce wig-wearing from their pulpits. The question could not be settled, since the ministers themselves could not agree. John Wilson, the zealous Boston minister, wore one, and John Cotton (see page 42); while Rev. Mr. Noyes preached long and often against the fashion. John Eliot, the noble preacher and missionary to

Daniel Waldo.

the Indians, found time even in the midst of his arduous and incessant duties to deliver many a blast against " prolix locks," — "with boiling zeal," as

Cotton Mather said, — and he labelled them a " luxurious feminine protexity " ; but lamented late in life that " the lust for wigs is become insuperable." He thought the horrors in King Philip's War were a direct punishment from God for wig-wearing. Increase Mather preached warmly against wigs, calling them " Horrid Bushes of Vanity," and saying that " such Apparel is contrary to the light of Nature, and to express Scripture," and that " Monstrous Periwigs such as some of our church members indulge in make them resemble ye locusts that came out of ye Bottomless Pit."

Rev. George Weeks preached a sermon on impropriety in clothes. He said in regard to wig-wearing : —

" We have no warrant in the word of God, that I know of, for our wearing of Periwigs except it be in extraordinary cases. Elisha did not cover his head with a Perriwigg altho' it was bald. To see the greater part of Men in some congregations wearing Perriwiggs is a matter of deep lamentation. For either all these men had a necessity to cut off their Hair or else not. If they had a necessity to cut off their Hair then we have reason to take up a lamentation over the sin of our first Parents which hath occasioned so many Persons in our Congregation to be sickly, weakly, crazy Persons."

Long " Ruffianly " or " Russianly " (I know not which word is right) hair equally worried the parsons. President Chauncey of Harvard College preached upon it, for the college undergraduates were vexingly addicted to prolix locks. Rev. Mr. Wigglesworth's sermon on the subject has often been

reprinted, and is full of logical arguments. This
offence was named on the list of existing evils which
was made by the general court: that "the men wore
long hair like women's hair." Still, the Puritan magistrates, omnipotent as they were in small things,
did not dare to force the becurled citizens of the
little towns to cut their long love-locks, though they

bribed them to do so. A
Salem man was, in 1687, fined
10s. for a misdemeanor, but
"in case he shall cutt off his
long har of his head into a
sevill (civil?) frame, in the
mean time shall have abated
5s. of his fine." John Eliot
hated long, natural hair as well
as false hair. Rev. Cotton

Reverend John Marsh.

Mather said of him, in a very unpleasant figure of
speech, "The hair of them that professed religion
grew too long for him to swallow." His own hair
curled on his shoulders, and would seem long to us
to-day.

A climax of wig-hating was reached by one who
has been styled "The Last of the Puritans" —
Judge Samuel Sewall of Boston. Constant references in his diary show how this hatred influenced
his daily life. He despised wigs so long and so
deeply, he thought and talked and prayed upon
them, until they became to him of undue importance; they became godless emblems of iniquity;
an unutterable snare and peril.

We find Sewall copying with evident approval a

"scandalous bill" which had been "posted" on the
church in Plymouth in 1701.   In this a few lines
ran : —

> "Our churches are too genteel.
> Parsons grow trim and trigg
> With wealth, wine, and wigg,
>   And their crowns are covered with meal."

Bitter must have been his efforts to reconcile to
his conscience the sight of wigs upon the heads of

his parson friends, worn
boldly in the pulpit.   He
would refrain from attend-
ing a church where the parson wore a wig; and his
italicized praise of a dead
friend was that he "was a
true New-English man and
abominated periwigs."   A
Boston wig-maker died a
drunkard, and Sewall took
much melancholy satisfac-
tion in dilating upon it.

John Adams in Youth.

Cotton Mather and Sewall had many pious differences and personal jealousies.   The parson was a
handsome man (see his picture facing page 42), and
he was a harmlessly and naïvely vain man.   He
quickly adopted a "great bush of vanity"—and a
very personable appearance he makes in it.   Soon
we find him inveighing at length in the pulpit against
"those who strain at a gnat and swallow a camel,
those who were zealous against an innocent fashion
taken up and used by the best of men."   "'Tis sup-

posed he means wearing a Perriwigg," writes Sewall
after this sermon; " I expected not to hear a vindication of Perriwiggs in Boston pulpit by Mr. Mather."

Poor Sewall! his regard of wigs had a severe test
when he wooed Madam Winthrop late in life.   She
was a rich widow.   He had courted her vainly for a
second wife.   And now he " yearned for her deeply "
for a third wife, so he wrote.   And ere she would
consent or even discuss marriage she stipulated two
things: one, that he keep a coach; the other, that
he wear a periwig.   When all the men of dignity
and office in the colony were bourgeoning out in
great flowing perukes, she was naturally a bit averse
to an elderly lover in a skullcap or, as he often
wore, a hood.   His love did not make him waver;
he stoutly persisted in his refusal to assume a periwig.

His portrait in a velvet skullcap shows a fringe
of white curling hair with a few forehead locks.   I
fancy he was bald.   Here is his entry with regard to
young Parson Willard's wig, in the year 1701 : —

" Having last night heard that Josiah Willard had cut
off his hair (a very full head of hair) and put on a wig, I
went to him this morning.   When I told his mother what
I came about, she called him.   Whereupon I inquired of
him what extreme need had forced him to put off his own
hair and put on a wig ?   He answered, none at all; he said
that his hair was straight, and that it parted behind.

" He seemed to argue that men might as well shave their
hair off their head, as off their face.   I answered that boys
grew to be men before they had hair on their faces, and that
half of mankind never have any beards.   I told him that

God seems to have created our hair as a test, to see whether we can bring our minds to be content at what he gives us, or whether we would be our own carvers and come back to him for nothing more.   We might dislike our skin or nails, as he disliked his hair; but in our case no thanks are due to us that we cut them not off; for pain and danger restrain us.   Your duty, said I, is to teach men self-denial.   I told him, further, that it would be displeasing and burdensome to good men for him to wear a wig, and they that care not what men think of them, care not what God thinks of them.

"I told him that he must remember that wigs were condemned by a meeting of ministers at Northampton.   I told him of the solemnity of the covenant which he and I had lately entered into, which put upon me the duty of discoursing to him.

Jonathan Edwards, 2nd.

"He seemed to say that he would leave off his wig when his hair was grown again.   I spoke to his father of it a day or two afterwards and he thanked me for reasoning with his son.

"He told me his son had promised to leave off his wig when his hair was grown to cover his ears.   If the father had known of it, he would have forbidden him to cut off his hair.   His mother heard him talk of it, but was afraid to forbid him for fear he should do it in spite of her, and so be more faulty than if she had let him go his own way."

Soon nearly every parson in England and every colony wore wigs.   John Wesley alone wore what seems to be his own white hair curled under softly

at the ends.   Whitfield is in a portentous wig like
the one on Dr. Marsh (page 331).

In the time of Queen Anne, wigs had multiplied
vastly in variety as they had increased in size.   I
have been asked the difference between a peruke and
a wig.   Of course both, and the periwig, are simply
wigs; but the term " peruke " is in general applied
to a formal, richly curled wig; and the word " periwig " also conveys the distinction of a formal wig.
Of less dignity were riding-wigs, nightcap wigs, and
bag-wigs.   Bag-wigs are said to have had their origin

among French servants,
who tied up their hair in a
black leather bag as a speedy
way of dressing it, and to
keep it out of the way
when at other and disor-
dering duties.

In May, 1706, the Eng-
lish, led by Marlborough,
gained a great victory on
the battle-field of Ramillies,
and that gave the title to a
new wig described as " hav-

Patrick Henry.

ing a long, gradually diminishing, plaited tail, called
the ' Ramillie-tail,' which was tied with a great bow
at the top and a smaller one at the bottom."   The
hair also bushed out at both sides of the face.
The Ramillies wig shown in Hogarth's *Modern
Midnight Conversation* hanging against the wall,
is reproduced on page 340.   This wig was not at
first deemed full-dress.   Queen Anne was deeply

offended because Lord Bolingbroke, summoned hurriedly to her, appeared in a Ramillies wig instead of a full-bottomed peruke. The queen remarked that she supposed next time Lord Bolingbroke would come in his nightcap. It was the same offending nobleman who brought in the fashion of the mean little tie-wigs.

It is stated in Read's *Weekly Journal* of May 1, 1736, in an account of the marriage of the Prince of Wales, that the officers of the Horse and Foot Guards wore Ramillies periwigs when on parade, by his Majesty's order. We meet in the reign of George II other forms of wigs and other titles; the most popular was the pigtail wig. The pigtail of this was worn hanging down the back or tied up in a knot behind. This pigtail wig, worn for so many years, is shown on page 340. It was popular in the army for sixty years, but in 1804 orders were given for the pigtail to be reduced to seven inches in length, and finally, in 1808, to be cut off wholly, to the deep mourning of disciplinarians who deemed a soldier without a pigtail as hopeless as a Manx cat.

Bob-wigs, minor and major, came in during the reign of George II. The bob-wig was held to be a direct imitation of the natural hair, though, of course, it deceived no one; it was used chiefly by poorer folk. The 'prentice minor bob was close and short, the citizen's bob major, or Sunday buckle, had several rows of curls. All these came to America by the hundreds — yes, by the thousands. Every profession and almost every calling had its peculiar wig. The caricatures of the period represent full-

"King" Carter. Died 1732.

fledged lawyers with a towering frontlet and a long bag at the back tied in the middle; while students of the university have a wig flat on the top, to accommodate their stiff, square-cornered hats, and a great bag like a lawyer's wig at the back.

"When the law lays down its full-bottom'd periwig you will find less wisdom in bald pates than you are aware of," says the *Choleric Man*. This lawyer's wig is the only one which has not been changed or abandoned. You may see

Judge Benjamin Lynde.

it here, on the head of Judge Benjamin Lynde of Salem. He died in 1745. Carlyle sneers:—

"Has not your Red hanging-individual a horsehair wig, squirrel-skins, and a plush-gown — whereby all Mortals know that he is a JUDGE?"

In the reigns of Anne and William and Mary perukes grew so vast and cumbersome that a wig was invented for travelling and for undress wear, and was called the "Campaign wig." It would not seem very simple since it was made full and curled to the front, and had, so writes a contemporary, Randle Holme, in his *Academy of Armory*, 1684, "knots and bobs a-dildo on each side and a curled forehead."

A campaign wig from Holme's drawing is shown on page 340.

There are constant references in old letters and in early literature in America which alter much the dates assigned by English authorities on costume: thus, knowing not of Randle Holme's drawing, Sydney writes that the name "campaign" was applied to a wig, the name and fashion of which came to England from France in 1702. In the Letter-book of William Byrd of Westover, Virginia, in a letter written in June, 1690, to Perry and Lane, his English factors in London, he says, " I have by Tonner sent my long Periwig which I desire you to get made into a Campagne and send mee." This was twelve years earlier than Sydney's date. Fitz-John Winthrop wrote to England in 1695 for " two wiggs one a campane the other short." The portrait of Fitz-John Winthrop shows a prodigious imposing wig, but it has no " knots or bobs a-dildo on each side," though the forehead is curled ; it is a fine example of a peruke.

I cannot attempt even to name all the wigs, much less can I describe them ; Hawthorne gave " the tie," the " Brigadier," the " Major," the " Ramillies," the grave " Full-bottom," the giddy " Feather-top." To these and others already named in this chapter I can add the " Neck-lock," the " Allonge," the " Lavant," the " Vallancy," the " Grecian fly wig," the " Beau-peruke," the " Long-tail," the " Fox-tail," the " Cut-wig," the " Scratch," the " Twist-wig."

Others named in 1753 in the *London Magazine* were the " Royal bird," the " Rhinoceros," the

" Corded Wolf's-paw," " Count Saxe's mode," the " She-dragon," the " Jansenist," the " Wild-boar's-back," the " Snail-back," the " Spinach-seed." These titles were literal translations of French wig-names.

Another wig-name was the " Gregorian." We read in *The Honest Ghost*, 1658, " Pulling a little down his Gregorian, which was displac't a little by his hastie taking off his beaver." This wig was named from the inventor, one Gregory, " the famous peruke-maker who is buryed at St. Clements Danes Church." In Cotgrave's *Dictionary* pe-rukes are called Gregorians.

John Rutledge.

In the prologue to *Haut Ton*, written by George Col-man, these wigs are named : —

> " The Tyburn scratch, thick Club and Temple tyes,
> The Parson's Feather-top, frizzed, broad and high.
> The coachman's Cauliflower, built tier on tier."

There was also the " Minister's bob," " Curley roys," " Airy levants," and " I — perukes." The " Dalmahoy " was a bushy bob-wig.

When Colonel John Carter died, he left to his brother Robert his cane, sword, and periwig. I believe this to be the very Vallancy periwig which, in all its snowy whiteness and air of extreme fashion, graces the head of the handsome young fellow as he is shown facing page 212. Even the portrait shares

the fascination which the man is said to have had
for every woman.   I have a copy of it now standing
on my desk, where I can glance at him as I write;
and pleasant company have I found the gay young
Virginian — the best of company.   It is good to

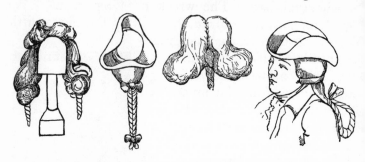

Campaign, Ramillies, Bob, and Pigtail Wigs.

have a companion so handsome of feature, so personable of figure, so laughing, care free, and debo-
nair — isn't it, King Robert?

These snowy wigs at a later date were called
Adonis wigs.

The cost of a handsome wig would sometimes
amount to thirty, forty, and fifty guineas, though
Swift grumbled at paying three guineas, and the ex-
ceedingly correct Mr. Pepys bought wigs at two and
three pounds.   It is not strange that they were often
stolen.   Gay, in his *Trivia*, thus tells the manner of
their disappearance : —

> " Nor is the flaxen wig with safety worn ;
>   High on the shoulder, in a basket borne,
>   Lurks the sly boy, whose hand to rapine bred,
>   Plucks off the curling honors of the head."

In America wigs were deemed rich spoils for the sneak-thief.

There was a vast trade in second-hand wigs. 'Tis said there was in Rosemary Lane in London a constantly replenished "Wig lottery." It was, rather, a wig grab-bag. The wreck of gentility paid his last sixpence for appearances, dipped a long arm into a hole in a cask, and fished out his wig. It might be half-decent, or it might be fit only to polish shoes — worse yet, it might have been used already for that purpose. The lowest depths of everything were found in London. I doubt if we had any Rosemary Lane wig lotteries in New York, or Philadelphia, or Boston.

An answer to a query in a modern newspaper gives the word "caxon" as descriptive of a dress-wig. It was in truth a term for a wig, but it was a cant term, a slang phrase for the worst possible wig; thus Charles Lamb wrote: —

Rev. William Welsteed.

"He had two wigs both pedantic but of different omen. The one serene, smiling, fresh-powdered, betokening a mild day. The other an old discoloured, unkempt, angry caxon denoting frequent and bloody execution."

All these wigs, even the bob-wig, were openly artificial. The manner of their make, their bindings, their fastening, as well as their material, completely destroyed any illusion which could possibly have been entertained as to their being a luxuriant crop of natural hair.

No one was ashamed of wearing a wig. On the contrary, a person with any sense of dignity was ashamed of being so unfashionable as to wear his own hair. It was a glorious time for those to whom Nature had been niggardly. A wig was as frankly extraneous as a hat. No attempt was made to imitate the roots of the hairs, or the parting. The hair was attached openly, and bound with a high-colored, narrow ribbon. Here is an advertisement from the *Boston News Letter* of August 14, 1729 : —

"Taken from the shop of Powers Mariott, Barber, a light Flaxen Natural Wigg parted from the forehead to the Crown. The Narrow Ribband is of a Red Pink Color, the Caul is in rows of Red, Green and White Ribband."

Another "peruke-maker" lost a Flaxen "Natural" wig bound with peach-colored ribbon ; while in 1755 Barber Coes, of Marblehead, lost "feather-tops" bound with various ribbons. Some had three colors on one wig — pink, green and purple. A goat's-hair wig bound with red and purple, with green ribbons striping the caul, must have been a pretty and dignified thing on an old gentleman's head. One of the most curious materials for a wig was fine wire, of which Wortley Montague's wig was made.

We read in many histories of costume, among them Miss Hill's recent history of English dress, that Quakers did not wear wigs. This is widely incorrect. Many Quakers wore most fashionably made wigs. William Penn wrote from England

Thomas Hopkinson.

to his steward, telling him to allow Deputy Governor Lloyd to wear his (Penn's) wigs. I suppose he wished his deputy to cut a good figure.

From the *New York Gazette* of May 9, 1737, we learn of a thief's stealing "one gray Hair Wig, not the worse for wearing, one Pale Hair Wig, not worn five times, marked V. S. E., one brown Natural wig, One old wig of goat's hair put in buckle." Buckle meant to curl, and derivatively a wig was in buckle when it was rolled for curling. Roulettes or bilbouquettes for buckling a wig were little rollers of pipe clay. The hair was twisted up in them, and papers bound over them to fix them in place. The roulettes could be put in buckle hot, or they could be rolled cold and the whole wig heated. The latter was not favored; it damaged the wig. Moreover, a careless barber had often roasted a forgotten wig which he had put in buckle and in an oven.

The *New York Gazette* of May 12, 1750, had this alluring advertisement: —

"This is to acquaint the Public, that there is lately arrived from London the Wonder of the World, *an Honest* Barber and Peruke Maker, who might have worked for the King, if his Majesty would have employed him: It was not for the want of Money he came here, for he had enough of that at Home, nor for the want of Business, that he advertises himself, BUT to acquaint the Gentlemen and Ladies, that *Such a Person is now in Town*, living near *Rosemary Lane* where Gentlemen and Ladies may be supplied with Goods as follows, viz.: Tyes, Full-Bottoms, Majors, Spencers, Fox-Tails, Ramalies, Tacks, cut and bob

Perukes: Also Ladies Tatematongues and Towers after the
Manner that is now wore at Court. *By their Humble and
Obedient Servant*,

" John Still."

"Perukes," says Malcolm, in his *Manners and
Customs*, "were an highly important article in 1734."
Those of right gray human hair were four guineas
each; light grizzle ties, three guineas; and other
colors in proportion, to twenty-five shillings. Right

gray human hair cue pe-
rukes, from two guineas to
fifteen shillings each, was the
price of dark ones; and right
gray bob perukes, two guineas and a half to fifteen
shillings, the price of dark
bobs. Those mixed with
horsehair were much lower.
Prices were a bit higher
in America. It was held

Reverend Dr. Barnard.

that better wigs were made in England than in
America or France; so the letter-books and agent's-
lists of American merchants are filled with orders
for English wigs.

Imperative orders for the earliest and extremest
new fashions stood from year to year on the lists of
fashionable London wig-makers; and these constant
orders came from Virginia gentlemen and Massachusetts magistrates, — not a few, too, from the parsons, — scantly paid as they were. The smaller
bob-wigs and tie-wigs were precisely the same in
both countries, and I am sure were no later in

assumption in America than was necessitated by the
weeks occupied in coming across seas.

Throughout the seventeenth century all classes of
men in American towns wore wigs. Negro slaves
flaunted white horsehair wigs, goat's-hair bob-wigs,
natural wigs, all the plainer wigs, and all the more
costly sorts when these were half worn and second-
hand. Soldiers wore wigs; and in the *Massachusetts
Gazette* of the year 1774 a runaway negro is described as wearing a curl of hair tied around his head
to imitate a scratch wig; with his woolly crown this
dangling curl must have been the height of absurdity.

It is not surprising to find in the formal life of the
English court the poor little tormented, sickly, sad
child of Queen Anne wearing, before he was seven
years old, a large full-bottomed wig; but it is
curious to see the portraits of American children
rigged up in wigs (I have half a dozen such), and
to find likewise an American gentleman (and not
one of wealth either) paying £9 apiece for wigs for
three little sons of seven, nine, and eleven years of
age. This lavish parent was Enoch Freeman, who
lived in Portland, Maine, in 1754.

Wigs were objects of much and constant solicitude
and care; their dressing was costly, and they wore
out readily. Barbers cared for them by the month
or year, visiting from house to house. Ten pounds
a year was not a large sum to be paid for the care of
a single wig. Men of dignity and careful dress had
barbers' bills of large amount, such men as Governor
John Hancock, Governor Hutchinson, and Governor Belcher. On Saturday afternoons the barbers'

boys were seen flying through the narrow streets, wig-box in hand, hurrying to deliver all the dressed wigs ere sunset came.

No doubt the constant wearing of such hot, heavy head-covering made the hair thin and the head bald; thus wigs became a necessity. Men had their heads very closely covered of old, and caught cold at a breath. Pepys took cold throwing off his hat while at dinner. If the wig were removed even within doors a close cap or hood at once took its place, or, as I tell elsewhere, a turban of some rich stuff. In America, in the Southern states, where people were poor and plantations scattered, all men did not wear wigs. A writer in the *London Magazine* in 1745 tells of this country carelessness of dress. He says that except some of the "very Elevated Sort" few wore perukes; so that at first sight "all looked as if about to go to bed," for all wore caps. Common people wore woollen caps; richer ones donned caps of white cotton or Holland linen. These were worn even when riding fifty miles from home. He adds, "It may be cooler for aught I know; but methinks 'tis very ridiculous." So wonted were his eyes to perukes, that his only thought of caps was that they were "ridiculous." Nevertheless, when a shipload of servants, bond-servants who might be stolen when in drink, or lured under false pretences, might be convicts, or honest workmen, — when these transports were set up in respectability, — scores of new wigs of varying degrees of dignity came across seas with them. Many an old caxon or "gossoon" — a wig worn yellow with age — ended its days on the pate of a redemptioner, who thereby acquired dignity and was more likely to be bought as a schoolmaster. Truly our ancestors were not squeamish, and it is well they were not, else they would have squeamed from morning till night at the sights, and sounds, and things, and dirt around them. But these be parlous words; they had the senses and feelings of their day — suited to the surroundings of their day. In one thing they can be envied. Knowing not of germs and microbes, dreaming not of antiseptics and fumigation, they could be happy in blissful unconsciousness of menacing environment — a blessing wholly denied to us.

Andrew Ellicott.

When James Murray came from Scotland in 1735 he went up the Cape Fear River in North Carolina to the struggling settlements of Brunswick. The stock of wigs which he brought as one of the commodities of his trade had absolutely no market. In 1751 he wrote thus to his London wig-maker : —

"We deal so much in caps in this country that we are almost as careless of the outside as of the inside of our heads. I have had but one wig since the last I had of you, and yours has outworn it. Now I am near out, and you may make me a new grisel Bob."

Nevertheless, in 1769, when he was roughly handled in Boston on account of his Tory utterances, his head, though he was but fifty-six, was bald from wig-wearing. His spirited recital runs thus : —

" The crowd intending sport, remained. As I was pressing out, my Wig was pulled off and a pate shaved by Time and the barber was left exposed. This was thought a signal and prelude to further insult ; which would probably have taken place but for hindering the cause. Going along in this plight, surrounded by the crowd, in the dark, a friend hold of either arm supporting me, while somebody behind kept nibbling at my sides and endeavouring of treading the reforming justice out of me by the multitude. My wig dishevelled, was borne on a staff behind. My friends and supporters offered to house me, but I insisted on going home in the present trim, and was landed in safety."

Patriotic Boston barbers found much satisfaction in ill treating the wigs of their Tory customers and patrons. William Pyncheon, a Salem Tory, wrote a few years later : —

" The tailors and barbers, in their squinting and fleering at our clothes, and especially our wiggs, begin to border on malevolence. Had not the caul of my wigg been of uncommon stuff and workmanship, I think my barber would have had it in pieces : his dressing it greatly resembles the farmer dressing his flax, the latter of the two being the gentlest in his motions."

Worcester Tories, among them Timothy Paine, had their wigs pulled off in public. Mr. Paine at once gave his dishonored wig to one of his negro slaves, and never after resumed wig-wearing.

CHAPTER XII

THE BEARD

" *Though yours be sorely lugg'd and torn*
  It does your Visage more adorn
  Than if 'twere prun'd, and starch'd, and launder'd
  And cut square by the Russian standard."

— " Hudibras," SAMUEL BUTLER.

" *Now of beards there be such company*
    And fashions such a throng
  That it is very hard to handle a beard
    Tho' it be never so long.

" *'Tis a pretty sight and a grave delight*
    That adorns both young and old
  A well thatch't face is a comely grace
    And a shelter from the cold."

— " Le Prince d'Amour," 1660.

CHAPTER XII

THE BEARD

EN'S hair on their heads hath ever been at odds with that on their face. If the head were well covered and the hair long, then the face was smooth shaven. William the Conqueror had short hair and a beard, then came a long-haired king, then a cropped one; Edward IV's subjects had long hair and closely cut beards. Henry VII fiercely forbade beards. The great sovereign Henry VIII ordered short hair like the French, and wore a beard. Through Elizabeth's day and that of James the beard continued. Not until great perukes overshadowed the whole face did the beard disappear. It vanished for a century as if men were beardless; but after men began to wear short hair in the early years of the nineteenth century, bearded men appeared. A few German mystics who had come to America full-bearded were stared at like the elephant, and a sight of them was recorded in a diary as a great event.

There is no doubt that, to the general reader, the ordinary thought of the Puritan is with a beard, a face and figure much like the Hogarth illustrations of Hudibras — one of the " Presbyterian true Blue,"

"the stubborn crew of Errant Saints,"—without the grotesquery of face and feature, perhaps, but certainly with all the plainness and gracelessness of

Herbert Westphaling, Bishop of Hereford.

dress and the commonplace beard.   The wording of Hudibras also figures the popular conception:—

> "His tawny Beard was th' equal Grace
> Both of his Wisdom and his Face :
>
> *   *   *   *   *
>
> His Doublet was of sturdy Buff
> And tho' not Sword, was Cudgel-Proof.
> His Breeches were of rugged Woolen
> And had been at the Siege of Bullen."

In truth this is well enough as far as it runs and for one suit of clothing; but this was by no means a universal dress, nor was it a universal beard. Indeed beards were fearfully and wonderfully varied.

That humorous old rhymester, Taylor, the "Water Poet," may be quoted at length on the vanity thus: —

"And Some, to set their Love's-Desire on Edge
Are cut and prun'd, like to a Quickset Hedge.
Some like a Spade, some like a Forke, some square,
Some round, some mow'd like stubble, some starke bare;
Some sharpe, Stilletto-fashion, Dagger-like,
That may with Whispering a Man's Eyes unpike;
Some with the Hammer-cut, or Roman T.
Their Beards extravagant, reform'd must be.
Some with the Quadrate, some Triangle fashion;
Some circular, some ovall in translation;
Some Perpendicular in Longitude,
Some like a Thicket for their Crassitude,
That Heights, Depths, Breadths, Triform, Square, Ovall, Round
And Rules Geometrical in Beards are found."

Taylor's own beard was screw-shaped. I fancy he invented it.

The Anglo-Saxon beard was parted, and this double form remained for a long time. Sometimes there were two twists or two long forks.

A curious pointed beard, a beard in two curls, is shown on page 225, on James Douglas, Earl of Morton. A still more strangely kept one, pointed in the middle of the chin, and kept in two rolls which roll toward the front, is upon the aged herald, on page 354.

Richard II had a mean beard, — two little tufts

on the chin known as " the mouse-eaten beard, here
a tuft, there a tuft." The round beard " like a half
a Holland cheese" is always seen in the depictions
of Falstaff; "a great round beard" we know he
had. This was easily trimmed, but others took so
much time and attention that pasteboard boxes were

The Herald Vandum.

made to tie over them
at night, that they
might be unrumpled in
the morning.

In the reign of Eliza-
beth and of James I a
beard and whiskers or
mustache were univer-
sally worn. In the
time of Charles I the
general effect of beard
and mustache was trian-
gular, with the mouth
in the centre, as in the
portrait of Waller on
page 37.

A beard of some form was certainly universal in
1620. Often it was the orderly natural growth shown
on Winthrop's face; a smaller tuft on the chin with
a mustache also was much worn. Many ministers
in America had this chin-tuft. Among them were
John Eliot and John Davenport. The Stuarts wore
a pointed beard, carefully trimmed, and a mustache;
but the natural beard seems to have disappeared with
the ruff. Charles II clung for a time to a mustache;
his portrait by Mary Beale has one; but with the

great development of the periwig came a smooth
face.   This continued until the nineteenth century
brought a fashion of bearded men again; a fashion
which was so abhorred, so reviled, so openly warred
with that I know of the bequest of a large estate with
the absolute and irrevocable condition that the in-
heritor should never wear a beard of any form.

The hammer cut was of the reign of Charles I.
It was T-shaped.   In the play, *The Queen of
Corinth*, 1647, are the lines: —

> " He strokes his beard
> Which now he puts in the posture of a T,
> The Roman T.   Your T-beard is in fashion."

The spade beard is shown on page 356.   It was
called the " broad pendant," and was held to make
a man look like a warrior.   The sugar-loaf beard
was the natural form much worn by Puritans; by
natural I mean not twisted into any " strange antic
forms."   The swallow-tail cut (about 1600) is more
unusual, but was occasionally seen.

> " The stiletto-beard
> It makes me afeard
>   It is so sharp beneath.
> For he that doth place
> A dagger in his face
>   What wears he in his sheath ? "

An unusually fine stiletto beard is on the chin of
John Endicott (page 5).   It was distinctly a soldier's
beard.   Endicott was major-general of the colonial
forces and a severe disciplinarian.   Shakespere, in

Henry V, speaks of "a beard of the General's cut."
It was worn by the Earl of Southampton (see facing
page 190), and perhaps Endicott favored it on that
account. The pique-devant beard or "pick-a-devant
beard, O Fine Fashion," was much worn. A good
moderate example may be seen upon Cousin Kilvert,

with doublet and band, in the
print on page 41. An extreme
type was the beard of Robert Greene, the Elizabethan
dramatist, "A jolly long red
peake like the spire of a steeple,
which he wore continually,
whereat a man might hang a
jewell; it was so sharp and
pendent."

Scotch Beard.

The word "peak" was constantly used for a beard,
and also the words "spike" and "spear." A barber is
represented in an old play as asking whether his cus-
tomer will "have his peak cut short and sharp; or
amiable like an inamorato, or broad pendant like a
spade; to be terrible like a warrior and a soldado;
to have his appendices primed, or his mustachios
fostered to turn about his eares like ye branches of
a vine."

A broad square-cut beard spreading at the ends
like an open fan is the "cathedral beard" of Randle
Holme, "so called because grave men of the church
did wear it." It is often seen in portraits. One
of these is shown on page 357.

In the *Life of Mrs. Elizabeth Thomas*, 1731, she
writes of her grandfather, a Turkey-merchant : —

" He was very nice in the Mode of his Age — his Valet being some hours every morning in *Starching* his *Beard* and Curling his Whiskers during which Time a Gentleman whom he maintain'd as Companion always read to him upon some useful subject."

So we may believe they really " starched " their beards, stiffened them with some dressing.

Dr. William Slater.
Cathedral Beard.

Taylor, the " Water Poet " (1640), says of beards : —

" Some seem as they were starched stiff and fine
Like to the Bristles of some Angry Swine."

Dr. John Dee. 1600.

Dr. Dee's extraordinary beard I can but regard as an affectation of singularity, assumed doubtless to attract attention, and to be a sign of unusual parts. Aubrey, his friend, calls him " a very handsome man ; of very fair, clear, sanguine complexion, with a long beard as white as milke. He was tall and slender. He wore a gowne like an artist's gowne ; with hanging sleeves and a slitt. A mighty good man he was." The word "artist" then meant artisan; and in this reference means a smock like a workman's.

A name seen often in Winthrop's letters is that of Sir Kenelm Digby. He was an intimate correspondent of John Winthrop the second, and it would not be strange if he did many errands for Winthrop in England besides purchasing drugs. His portrait, and a lugubrious one it is, is one of the few of his day which shows an untrimmed beard. Aubrey says of him that after the death of his wife he wore "a long mourning cloak, a high cornered hatt, his beard unshorn, look't like a hermit; as signs of sorrow for his beloved wife. He had something of the sweetness of his mother's face." This sweetness is, however, not to be perceived in his unattractive portrait.

CHAPTER XIII

PATTENS, CLOGS, AND GOLOE-SHOES

" *Q. Why is a Wife like a Patten?*
A. Both are Clogs."

— Old Riddle.

CHAPTER XIII

PATTENS, CLOGS, AND GOLOE-SHOES

WHEN this old pigskin trunk was new, the men who fought in the Revolution were young. Here is the date, "1756," and the initials in brass-headed nails, "J. E. H." It was a bride's trunk, the trunk of Elizabeth, who married John; and it was marked after the manner of marking the belongings of married folk in her day. It is curious in shape, spreading out wide at the top; for it was made to fit a special place in an old coach. I have told the story of that ancient coach in my *Old Narragansett*: the tale of the ignoble end of its days, the account of its fall from transportation of this happy bride and bridegroom, through years of stately use and formal dignity to more years of happy desuetude as a children's cubby-house; and finally its ignominy as a roosting-place, and hiding-place, and laying-place, and setting-place of misinformed and misguided hens. Under the coachman's seat, where the two-score dark-blue Staffordshire pie-plates were found on the day of the annihilation of the coach, was the true resting-place of this trunk. It was a hidden spot, for the trunk was small, and was intended to hold only treasures. It holds them still, though they are not the silver-plate, the round watches, the narrow laces, and the precious camel's-hair scarf.   It now holds treasured relics of the olden time; trifles, but not unconsidered ones; much esteemed trifles are they, albeit not in form or shape or manner of being fit to rest in parlor cabinets or on tables, but valued, nevertheless, valued for that most intangible of qualities — association.

Iron and Leather Pattens.   1760.

Here is one little "antick."   It is an ample bag with the neat double drawing-strings of our youth; a bag, nay, a pocket.   It once hung by the side of some one of my forbears, perhaps Elizabeth of the brass-nailed initials.   It was a much-esteemed pocket, though it is only of figured cotton or chiney; but those stuffs were much sought after when this old trunk was new.   The pocket has served during recent years as a cover for two articles of footwear which many "of the younger sort" to-day have never seen — they are pattens.   "Clumsy, ugly pattens" we find them frequently stigmatized in the

severe words of the early years of the nineteenth
century, but there is nothing ugly or clumsy about
this pair.   The sole is of some black, polished
wood — it is heavy enough for ebony; the straps
are of strong leather neatly stitched; the buckles
are polished brass, and brass nails fasten the leather
to the wooden soles.   These soles are cut up high
in a ridge to fit under the instep of a high-heeled

Oak, Iron, and Leather Clogs. 1790.

shoe; for it was a very little lady who wore these
pattens, — Elizabeth, — and her little feet always
stood in the highest heels.   She was active, kindly,
and bountiful.   She lived to great age, and she could
and did walk many miles a day until the last year
of her life.   She is recalled as wearing a great scarlet
cloak with a black silk quilted hood on cold winter
days, when she visited her neighbors with kindly
words, and housewifely, homely gifts, conveyed in
an ample basket.   The cloak was made precisely
like the scarlet cloak shown facing page 258, and had
a like hood.   She was brown-eyed, and her dark

hair was never gray even in extreme old age; nor
was the hair of her granddaughter, another Elizabeth, my grandmother. Trim and erect of figure,
and precise and neat of dress, wearing, on account
of this neatness, shorter petticoats, when walking,
than was the mode of her day, and also through
this neatness clinging to the very last to these
cleanly, useful, quaint pattens. Her black hood,
frilled white cap, short, quilted petticoat, high-heeled
shoes, and the shining ebony and brass pattens,
and over all the great, full scarlet cloak, — all these
made her an unusual and striking figure against the
Wayland landscape, the snowy fields and great
sombre pine trees of Heard's Island, as she trod
trimly, in short pattened steps that crackled the
kittly-benders in the shadowed roads, or sunk softly
in the shallow mud of the sunny lanes on a snow-
melting day in late winter. Would I could paint
the picture as I see it!

These pattens in the old trunk are prettier than
most pattens which have been preserved. In general, they are rather shabby things. I have another
pair — more commonplace, which chance to exist;
they were not saved purposely. They are pictured
on page 362.

There is a most ungallant old riddle, "Why is a
wife like a patten?" The answer reads, "Because
both are clogs." A very courteous bishop was once
asked this uncivil query, and he answered without
a moment's hesitation, "Because both elevate the
soul (sole)." Pattens may be clogs, yet there is a
difference. After much consultation of various

authorities, and much discussion in the columns
of various querying journals, I make this decision
and definition.   Pattens are thick, wooden soles
roughly shaped in the outline of the human foot (in
the shoemaker's notion of that member), mounted

English Clogs.

on a round or oval ring of iron, fixed by two or
three pins to the sole, in such a way that when the
patten is worn the sole of the wearer's foot is about
two inches above the ground.   A heel-piece with
buckles and straps, strings or buttons and leather
loops, and a strap over the toe, retain the patten
in place upon the foot when the wearer trips along.
(See page 362.)   Clogs serve the same purpose, but
are simply wooden soles tipped and shod with iron.
These also have heel-pieces and straps of various
materials — from the heavy serviceable leather shown
in the clogs on pages 363 and 365 to the fine brocade
clogs made and worn by two brides and pictured on
page 368.   Dainty brass tips and colored morocco
straps made a really refined pair of clogs.   Poplar
wood was deemed the best wood for pattens and
clogs.   Sometimes the wooden sole was thin, and

was cut at the line under the instep in two pieces and hinged. These hinges were held to facilitate walking. Children also wore clogs. (See page 370.) Clogs, as worn by English and American folk, did not raise the wearer as high above the mud and mire as did pattens, but I have seen Turkish clogs that were ten inches high. Chopines were worn by Englishwomen to make them look taller. Three are shown on page 367. Lady Falkland was short and stout, and wore them for years to increase her apparent height; so she states in her memoirs.

It is a curious philological study that, while the words "clogs" and "pattens" for a time were constantly heard, the third name which has survived till to-day is the oldest of all — "galoshes." Under the many spellings, galoe-shoes, goloshes, gallage, galoche, and gallosh, it has come down to us from the Middle Ages. It is spelt galoches in *Piers Plowman*. In a *Compotus* or household account of the Countess of Derby in 1388 are entries of botews (boots), souters (slippers), and "one pair of galoches, 14 *d.*" Clogs, or galoches, were known in the days of the Saxons, when they were termed "wife's shoes."

A "galage" was a shoe "which has nothing on the feet but a latchet"; it was simply a clog. In February, 1687, Judge Sewall notes, "Send my mothers Shoes & Golowshoes to carry to her." In 1736 Peter Faneuil sent to England for "Galoushoes" for his sister. Another foot-covering for slippery, icy walking is named by Judge Sewall.

He wrote on January 19, 1717, "Great rain and
very Slippery; was fain to wear Frosts." These
frosts were what had been called on horses, "frost
nails," or calks. They were simply spiked soles
to help the wearer to walk on ice. A pair may
be seen at the Deerfield Memorial Hall. Another pair is of half-soles with sharp ridges of
iron, set, one the length of the half-sole, the other
across it.

For a time clogs seem to have been in constant
use in America; frail morocco slippers and thin

Chopines, Seventeenth Century. In the Ashmolean Museum.

prunella and callimanco shoes made them necessary,
as did also the unpaved streets. Heavy-soled shoes
were unknown for women's wear. Women walked
but short distances. In the country they always
rode. We find even Quaker women warned in
1720 not to wear "Shoes of light Colours bound
with Differing Colours, and heels White or Red,
with White bands, and fine Coloured Clogs and
Strings, and Scarlet and Purple Stockings and
Petticoats made Short to expose them"—a rather
startling description of footwear. Again, in 1726,
in Burlington, New Jersey, Friends were asked to
be "careful to avoid wearing of Stript Shoos, or

Red and White Heel'd Shoos, or Clogs, or Shoos trimmed with Gawdy Colours."

Ann Warder, an English Quaker, was in Philadelphia, 1786 to 1789, and kept an entertaining journal, from which I make this quotation : —

"Got B. Parker to go out shopping with me. On our way happened of Uncle Head, to whom I complained bitterly of the dirty streets, declaring if I could purchase a

Brides' Clogs of Brocade and Sole Leather.

pair of pattens, the singularity I would not mind. Uncle soon found me up an apartment, out of which I took a pair and trotted along quite Comfortable, crossing some streets with the greatest ease, which the idea of had troubled me. My little companion was so pleased, that she wished some also, and kept them on her feet to learn to walk in them most of the remainder of the day."

Fairholt, in his book upon costume, says, "Pattens date their origin to the reign of Anne." Like many other dates and statements given by this author, this is wholly wrong. In *Purchas', his Pilgrimage*, 1613, is this sentence, "Clogges or Pattens to keep them out of the dust they may not burden themselves with," showing that the name and thing was the same then as to-day.

Charles Dibdin has a song entitled, *The Origin of the Patten.* Fair Patty went out in the mud and the mire, and her thin shoes

Clogs of "Pennsylvania Dutch."

speedily were wet. Then she became hoarse and could not sing, while her lover longed for the sweet sound of her voice.

> " My anvil glow'd, my hammer rang,
>   Till I had form'd from out the fire
>   To bear her feet above the mire,
>   A platform for my blue-eyed Patty.
>   Again was heard each tuneful close,
>   My fair one in the patten rose,
>   Which takes its name from blue-eyed Patty."

This fanciful derivation of the word was not an original thought of Dibdin. Gay wrote in his *Trivia,* 1715 :—

> " The patten now supports each frugal dame
>   That from the blue-eyed Patty takes the name."

In reality, patten is derived from the French word *patin*, which has a varied meaning of the sole of a shoe or a skate.

Pattens were noisy, awkward wear. A writer of the day of their universality wrote, "Those ugly,

noisy, ferruginous, ancle-twisting, foot-cutting, clink-
ing things called women's pattens." Notices were
set in church porches enjoining the removal of
women's pattens, which, of course, should never
have been worn into church during service-time.

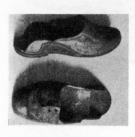

Children's Clogs.   1730.

It may have disappeared to-
day, but four years ago, on the
door of Walpole St. Peters,
near Wisbeck, England, hung
a board which read, " People who enter this church are
requested to take off their pattens." A friend in Northamp-
tonshire, England, writes me
that pattens are still seen on
muddy days in remote English villages in that shire.

Men wore pattens in early days.   And men did
and do wear clogs in English mill-towns.

There were also horse pattens or horse clogs
which horses wore through deep, muddy roads; I
have an interesting photograph of a pair found in
Northampton.

CHAPTER XIV

BATTS AND BROAGS, BOOTS AND SHOES

" By my Faith ! Master Inkpen, thou hast put thy foot in it !
Tis a pretty subject and a strange one, and a vast one, but
we'll leave it never a sole to stand on. The proverb hath
' There's naught like leather,' but my Lady answers ' Save
silk.' "

—Old Play.

CHAPTER XIV

BATTS AND BROAGS, BOOTS AND SHOES

NE of the first sumptuary laws in New England declared that men of mean estate should not walk abroad in immoderate great boots. It was a natural prohibition where all extravagance in dress was reprehended and restrained. The "great boots" which had been so vast in the reign of James I seemed to be spreading still wider in the reign of Charles. I have an old "Discourse" on leather dated 1629, which states fully the condition of things. Its various headings read, "The general Use of Leather;" "The general Abuse thereof;" "The good which may arise from the Reformation;" "The several Statutes made in that behalf by our ancient Kings;" and lastly a "Petition to the High Court of Parliament." It is all most informing; for instance, in the trades that might want work were it not for leather are named not only "shoemakers, cordwainers, curriers, etc.," but many now obsolete. The list reads: —

" Book binders.	Budget makers.
Saddlers.	Trunk makers.
Upholsterers.	Belt makers.

Case makers.	Box makers.
Wool-card makers.	Cabinet makers.
Shuttle makers.	Bottle and Jack makers.
Hawks-hood makers	Gridlers.
Scabbard-makers.	Glovers."

Unwillingly the author added " those *upstart trades* — Coach Makers, and Harness Makers for Coach Horses." It was really feared, by this sensible gentleman-writer — and many others — that if many carriages and coaches were used, shoemakers would suffer because so few shoes would be worn out.

From the statutes which are rehearsed we learn that the footwear of the day was " boots, shoes, buskins, startups, slippers, or pantofles." Stubbes said : —

" They have korked shooes puisnets pantoffles, some of black velvet, some of white some of green, some of yellow, some of Spanish leather, some of English leather stitched with Silke and embroidered with Gold & Silver all over the foot."

A very interesting book has been published by the British Cordwainers' Guild, giving a succession of fine illustrations of the footwear of different times and nations. Among them are some handsome English slippers, shoes, jack-boots, etc. We have also in our museums, historical collections, and private families many fine examples ; but the difficulty is in the assigning of correct dates. Family tradition is absolutely wide of the truth — its fabulous dates are often a century away from the proper year.

The Copley Family Picture.

Buskins to the knee were worn even by royalty; Queen Elizabeth's still exist. Buskins were in wear when the colonies were settled. Richard Sawyer, of Windsor, Connecticut, had cloth buskins in 1648; and a hundred years later runaway servants wore

Wedding Slippers and Brocade. 1712.

them. One redemptioner is described as running off in "sliders and buskins." American buskins were a foot-covering consisting of a strong leather sole with cloth uppers and leggins to the knees, which were fastened with lacings. Startups were similar, but heavier. In Thynne's *Debate between Pride and Lowliness*, the dress of a countryman is described. It runs thus: —

> " A payre of startups had he on his feete
>   That lased were up to the small of the legge.
>   Homelie they are, and easier than meete ;
>   And in their soles full many a wooden pegge."

Thomas Johnson of Wethersfield, Connecticut, died in 1840. He owned " 1 Perre of Startups."

Slippers were worn even in the fifteenth century. In the *Paston Letters*, in a letter dated February 23, 1479, is this sentence, " In the whych lettre was VIII d with the whych I shulde bye a peyr of slyppers." Even for those days eightpence must have been a small price for slippers. In 1686, Judge Samuel Sewall wrote to a member of the Hall family thanking him for " The Kind Loving Token — the East Indian Slippers for my wife." Other colonial letters refer to Oriental slippers; and I am sure that Turkish slippers are worn by Lady Temple in her childish portrait, painted in company with her brother. Slip-shoes were evidently slippers — the word is used by Sewall; and slap-shoes are named by Randle Holme. Pantofles were also slippers, being apparently rather handsomer footwear than ordinary slippers or slip-shoes. They are in general specified as embroidered. Evelyn tells of the fine pantofles of the Pope embroidered with jewels on the instep.

So great was the use and abuse of leather that a petition was made to Parliament in 1629 to attempt to restrict the making of great boots. One sentence runs : —

" The wearing of Boots is not the Abuse ; but the generality of wearing and the manner of cutting Boots out with huge slovenly unmannerly immoderate tops. What over lavish spending is there in Boots and Shoes. To either of which is now added a French proud Superfluity of Leather.

"For the general Walking in Boots it is a Pride taken up by the Courtier and is descended to the Clown. The Merchant and Mechanic walk in Boots. Many of our

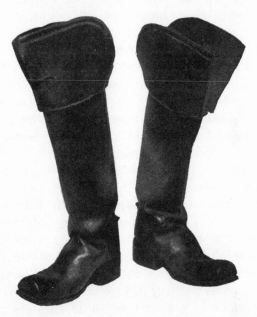

Jack-boots. Owned by Lord Fairfax of Virginia.

Clergy either in neat Boots or Shoes and Galloshoes. University Scholars maintain the Fashion likewise. Some Citizens out of a Scorn not to be Gentile go every day booted. Attorneys, Lawyers, Clerks, Serving Men, All Sorts of Men delight in this Wasteful Wantonness.

Wasteful I may well call it. One pair of boots eats up the leather of six reasonable pair of men's shoes."

Monstrous boots seem to have been the one fri-
volity in dress which the Puritans could not give up.
In the reign of Charles I boots were superb. The
tops were flaring, lined within with lace or embroidered or fringed; thus when turned down they
were richly ornamental. Fringes of leather, silk, or
cloth edged some boot-tops on the outside; the
leather itself was carved and gilded. The soldiers
and officers of Cromwell's army sometimes gave up
laces and fringes, but not the boot-tops. The Earl
of Essex, his general, had cloth fringes on his boots.
(See his portrait facing page 26; also the portrait
of Lord Fairfax, facing page 38.) In the court of
Charles II and Louis XIV of France the boot-tops
spread to absurd inconvenience. The toes of these
boots were very square, as were the toes of men's
and women's shoes. Children's shoes were of similar form. The singular shoes worn by John Quincy
and Robert Gibbes are precisely right-angled. It
was a sneer at the Puritans that they wore pointed
toes. The shoe-ties, roses, and buckles varied; but
the square toes lingered, though they were singularly
inelegant. On the feet of George I (see portrait facing page 184) the square-toed shoes are ugly indeed.

James I scornfully repelled shoe-roses when
brought to him for his wear; asking if they wished
to "make a ruffle-footed dove" of him. But soon
he wore the largest rosettes in court. Peacham tells
that some cost as much as £30 a pair, being then, of
course, of rare lace.

Friar Bacon's Brazen Head Prophecie, set into a
"Plaie" or Rhyme, has these verses (1604) : —

Joshua Warner.

" Then Handkerchers were wrought
    With Names and true Love Knots ;
And not a wench was taught
    A false Stitch in her spots ;
When Roses in the Gardaines grew
And not in Ribons on a Shoe.

" *Now* Sempsters few are taught
    The true Stitch in their Spots ;
And Names are sildome wrought
    Within the true love knots ;
And Ribon Roses takes such Place
That Garden Roses want their Grace."

Shoes of buff leather, slashed, were the very height of the fashion in the first years of the seventeenth century. They can be seen on the feet of Will Sommers in his portrait. Through the slashes showed bright the scarlet or green stockings of cloth or yarn. Bright-colored shoe-strings gave additional gaudiness. Green shoe-strings, spangled, gilded shoe-strings, shoes of " dry-neat-leather tied with red ribbons," " russet boots," " white silken shoe strings," — all were worn.

Red heels appear about 1710. In Hogarth's original paintings they are seen. Women wore them extensively in America.

The jack-boots of Stuart days seem absolutely imperishable. They are of black, jacked leather like the leather bottles and black-jacks from which Englishmen drank their ale. So closely are they alike that I do not wonder a French traveller wrote home that Englishmen drank from their boots. These jack-boots were as solid and unpliable as iron,

Shoe and Knee Buckles.

square-toed and clumsy of shape. A pair in perfect preservation which belonged to Lord Fairfax in Virginia is portrayed on page 377. Had all colonial gentlemen worn jack-boots, the bootmakers and shoemakers would have been ruined, for a pair would last a lifetime.

In 1767 we find William Cabell of Virginia paying these prices for his finery : —

	£	s.	d.
1 Pair single channelled boots with straps .	1	2	
1 Pair Strong Buckskin Breeches	1	10	
2 Pairs Fashionable Chain Silver Spurs . .	2	10	
1 Pair Silver Buttons		6	

	£	s.	d.
1 fine Magazine Blue Cloth Housing laced .		12	
1 Strong Double Bridle		4	6
6 Pair Men's fine Silk Hose	4	4	
Buttons & trimmings for a coat	5	2	

New England dandies wore, as did Monsieur A-la-mode : —

> " A pair of smart pumps made up of grain'd leather,
>   So thin he can't venture to tread on a feather."

Buckles were made of pinchbeck, an alloy of four parts of copper and one part of zinc, invented by Christopher Pinchbeck, a London watchmaker of the eighteenth century. Buckles were also "plaited" and double " plaited " with gold and silver (which was the general spelling of plated). Plated buckles were cast in pinchbeck, with a pattern on the surface. A silver coating was laid over this. These buckles were set with marcasite, garnet, and paste jewels; sometimes they were of gold with real diamonds. But much imitation jewellery was worn by all people even of great wealth. Perhaps imitation is an incorrect word. The old paste jewels made no assertion of being diamonds. Steel cut in facets and combined with gold, made beautiful buckles. A number of rich shoe and garter buckles, owned in Salem, are shown on page 380.

These old buckles were handsome, costly, dignified; they were becoming; they were elegant. Nevertheless, the fashionable world tired of its expensive and appropriate buckles; they suddenly were deemed inconveniently large, and plain shoe-strings took their place. This caused great commotion and ruin among the buckle-makers, who, with the fatuity of other tradespeople — the wig-makers, the hair-powder makers — in like calamitous changes of fashion, petitioned the Prince of Wales, in 1791, to do something to revive their vanishing trade. But it was like placing King Canute against the advancing waves of the sea.

When the Revolutionists in France set about altering and simplifying costume, they did away

Wedding Slippers.

with shoe-buckles, and fastened their shoes with plain strings. Minister Roland, one day in 1793, was about to present himself to Louis XVI while he was wearing shoes with strings. The old Master of Ceremonies, scandalized at having to introduce a person in such a state of undress, looked despairingly at Dumouriez, who was present. Dumouriez replied with an equally hopeless gesture, and the words, " Hélas! oui, monsieur, tout est perdu."

President Jefferson, with his hateful French notions, made himself especially obnoxious to conservative American folk by giving up shoe-buckles. I read in the *New York Evening Post* that when he received the noisy bawling band of admirers who brought. into the White House the Mammoth Cheese (one of the most vulgar exhibitions ever seen in this country), he was "dressed in his suit of customary black, with shoes that laced tight round the ankle and closed with a neat leathern string."

When shoe-strings were established and trousers were becoming popular, there seemed to be a time of indecision as to the dress of the legs below the short pantaloons and above the stringed shoes. That point of indefiniteness was filled promptly with top-boots. First, black tops appeared; then came tops of fancy leather, of which yellow was the favorite. Gilt tassels swung pleasingly from the colored tops. Silken tassels — home made — were worn. I have a letter from a young American macaroni to his sweetheart in which he thanks her for her "heart-filling boot-tossels" — which seems to me a very cleverly flattering adjective. He adds: "Did those rosy fingers twist the silken strands, and knot them with thought of the wearer? I wish you was loveing enough to tye some threads of your golden hair into the tossells, but I swear I cannot find never a one." The conjunction of two negatives in this manner was common usage a hundred years ago; while "you was" may be found in the writings of our greatest authors of that date.

In one attribute, women's footwear never varied in the two centuries of this book's recording. It was always thin-soled and of light material; never adequate for much "walking abroad" or for any wet weather. In fact, women have never worn heavy walking-boots until our own day. Whether high-heeled or no-heeled they were always thin.

The curious "needle-pointed" slippers which are pictured on page 375 were the bridal slippers at the wedding of Cornelia de Peyster, who married Oliver Teller in 1712. Several articles of her dress still exist; and the background of the slippers is a breadth of the superb yellow and silver brocade wedding gown worn at the same time.

When we have the tiny pages of the few newspapers to turn to, we learn a little of women's shoes. There were advertisements in 1740 of "mourning shoes," "fine silk shoes," "flowered russet shoes," "white callimanco shoes," "black shammy shoes," "girls' flowered russet shoes," "shoes of black velvet, white damask, red morocco, and red everlasting." "Damask worsted shoes in red, blue, green, pink color and white," in 1751. There were satinet patterns for ladies' shoes embroidered with flowers in the vamp. The heels were "high, cross-cut, common, court, and wurtemburgh." Some shoes were white with russet bands. "French fall" shoes were worn both by women and men for many years.

On page 382 is a pair of beautiful brocade wedding shoes. The heels are not high. Another pair was made of the silken stuff of the beautiful sacque

Mrs. Abigail Bromfield Rogers.

worn by Mrs. Carroll. These have high heels running down to a very small heel-base. In the works of Hogarth we may find many examples of women's shoes. In all the old shoes I have seen, made about the time of the American Revolution, the maker's name is within and this legend, " Rips

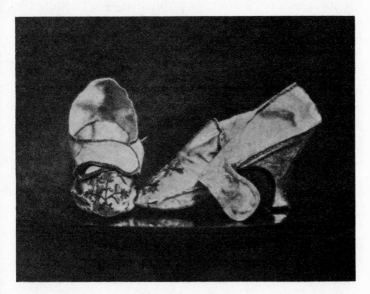

Mrs. Carroll's Slippers.

mended free." Many heels were much higher and smaller than any given in this book.

It is astonishing to read the advocacy and eulogy given by sensible gentlemen to these extreme heels. Watson, the writer of the *Annals of Philadelphia*, extolled their virtues — that they threw the weight of the wearer on the ball of the foot and spread it

out for a good support.   He deplores the flat feet
of 1830.

In 1790 heels disappeared ; sandal-shapes were
the mode.   The quarters were made low, and instead of a buckle was a tiny bow or a pleated ribbon
edging.   In 1791 " the exact size " of the shoe of
the Duchess of York was published — a fashionable
fad which our modern sensation hunters have not
bethought themselves of.   It was $5\frac{3}{4}$ inches in
length ; the breadth of sole, $1\frac{3}{4}$ inches.   It was a
colored print, and shows that the lady's shoe was
of green silk spotted with gold stars, and bound
with scarlet silk.   The sole is thicker at the back,
forming a slight uplift which was not strictly a heel.
Of course, this was a tiny foot, but we do not know
the height of the duchess.

I have seen the remains of a charming pair of
court shoes worn in France by a pretty Boston girl.
These had been embroidered with paste jewels,
" diamonds " ; while to my surprise the back seam
of both shoes was outlined with paste emeralds.   I
find that this was the mode of the court of Marie
Antoinette.   The queen and her ladies wore these
in real jewels, and in affectation wore no jewels elsewhere.

In Mrs. Gaskell's *My Lady Ludlow* we are told
that my lady would not sanction the mode of the
beginning of the century which " made all the fine
ladies take to making shoes."   Mrs. Blundell, in
one of her novels, sets her heroine (about 1805) at
shoe-making.   The shoes of that day were very thin
of material, very simple of shape, were heelless, and

in many cases closely approached a sandal.   A pair
worn by my great-aunt at that date is shown on this
page.   American women certainly had tiny feet.
This aunt was above the average height, but her
shoes are no larger than the number known to-day
as " Ones "— a size about large enough for a girl
ten years old.

It was not long after English girls were making
shoes that Yankee girls were shaping and binding

White Kid Slippers.   1815.

them in New England.   I have seen several old
letters which gave rules for shaping and directions
for sewing party-shoes of thin light kid and silk.
It is not probable that any heavy materials were ever
made up by women at home.   Sandals also were
worn, and made by girls for their own wear from
bits of morocco and kid.

In the early years of the century the thin, silk hose
and low slippers of the French fashions proved almost
unendurable in our northern winters.   One wearer
of the time writes, " Many a time have I walked
Broadway when the pavement sent almost a death
chill to my heart."   The Indians then furnished an
article of dress which must have been grateful indeed,

pretty moccasins edged with fur, to be worn over the thin slippers.

An old lady recalled with precision that the first boots for women's wear came in fashion in 1828; they were laced at the side. Garters and boots both had fringes at the top.

A CATALOGUE OF SELECTED DOVER BOOKS
IN ALL FIELDS OF INTEREST

A CATALOGUE OF SELECTED DOVER BOOKS
IN ALL FIELDS OF INTEREST

WHAT IS SCIENCE?, *N. Campbell*
The role of experiment and measurement, the function of mathematics, the nature of scientific laws, the difference between laws and theories, the limitations of science, and many similarly provocative topics are treated clearly and without technicalities by an eminent scientist. "Still an excellent introduction to scientific philosophy," H. Margenau in *Physics Today*. "A first-rate primer . . . deserves a wide audience," *Scientific American*. 192pp. 5⅜ x 8.
60043-2 Paperbound $1.25

THE NATURE OF LIGHT AND COLOUR IN THE OPEN AIR, *M. Minnaert*
Why are shadows sometimes blue, sometimes green, or other colors depending on the light and surroundings? What causes mirages? Why do multiple suns and moons appear in the sky? Professor Minnaert explains these unusual phenomena and hundreds of others in simple, easy-to-understand terms based on optical laws and the properties of light and color. No mathematics is required but artists, scientists, students, and everyone fascinated by these "tricks" of nature will find thousands of useful and amazing pieces of information. Hundreds of observational experiments are suggested which require no special equipment. 200 illustrations; 42 photos. xvi + 362pp. 5⅜ x 8.
20196-1 Paperbound $2.75

THE STRANGE STORY OF THE QUANTUM, AN ACCOUNT FOR THE GENERAL READER OF THE GROWTH OF IDEAS UNDERLYING OUR PRESENT ATOMIC KNOWLEDGE, *B. Hoffmann*
Presents lucidly and expertly, with barest amount of mathematics, the problems and theories which led to modern quantum physics. Dr. Hoffmann begins with the closing years of the 19th century, when certain trifling discrepancies were noticed, and with illuminating analogies and examples takes you through the brilliant concepts of Planck, Einstein, Pauli, Broglie, Bohr, Schroedinger, Heisenberg, Dirac, Sommerfeld, Feynman, etc. This edition includes a new, long postscript carrying the story through 1958. "Of the books attempting an account of the history and contents of our modern atomic physics which have come to my attention, this is the best," H. Margenau, Yale University, in *American Journal of Physics*. 32 tables and line illustrations. Index. 275pp. 5⅜ x 8.
20518-5 Paperbound $2.00

GREAT IDEAS OF MODERN MATHEMATICS: THEIR NATURE AND USE, *Jagjit Singh*
Reader with only high school math will understand main mathematical ideas of modern physics, astronomy, genetics, psychology, evolution, etc. better than many who use them as tools, but comprehend little of their basic structure. Author uses his wide knowledge of non-mathematical fields in brilliant exposition of differential equations, matrices, group theory, logic, statistics, problems of mathematical foundations, imaginary numbers, vectors, etc. Original publication. 2 appendixes. 2 indexes. 65 ills. 322pp. 5⅜ x 8.
20587-8 Paperbound $2.50

THE MUSIC OF THE SPHERES: THE MATERIAL UNIVERSE—FROM ATOM TO QUASAR, SIMPLY EXPLAINED, *Guy Murchie*
Vast compendium of fact, modern concept and theory, observed and calculated data, historical background guides intelligent layman through the material universe. Brilliant exposition of earth's construction, explanations for moon's craters, atmospheric components of Venus and Mars (with data from recent fly-by's), sun spots, sequences of star birth and death, neighboring galaxies, contributions of Galileo, Tycho Brahe, Kepler, etc.; and (Vol. 2) construction of the atom (describing newly discovered sigma and xi subatomic particles), theories of sound, color and light, space and time, including relativity theory, quantum theory, wave theory, probability theory, work of Newton, Maxwell, Faraday, Einstein, de Broglie, etc. "Best presentation yet offered to the intelligent general reader," *Saturday Review*. Revised (1967). Index. 319 illustrations by the author. Total of xx + 644pp. 5⅜ x 8½.
21809-0, 21810-4   Two volume set, paperbound $5.00

FOUR LECTURES ON RELATIVITY AND SPACE, *Charles Proteus Steinmetz*
Lecture series, given by great mathematician and electrical engineer, generally considered one of the best popular-level expositions of special and general relativity theories and related questions. Steinmetz translates complex mathematical reasoning into language accessible to laymen through analogy, example and comparison. Among topics covered are relativity of motion, location, time; of mass; acceleration; 4-dimensional time-space; geometry of the gravitational field; curvature and bending of space; non-Euclidean geometry. Index. 40 illustrations. x + 142pp. 5⅜ x 8½.   61771-8 Paperbound $1.50

HOW TO KNOW THE WILD FLOWERS, *Mrs. William Starr Dana*
Classic nature book that has introduced thousands to wonders of American wild flowers. Color-season principle of organization is easy to use, even by those with no botanical training, and the genial, refreshing discussions of history, folklore, uses of over 1,000 native and escape flowers, foliage plants are informative as well as fun to read. Over 170 full-page plates, collected from several editions, may be colored in to make permanent records of finds. Revised to conform with 1950 edition of Gray's Manual of Botany. xlii + 438pp. 5⅜ x 8½.   20332-8 Paperbound $2.50

MANUAL OF THE TREES OF NORTH AMERICA, *Charles Sprague Sargent*
Still unsurpassed as most comprehensive, reliable study of North American tree characteristics, precise locations and distribution. By dean of American dendrologists. Every tree native to U.S., Canada, Alaska; 185 genera, 717 species, described in detail—leaves, flowers, fruit, winterbuds, bark, wood, growth habits, etc. plus discussion of varieties and local variants, immaturity variations. Over 100 keys, including unusual 11-page analytical key to genera, aid in identification. 783 clear illustrations of flowers, fruit, leaves. An unmatched permanent reference work for all nature lovers. Second enlarged (1926) edition. Synopsis of families. Analytical key to genera. Glossary of technical terms. Index. 783 illustrations, 1 map. Total of 982pp. 5⅜ x 8.
20277-1, 20278-X Two volume set, paperbound $6.00

It's Fun to Make Things From Scrap Materials,
Evelyn Glantz Hershoff

What use are empty spools, tin cans, bottle tops? What can be made from rubber bands, clothes pins, paper clips, and buttons? This book provides simply worded instructions and large diagrams showing you how to make cookie cutters, toy trucks, paper turkeys, Halloween masks, telephone sets, aprons, linoleum block- and spatter prints — in all 399 projects! Many are easy enough for young children to figure out for themselves; some challenging enough to entertain adults; all are remarkably ingenious ways to make things from materials that cost pennies or less! Formerly "Scrap Fun for Everyone." Index. 214 illustrations. 373pp. 5⅜ x 8½.   21251-3 Paperbound $2.00

Symbolic Logic and The Game of Logic, *Lewis Carroll*

"Symbolic Logic" is not concerned with modern symbolic logic, but is instead a collection of over 380 problems posed with charm and imagination, using the syllogism and a fascinating diagrammatic method of drawing conclusions. In "The Game of Logic" Carroll's whimsical imagination devises a logical game played with 2 diagrams and counters (included) to manipulate hundreds of tricky syllogisms. The final section, "Hit or Miss" is a lagniappe of 101 additional puzzles in the delightful Carroll manner. Until this reprint edition, both of these books were rarities costing up to $15 each. Symbolic Logic: Index. xxxi + 199pp. The Game of Logic: 96pp. 2 vols. bound as one. 5⅜ x 8.
20492-8 Paperbound $2.50

Mathematical Puzzles of Sam Loyd, Part I
selected and edited by M. Gardner

Choice puzzles by the greatest American puzzle creator and innovator. Selected from his famous collection, "Cyclopedia of Puzzles," they retain the unique style and historical flavor of the originals. There are posers based on arithmetic, algebra, probability, game theory, route tracing, topology, counter and sliding block, operations research, geometrical dissection. Includes the famous "14-15" puzzle which was a national craze, and his "Horse of a Different Color" which sold millions of copies. 117 of his most ingenious puzzles in all. 120 line drawings and diagrams. Solutions. Selected references. xx + 167pp. 5⅜ x 8.
20498-7 Paperbound $1.35

String Figures and How to Make Them, *Caroline Furness Jayne*

107 string figures plus variations selected from the best primitive and modern examples developed by Navajo, Apache, pygmies of Africa, Eskimo, in Europe, Australia, China, etc. The most readily understandable, easy-to-follow book in English on perennially popular recreation. Crystal-clear exposition; step-by-step diagrams. Everyone from kindergarten children to adults looking for unusual diversion will be endlessly amused. Index. Bibliography. Introduction by A. C. Haddon. 17 full-page plates, 960 illustrations. xxiii + 401pp. 5⅜ x 8½.
20152-X Paperbound $2.50

Paper Folding for Beginners, *W. D. Murray and F. J. Rigney*

A delightful introduction to the varied and entertaining Japanese art of origami (paper folding), with a full, crystal-clear text that anticipates every difficulty; over 275 clearly labeled diagrams of all important stages in creation. You get results at each stage, since complex figures are logically developed from simpler ones. 43 different pieces are explained: sailboats, frogs, roosters, etc. 6 photographic plates. 279 diagrams. 95pp. 5⅝ x 8⅜.
20713-7 Paperbound $1.00

PRINCIPLES OF ART HISTORY,
H. Wölfflin
Analyzing such terms as "baroque," "classic," "neoclassic," "primitive," "picturesque," and 164 different works by artists like Botticelli, van Cleve, Dürer, Hobbema, Holbein, Hals, Rembrandt, Titian, Brueghel, Vermeer, and many others, the author establishes the classifications of art history and style on a firm, concrete basis. This classic of art criticism shows what really occurred between the 14th-century primitives and the sophistication of the 18th century in terms of basic attitudes and philosophies. "A remarkable lesson in the art of seeing," *Sat. Rev. of Literature*. Translated from the 7th German edition. 150 illustrations. 254pp. 6⅛ x 9¼. 20276-3 Paperbound $2.50

PRIMITIVE ART,
Franz Boas
This authoritative and exhaustive work by a great American anthropologist covers the entire gamut of primitive art. Pottery, leatherwork, metal work, stone work, wood, basketry, are treated in detail. Theories of primitive art, historical depth in art history, technical virtuosity, unconscious levels of patterning, symbolism, styles, literature, music, dance, etc. A must book for the interested layman, the anthropologist, artist, handicrafter (hundreds of unusual motifs), and the historian. Over 900 illustrations (50 ceramic vessels, 12 totem poles, etc.). 376pp. 5⅜ x 8.   20025-6 Paperbound $2.50

THE GENTLEMAN AND CABINET MAKER'S DIRECTOR,
Thomas Chippendale
A reprint of the 1762 catalogue of furniture designs that went on to influence generations of English and Colonial and Early Republic American furniture makers. The 200 plates, most of them full-page sized, show Chippendale's designs for French (Louis XV), Gothic, and Chinese-manner chairs, sofas, canopy and dome beds, cornices, chamber organs, cabinets, shaving tables, commodes, picture frames, frets, candle stands, chimney pieces, decorations, etc. The drawings are all elegant and highly detailed; many include construction diagrams and elevations. A supplement of 24 photographs shows surviving pieces of original and Chippendale-style pieces of furniture. Brief biography of Chippendale by N. I. Bienenstock, editor of *Furniture World*. Reproduced from the 1762 edition. 200 plates, plus 19 photographic plates. vi + 249pp. 9⅛ x 12¼.   21601-2 Paperbound $4.00

AMERICAN ANTIQUE FURNITURE: A BOOK FOR AMATEURS,
Edgar G. Miller, Jr.
Standard introduction and practical guide to identification of valuable American antique furniture. 2115 illustrations, mostly photographs taken by the author in 148 private homes, are arranged in chronological order in extensive chapters on chairs, sofas, chests, desks, bedsteads, mirrors, tables, clocks, and other articles. Focus is on furniture accessible to the collector, including simpler pieces and a larger than usual coverage of Empire style. Introductory chapters identify structural elements, characteristics of various styles, how to avoid fakes, etc. "We are frequently asked to name some book on American furniture that will meet the requirements of the novice collector, the beginning dealer, and . . . the general public. . . . We believe Mr. Miller's two volumes more completely satisfy this specification than any other work," *Antiques*. Appendix. Index. Total of vi + 1106pp. 7⅞ x 10¾.
                21599-7, 21600-4 Two volume set, paperbound $10.00

CATALOGUE OF DOVER BOOKS

The Bad Child's Book of Beasts, More Beasts for Worse Children, and A Moral Alphabet, *H. Belloc*
Hardly and anthology of humorous verse has appeared in the last 50 years without at least a couple of these famous nonsense verses. But one must see the entire volumes — with all the delightful original illustrations by Sir Basil Blackwood — to appreciate fully Belloc's charming and witty verses that play so subacidly on the platitudes of life and morals that beset his day — and ours. A great humor classic. Three books in one. Total of 157pp. 5⅜ x 8.
20749-8 Paperbound $1.25

The Devil's Dictionary, *Ambrose Bierce*
Sardonic and irreverent barbs puncturing the pomposities and absurdities of American politics, business, religion, literature, and arts, by the country's greatest satirist in the classic tradition. Epigrammatic as Shaw, piercing as Swift, American as Mark Twain, Will Rogers, and Fred Allen, Bierce will always remain the favorite of a small coterie of enthusiasts, and of writers and speakers whom he supplies with "some of the most gorgeous witticisms of the English language" (H. L. Mencken). Over 1000 entries in alphabetical order. 144pp. 5⅜ x 8.
20487-1 Paperbound $1.25

The Complete Nonsense of Edward Lear.
This is the only complete edition of this master of gentle madness available at a popular price. *A Book of Nonsense, Nonsense Songs, More Nonsense Songs and Stories* in their entirety with all the old favorites that have delighted children and adults for years. The Dong With A Luminous Nose, The Jumblies, The Owl and the Pussycat, and hundreds of other bits of wonderful nonsense. 214 limericks, 3 sets of Nonsense Botany, 5 Nonsense Alphabets, 546 drawings by Lear himself, and much more. 320pp. 5⅜ x 8. 20167-8 Paperbound $1.75

The Wit and Humor of Oscar Wilde, *ed. by Alvin Redman*
Wilde at his most brilliant, in 1000 epigrams exposing weaknesses and hypocrisies of "civilized" society. Divided into 49 categories—sin, wealth, women, America, etc.—to aid writers, speakers. Includes excerpts from his trials, books, plays, criticism. Formerly "The Epigrams of Oscar Wilde." Introduction by Vyvyan Holland, Wilde's only living son. Introductory essay by editor. 260pp. 5⅜ x 8.
20602-5 Paperbound $1.50

A Child's Primer of Natural History, *Oliver Herford*
Scarcely an anthology of whimsy and humor has appeared in the last 50 years without a contribution from Oliver Herford. Yet the works from which these examples are drawn have been almost impossible to obtain! Here at last are Herford's improbable definitions of a menagerie of familiar and weird animals, each verse illustrated by the author's own drawings. 24 drawings in 2 colors; 24 additional drawings. vii + 95pp. 6½ x 6. 21647-0 Paperbound $1.00

The Brownies: Their Book, *Palmer Cox*
The book that made the Brownies a household word. Generations of readers have enjoyed the antics, predicaments and adventures of these jovial sprites, who emerge from the forest at night to play or to come to the aid of a deserving human. Delightful illustrations by the author decorate nearly every page. 24 short verse tales with 266 illustrations. 155pp. 6⅝ x 9¼.
21265-3 Paperbound $1.50

THE PRINCIPLES OF PSYCHOLOGY,
William James
The full long-course, unabridged, of one of the great classics of Western literature and science. Wonderfully lucid descriptions of human mental activity, the stream of thought, consciousness, time perception, memory, imagination, emotions, reason, abnormal phenomena, and similar topics. Original contributions are integrated with the work of such men as Berkeley, Binet, Mills, Darwin, Hume, Kant, Royce, Schopenhauer, Spinoza, Locke, Descartes, Galton, Wundt, Lotze, Herbart, Fechner, and scores of others. All contrasting interpretations of mental phenomena are examined in detail—introspective analysis, philosophical interpretation, and experimental research. "A classic," *Journal of Consulting Psychology.* "The main lines are as valid as ever," *Psychoanalytical Quarterly.* "Standard reading . . . a classic of interpretation," *Psychiatric Quarterly.* 94 illustrations. 1408pp. 5⅜ x 8.
20381-6, 20382-4 Two volume set, paperbound $6.00

VISUAL ILLUSIONS: THEIR CAUSES, CHARACTERISTICS AND APPLICATIONS,
M. Luckiesh
"Seeing is deceiving," asserts the author of this introduction to virtually every type of optical illusion known. The text both describes and explains the principles involved in color illusions, figure-ground, distance illusions, etc. 100 photographs, drawings and diagrams prove how easy it is to fool the sense: circles that aren't round, parallel lines that seem to bend, stationary figures that seem to move as you stare at them — illustration after illustration strains our credulity at what we see. Fascinating book from many points of view, from applications for artists, in camouflage, etc. to the psychology of vision. New introduction by William Ittleson, Dept. of Psychology, Queens College. Index. Bibliography. xxi + 252pp. 5⅜ x 8½.
21530-X Paperbound $1.75

FADS AND FALLACIES IN THE NAME OF SCIENCE,
Martin Gardner
This is the standard account of various cults, quack systems, and delusions which have masqueraded as science: hollow earth fanatics. Reich and orgone sex energy, dianetics, Atlantis, multiple moons, Forteanism, flying saucers, medical fallacies like iridiagnosis, zone therapy, etc. A new chapter has been added on Bridey Murphy, psionics, and other recent manifestations in this field. This is a fair, reasoned appraisal of eccentric theory which provides excellent inoculation against cleverly masked nonsense. "Should be read by everyone, scientist and non-scientist alike," R. T. Birge, Prof. Emeritus of Physics, Univ. of California; Former President, American Physical Society. Index. x + 365pp. 5⅜ x 8.
20394-8 Paperbound $2.00

ILLUSIONS AND DELUSIONS OF THE SUPERNATURAL AND THE OCCULT,
D. H. Rawcliffe
Holds up to rational examination hundreds of persistent delusions including crystal gazing, automatic writing, table turning, mediumistic trances, mental healing, stigmata, lycanthropy, live burial, the Indian Rope Trick, spiritualism, dowsing, telepathy, clairvoyance, ghosts, ESP, etc. The author explains and exposes the mental and physical deceptions involved, making this not only an exposé of supernatural phenomena, but a valuable exposition of characteristic types of abnormal psychology. Originally titled "The Psychology of the Occult." 14 illustrations. Index. 551pp. 5⅜ x 8. 20503-7 Paperbound $3.50

FAIRY TALE COLLECTIONS, *edited by Andrew Lang*
Andrew Lang's fairy tale collections make up the richest shelf-full of traditional children's stories anywhere available. Lang supervised the translation of stories from all over the world—familiar European tales collected by Grimm, animal stories from Negro Africa, myths of primitive Australia, stories from Russia, Hungary, Iceland, Japan, and many other countries. Lang's selection of translations are unusually high; many authorities consider that the most familiar tales find their best versions in these volumes. All collections are richly decorated and illustrated by H. J. Ford and other artists.

THE BLUE FAIRY BOOK. 37 stories. 138 illustrations. ix + 390pp. 5⅜ x 8½.
21437-0 Paperbound $1.95

THE GREEN FAIRY BOOK. 42 stories. 100 illustrations. xiii + 366pp. 5⅜ x 8½.
21439-7 Paperbound $2.00

THE BROWN FAIRY BOOK. 32 stories. 50 illustrations, 8 in color. xii + 350pp. 5⅜ x 8½.
21438-9 Paperbound $1.95

THE BEST TALES OF HOFFMANN, *edited by E. F. Bleiler*
10 stories by E. T. A. Hoffmann, one of the greatest of all writers of fantasy. The tales include "The Golden Flower Pot," "Automata," "A New Year's Eve Adventure," "Nutcracker and the King of Mice," "Sand-Man," and others. Vigorous characterizations of highly eccentric personalities, remarkably imaginative situations, and intensely fast pacing has made these tales popular all over the world for 150 years. Editor's introduction. 7 drawings by Hoffmann. xxxiii + 419pp. 5⅜ x 8½.
21793-0 Paperbound $2.25

GHOST AND HORROR STORIES OF AMBROSE BIERCE,
edited by E. F. Bleiler
Morbid, eerie, horrifying tales of possessed poets, shabby aristocrats, revived corpses, and haunted malefactors. Widely acknowledged as the best of their kind between Poe and the moderns, reflecting their author's inner torment and bitter view of life. Includes "Damned Thing," "The Middle Toe of the Right Foot," "The Eyes of the Panther," "Visions of the Night," "Moxon's Master," and over a dozen others. Editor's introduction. xxii + 199pp. 5⅜ x 8½.
20767-6 Paperbound $1.50

THREE GOTHIC NOVELS, *edited by E. F. Bleiler*
Originators of the still popular Gothic novel form, influential in ushering in early 19th-century Romanticism. Horace Walpole's *Castle of Otranto*, William Beckford's *Vathek*, John Polidori's *The Vampyre*, and a *Fragment* by Lord Byron are enjoyable as exciting reading or as documents in the history of English literature. Editor's introduction. xi + 291pp. 5⅜ x 8½.
21232-7 Paperbound $2.00

BEST GHOST STORIES OF LEFANU, *edited by E. F. Bleiler*
Though admired by such critics as V. S. Pritchett, Charles Dickens and Henry James, ghost stories by the Irish novelist Joseph Sheridan LeFanu have never become as widely known as his detective fiction. About half of the 16 stories in this collection have never before been available in America. Collection includes "Carmilla" (perhaps the best vampire story ever written), "The Haunted Baronet," "The Fortunes of Sir Robert Ardagh," and the classic "Green Tea." Editor's introduction. 7 contemporary illustrations. Portrait of LeFanu. xii + 467pp. 5⅜ x 8.
20415-4 Paperbound $2.50

EASY-TO-DO ENTERTAINMENTS AND DIVERSIONS WITH COINS, CARDS, STRING, PAPER AND MATCHES, *R. M. Abraham*

Over 300 tricks, games and puzzles will provide young readers with absorbing fun. Sections on card games; paper-folding; tricks with coins, matches and pieces of string; games for the agile; toy-making from common household objects; mathematical recreations; and 50 miscellaneous pastimes. Anyone in charge of groups of youngsters, including hard-pressed parents, and in need of suggestions on how to keep children sensibly amused and quietly content will find this book indispensable. Clear, simple text, copious number of delightful line drawings and illustrative diagrams. Originally titled "Winter Nights' Entertainments." Introduction by Lord Baden Powell. 329 illustrations. v + 186pp. 5⅜ x 8½. 20921-0 Paperbound $1.25

AN INTRODUCTION TO CHESS MOVES AND TACTICS SIMPLY EXPLAINED, *Leonard Barden*

Beginner's introduction to the royal game. Names, possible moves of the pieces, definitions of essential terms, how games are won, etc. explained in 30-odd pages. With this background you'll be able to sit right down and play. Balance of book teaches strategy — openings, middle game, typical endgame play, and suggestions for improving your game. A sample game is fully analyzed. True middle-level introduction, teaching you all the essentials without oversimplifying or losing you in a maze of detail. 58 figures. 102pp. 5⅜ x 8½. 21210-6 Paperbound $1.25

LASKER'S MANUAL OF CHESS, *Dr. Emanuel Lasker*

Probably the greatest chess player of modern times, Dr. Emanuel Lasker held the world championship 28 years, independent of passing schools or fashions. This unmatched study of the game, chiefly for intermediate to skilled players, analyzes basic methods, combinations, position play, the aesthetics of chess, dozens of different openings, etc., with constant reference to great modern games. Contains a brilliant exposition of Steinitz's important theories. Introduction by Fred Reinfeld. Tables of Lasker's tournament record. 3 indices. 308 diagrams. 1 photograph. xxx + 349pp. 5⅜ x 8. 20640-8 Paperbound $2.50

COMBINATIONS: THE HEART OF CHESS, *Irving Chernev*

Step-by-step from simple combinations to complex, this book, by a well-known chess writer, shows you the intricacies of pins, counter-pins, knight forks, and smothered mates. Other chapters show alternate lines of play to those taken in actual championship games; boomerang combinations; classic examples of brilliant combination play by Nimzovich, Rubinstein, Tarrasch, Botvinnik, Alekhine and Capablanca. Index. 356 diagrams. ix + 245pp. 5⅜ x 8½. 21744-2 Paperbound $2.00

HOW TO SOLVE CHESS PROBLEMS, *K. S. Howard*

Full of practical suggestions for the fan or the beginner — who knows only the moves of the chessmen. Contains preliminary section and 58 two-move, 46 three-move, and 8 four-move problems composed by 27 outstanding American problem creators in the last 30 years. Explanation of all terms and exhaustive index. "Just what is wanted for the student," Brian Harley. 112 problems, solutions. vi + 171pp. 5⅜ x 8. 20748-X Paperbound $1.50

SOCIAL THOUGHT FROM LORE TO SCIENCE,
H. E. Barnes and H. Becker
An immense survey of sociological thought and ways of viewing, studying, planning, and reforming society from earliest times to the present. Includes thought on society of preliterate peoples, ancient non-Western cultures, and every great movement in Europe, America, and modern Japan. Analyzes hundreds of great thinkers: Plato, Augustine, Bodin, Vico, Montesquieu, Herder, Comte, Marx, etc. Weighs the contributions of utopians, sophists, fascists and communists; economists, jurists, philosophers, ecclesiastics, and every 19th and 20th century school of scientific sociology, anthropology, and social psychology throughout the world. Combines topical, chronological, and regional approaches, treating the evolution of social thought as a process rather than as a series of mere topics. "Impressive accuracy, competence, and discrimination . . . easily the best single survey," *Nation.* Thoroughly revised, with new material up to 1960. 2 indexes. Over 2200 bibliographical notes. Three volume set. Total of 1586pp. 5⅜ x 8.
20901-6, 20902-4, 20903-2 Three volume set, paperbound $10.50

A HISTORY OF HISTORICAL WRITING, *Harry Elmer Barnes*
Virtually the only adequate survey of the whole course of historical writing in a single volume. Surveys developments from the beginnings of historiography in the ancient Near East and the Classical World, up through the Cold War. Covers major historians in detail, shows interrelationship with cultural background, makes clear individual contributions, evaluates and estimates importance; also enormously rich upon minor authors and thinkers who are usually passed over. Packed with scholarship and learning, clear, easily written. Indispensable to every student of history. Revised and enlarged up to 1961. Index and bibliography. xv + 442pp. 5⅜ x 8½.
20104-X Paperbound $3.00

JOHANN SEBASTIAN BACH, *Philipp Spitta*
The complete and unabridged text of the definitive study of Bach. Written some 70 years ago, it is still unsurpassed for its coverage of nearly all aspects of Bach's life and work. There could hardly be a finer non-technical introduction to Bach's music than the detailed, lucid analyses which Spitta provides for hundreds of individual pieces. 26 solid pages are devoted to the B minor mass, for example, and 30 pages to the glorious St. Matthew Passion. This monumental set also includes a major analysis of the music of the 18th century: Buxtehude, Pachelbel, etc. "Unchallenged as the last word on one of the supreme geniuses of music," John Barkham, *Saturday Review Syndicate.* Total of 1819pp. Heavy cloth binding. 5⅜ x 8.
22278-0, 22279-9 Two volume set, clothbound $15.00

BEETHOVEN AND HIS NINE SYMPHONIES, *George Grove*
In this modern middle-level classic of musicology Grove not only analyzes all nine of Beethoven's symphonies very thoroughly in terms of their musical structure, but also discusses the circumstances under which they were written, Beethoven's stylistic development, and much other background material. This is an extremely rich book, yet very easily followed; it is highly recommended to anyone seriously interested in music. Over 250 musical passages. Index. viii + 407pp. 5⅜ x 8.
20334-4 Paperbound $2.50

THE TIME STREAM
John Taine
Acknowledged by many as the best SF writer of the 1920's, Taine (under the name Eric Temple Bell) was also a Professor of Mathematics of considerable renown. Reprinted here are *The Time Stream*, generally considered Taine's best, *The Greatest Game*, a biological-fiction novel, and *The Purple Sapphire*, involving a supercivilization of the past. Taine's stories tie fantastic narratives to frameworks of original and logical scientific concepts. Speculation is often profound on such questions as the nature of time, concept of entropy, cyclical universes, etc. 4 contemporary illustrations. v + 532pp. 5⅜ x 8⅜.
21180-0 Paperbound $3.00

SEVEN SCIENCE FICTION NOVELS,
H. G. Wells
Full unabridged texts of 7 science-fiction novels of the master. Ranging from biology, physics, chemistry, astronomy, to sociology and other studies, Mr. Wells extrapolates whole worlds of strange and intriguing character. "One will have to go far to match this for entertainment, excitement, and sheer pleasure . . ."*New York Times*. Contents: The Time Machine, The Island of Dr. Moreau, The First Men in the Moon, The Invisible Man, The War of the Worlds, The Food of the Gods, In The Days of the Comet. 1015pp. 5⅜ x 8.
20264-X Clothbound $5.00

28 SCIENCE FICTION STORIES OF H. G. WELLS.
Two full, unabridged novels, *Men Like Gods* and *Star Begotten*, plus 26 short stories by the master science-fiction writer of all time! Stories of space, time, invention, exploration, futuristic adventure. Partial contents: *The Country of the Blind, In the Abyss, The Crystal Egg, The Man Who Could Work Miracles, A Story of Days to Come, The Empire of the Ants, The Magic Shop, The Valley of the Spiders, A Story of the Stone Age, Under the Knife, Sea Raiders*, etc. An indispensable collection for the library of anyone interested in science fiction adventure. 928pp. 5⅜ x 8.
20265-8 Clothbound $5.00

THREE MARTIAN NOVELS,
Edgar Rice Burroughs
Complete, unabridged reprinting, in one volume, of Thuvia, Maid of Mars; Chessmen of Mars; The Master Mind of Mars. Hours of science-fiction adventure by a modern master storyteller. Reset in large clear type for easy reading. 16 illustrations by J. Allen St. John. vi + 490pp. 5⅜ x 8½.
20039-6.Paperbound $2.50

AN INTELLECTUAL AND CULTURAL HISTORY OF THE WESTERN WORLD,
Harry Elmer Barnes
Monumental 3-volume survey of intellectual development of Europe from primitive cultures to the present day. Every significant product of human intellect traced through history: art, literature, mathematics, physical sciences, medicine, music, technology, social sciences, religions, jurisprudence, education, etc. Presentation is lucid and specific, analyzing in detail specific discoveries, theories, literary works, and so on. Revised (1965) by recognized scholars in specialized fields under the direction of Prof. Barnes. Revised bibliography. Indexes. 24 illustrations. Total of xxix + 1318pp.
21275-0, 21276-9, 21277-7 Three volume set, paperbound $7.75

HEAR ME TALKIN' TO YA, *edited by Nat Shapiro and Nat Hentoff*
In their own words, Louis Armstrong, King Oliver, Fletcher Henderson, Bunk Johnson, Bix Beiderbecke, Billy Holiday, Fats Waller, Jelly Roll Morton, Duke Ellington, and many others comment on the origins of jazz in New Orleans and its growth in Chicago's South Side, Kansas City's jam sessions, Depression Harlem, and the modernism of the West Coast schools. Taken from taped conversations, letters, magazine articles, other first-hand sources. Editors' introduction. xvi + 429pp. 5⅜ x 8½.   21726-4 Paperbound $2.50

THE JOURNAL OF HENRY D. THOREAU
A 25-year record by the great American observer and critic, as complete a record of a great man's inner life as is anywhere available. Thoreau's Journals served him as raw material for his formal pieces, as a place where he could develop his ideas, as an outlet for his interests in wild life and plants, in writing as an art, in classics of literature, Walt Whitman and other contemporaries, in politics, slavery, individual's relation to the State, etc. The Journals present a portrait of a remarkable man, and are an observant social history. Unabridged republication of 1906 edition, Bradford Torrey and Francis H. Allen, editors. Illustrations. Total of 1888pp. 8⅜ x 12¼.
20312-3, 20313-1 Two volume set, clothbound $30.00

A SHAKESPEARIAN GRAMMAR, *E. A. Abbott*
Basic reference to Shakespeare and his contemporaries, explaining through thousands of quotations from Shakespeare, Jonson, Beaumont and Fletcher, North's *Plutarch* and other sources the grammatical usage differing from the modern. First published in 1870 and written by a scholar who spent much of his life isolating principles of Elizabethan language, the book is unlikely ever to be superseded. Indexes. xxiv + 511pp. 5⅜ x 8½. 21582-2 Paperbound $3.00

FOLK-LORE OF SHAKESPEARE, *T. F. Thistelton Dyer*
Classic study, drawing from Shakespeare a large body of references to supernatural beliefs, terminology of falconry and hunting, games and sports, good luck charms, marriage customs, folk medicines, superstitions about plants, animals, birds, argot of the underworld, sexual slang of London, proverbs, drinking customs, weather lore, and much else. From full compilation comes a mirror of the 17th-century popular mind. Index. ix + 526pp. 5⅜ x 8½.
21614-4 Paperbound $3.25

THE NEW VARIORUM SHAKESPEARE, *edited by H. H. Furness*
By far the richest editions of the plays ever produced in any country or language. Each volume contains complete text (usually First Folio) of the play, all variants in Quarto and other Folio texts, editorial changes by every major editor to Furness's own time (1900), footnotes to obscure references or language, extensive quotes from literature of Shakespearian criticism, essays on plot sources (often reprinting sources in full), and much more.

HAMLET, *edited by H. H. Furness*
Total of xxvi + 905pp. 5⅜ x 8½.
21004-9, 21005-7 Two volume set, paperbound $5.50

TWELFTH NIGHT, *edited by H. H. Furness*
Index. xxii + 434pp. 5⅜ x 8½.   21189-4 Paperbound $2.75

LA BOHEME BY GIACOMO PUCCINI,
translated and introduced by Ellen H. Bleiler
Complete handbook for the operagoer, with everything needed for full enjoyment except the musical score itself. Complete Italian libretto, with new, modern English line-by-line translation—the only libretto printing all repeats; biography of Puccini; the librettists; background to the opera, Murger's La Boheme, etc.; circumstances of composition and performances; plot summary; and pictorial section of 73 illustrations showing Puccini, famous singers and performances, etc. Large clear type for easy reading. 124pp. 5⅜ x 8½.
20404-9 Paperbound $1.50

ANTONIO STRADIVARI: HIS LIFE AND WORK (1644-1737),
W. Henry Hill, Arthur F. Hill, and Alfred E. Hill
Still the only book that really delves into life and art of the incomparable Italian craftsman, maker of the finest musical instruments in the world today. The authors, expert violin-makers themselves, discuss Stradivari's ancestry, his construction and finishing techniques, distinguished characteristics of many of his instruments and their locations. Included, too, is story of introduction of his instruments into France, England, first revelation of their supreme merit, and information on his labels, number of instruments made, prices, mystery of ingredients of his varnish, tone of pre-1684 Stradivari violin and changes between 1684 and 1690. An extremely interesting, informative account for all music lovers, from craftsman to concert-goer. Republication of original (1902) edition. New introduction by Sydney Beck, Head of Rare Book and Manuscript Collections, Music Division, New York Public Library. Analytical index by Rembert Wurlitzer. Appendixes. 68 illustrations. 30 full-page plates. 4 in color. xxvi + 315pp. 5⅜ x 8½.
20425-1 Paperbound $3.00

MUSICAL AUTOGRAPHS FROM MONTEVERDI TO HINDEMITH,
Emanuel Winternitz
For beauty, for intrinsic interest, for perspective on the composer's personality, for subtleties of phrasing, shading, emphasis indicated in the autograph but suppressed in the printed score, the mss. of musical composition are fascinating documents which repay close study in many different ways. This 2-volume work reprints facsimiles of mss. by virtually every major composer, and many minor figures—196 examples in all. A full text points out what can be learned from mss., analyzes each sample. Index. Bibliography. 18 figures. 196 plates. Total of 170pp. of text. 7⅞ x 10¾.
21312-9, 21313-7 Two volume set, paperbound $5.00

J. S. BACH,
Albert Schweitzer
One of the few great full-length studies of Bach's life and work, and the study upon which Schweitzer's renown as a musicologist rests. On first appearance (1911), revolutionized Bach performance. The only writer on Bach to be musicologist, performing musician, and student of history, theology and philosophy, Schweitzer contributes particularly full sections on history of German Protestant church music, theories on motivic pictorial representations in vocal music, and practical suggestions for performance. Translated by Ernest Newman. Indexes. 5 illustrations. 650 musical examples. Total of xix + 928pp. 5⅜ x 8½.
21631-4, 21632-2 Two volume set, paperbound $5.00

THE METHODS OF ETHICS, *Henry Sidgwick*
Propounding no organized system of its own, study subjects every major methodological approach to ethics to rigorous, objective analysis. Study discusses and relates ethical thought of Plato, Aristotle, Bentham, Clarke, Butler, Hobbes, Hume, Mill, Spencer, Kant, and dozens of others. Sidgwick retains conclusions from each system which follow from ethical premises, rejecting the faulty. Considered by many in the field to be among the most important treatises on ethical philosophy. Appendix. Index. xlvii + 528pp. 5⅜ x 8½.
21608-X Paperbound $3.00

TEUTONIC MYTHOLOGY, *Jakob Grimm*
A milestone in Western culture; the work which established on a modern basis the study of history of religions and comparative religions. 4-volume work assembles and interprets everything available on religious and folkloristic beliefs of Germanic people (including Scandinavians, Anglo-Saxons, etc.). Assembling material from such sources as Tacitus, surviving Old Norse and Icelandic texts, archeological remains, folktales, surviving superstitions, comparative traditions, linguistic analysis, etc. Grimm explores pagan deities, heroes, folklore of nature, religious practices, and every other area of pagan German belief. To this day, the unrivaled, definitive, exhaustive study. Translated by J. S. Stallybrass from 4th (1883) German edition. Indexes. Total of lxxvii + 1887pp. 5⅜ x 8½.
21602-0, 21603-9, 21604-7, 21605-5 Four volume set, paperbound $12.00

THE I CHING, *translated by James Legge*
Called "The Book of Changes" in English, this is one of the Five Classics edited by Confucius, basic and central to Chinese thought. Explains perhaps the most complex system of divination known, founded on the theory that all things happening at any one time have characteristic features which can be isolated and related. Significant in Oriental studies, in history of religions and philosophy, and also to Jungian psychoanalysis and other areas of modern European thought. Index. Appendixes. 6 plates. xxi + 448pp. 5⅜ x 8½.
21062-6 Paperbound $2.75

HISTORY OF ANCIENT PHILOSOPHY, *W. Windelband*
One of the clearest, most accurate comprehensive surveys of Greek and Roman philosophy. Discusses ancient philosophy in general, intellectual life in Greece in the 7th and 6th centuries B.C., Thales, Anaximander, Anaximenes, Heraclitus, the Eleatics, Empedocles, Anaxagoras, Leucippus, the Pythagoreans, the Sophists, Socrates, Democritus (20 pages), Plato (50 pages), Aristotle (70 pages), the Peripatetics, Stoics, Epicureans, Sceptics, Neo-platonists, Christian Apologists, etc. 2nd German edition translated by H. E. Cushman. xv + 393pp. 5⅜ x 8.
20357-3 Paperbound $3.00

THE PALACE OF PLEASURE, *William Painter*
Elizabethan versions of Italian and French novels from *The Decameron*, Cinthio, Straparola, Queen Margaret of Navarre, and other continental sources — the very work that provided Shakespeare and dozens of his contemporaries with many of their plots and sub-plots and, therefore, justly considered one of the most influential books in all English literature. It is also a book that any reader will still enjoy. Total of cviii + 1,224pp.
21691-8, 21692-6, 21693-4 Three volume set, paperbound $8.25

THE WONDERFUL WIZARD OF OZ, *L. F. Baum*
All the original W. W. Denslow illustrations in full color—as much a part of "The Wizard" as Tenniel's drawings are of "Alice in Wonderland." "The Wizard" is still America's best-loved fairy tale, in which, as the author expresses it, "The wonderment and joy are retained and the heartaches and nightmares left out." Now today's young readers can enjoy every word and wonderful picture of the original book. New introduction by Martin Gardner. A Baum bibliography. 23 full-page color plates. viii + 268pp. 5⅜ x 8.

20691-2 Paperbound $1.95

THE MARVELOUS LAND OF OZ, *L. F. Baum*
This is the equally enchanting sequel to the "Wizard," continuing the adventures of the Scarecrow and the Tin Woodman. The hero this time is a little boy named Tip, and all the delightful Oz magic is still present. This is the Oz book with the Animated Saw-Horse, the Woggle-Bug, and Jack Pumpkinhead. All the original John R. Neill illustrations, 10 in full color. 287pp. 5⅜ x 8.

20692-0 Paperbound $1.75

ALICE'S ADVENTURES UNDER GROUND, *Lewis Carroll*
The original *Alice in Wonderland*, hand-lettered and illustrated by Carroll himself, and originally presented as a Christmas gift to a child-friend. Adults as well as children will enjoy this charming volume, reproduced faithfully in this Dover edition. While the story is essentially the same, there are slight changes, and Carroll's spritely drawings present an intriguing alternative to the famous Tenniel illustrations. One of the most popular books in Dover's catalogue. Introduction by Martin Gardner. 38 illustrations. 128pp. 5⅜ x 8½.

21482-6 Paperbound $1.00

THE NURSERY "ALICE," *Lewis Carroll*
While most of us consider *Alice in Wonderland* a story for children of all ages, Carroll himself felt it was beyond younger children. He therefore provided this simplified version, illustrated with the famous Tenniel drawings enlarged and colored in delicate tints, for children aged "from Nought to Five." Dover's edition of this now rare classic is a faithful copy of the 1889 printing, including 20 illustrations by Tenniel, and front and back covers reproduced in full color. Introduction by Martin Gardner. xxiii + 67pp. 6⅛ x 9¼.

21610-1 Paperbound $1.75

THE STORY OF KING ARTHUR AND HIS KNIGHTS, *Howard Pyle*
A fast-paced, exciting retelling of the best known Arthurian legends for young readers by one of America's best story tellers and illustrators. The sword Excalibur, wooing of Guinevere, Merlin and his downfall, adventures of Sir Pellias and Gawaine, and others. The pen and ink illustrations are vividly imagined and wonderfully drawn. 41 illustrations. xviii + 313pp. 6⅛ x 9¼.

21445-1 Paperbound $2.00

Prices subject to change without notice.

Available at your book dealer or write for free catalogue to Dept. Adsci, Dover Publications, Inc., 180 Varick St., N.Y., N.Y. 10014. Dover publishes more than 150 books each year on science, elementary and advanced mathematics, biology, music, art, literary history, social sciences and other areas.